From its beginnings, the Church has presented itself as a human phenomenon that carries the divine within it. As a social fact, its reality given form by men and women, the Church has always affirmed that its existence surpasses the human reality of its components and that it stands as the continuation of the event of Christ's entry into human history. *Why the Church?*, the final volume in McGill-Queen's University Press's trilogy of Luigi Giussani's writings, explores the Church's definition of itself as both human and divine and evaluates the truth of this claim.

Giussani begins by focusing on the Church as a community composed of people who are aware of themselves as defined by the gift of the Spirit, from which they derive a new conception of existence, the fruit of conversion. He then describes the Church's developing self-awareness of its dual elements of the human and divine. Concerned with verifying the Church's claim to embody Christ, Giussani situates the locus of verification in human experience, arguing that a different type of life is born in those who try to live the life of the Church.

Why the Church? is a seminal study that will engage both the scholar and the general reader.

LUIGI GIUSSANI is professor emeritus of the Università Cattolica del Sacro Cuore in Milan, Italy, and is the founder of the Catholic lay movement Communion and Liberation, which is flourishing in Italy and has spread to over sixty countries throughout the world, including Canada, the United States, and Britain.

Why the Church?

LUIGI GIUSSANI

Translated by Viviane Hewitt

McGill-Queen's University Press
Montreal & Kingston · London · Ithaca

© McGill-Queen's University Press 2001
ISBN 0-7735-1654-9 (cloth)
ISBN 0-7735-1707-3 (paper)

Legal deposit first quarter 2001
Bibliothèque nationale du Québec

Printed in Canada on acid-free paper

McGill-Queen's University Press acknowledges the
financial support of the the Government of Canada
through the Book Publishing Industry Development
Program (BPIDP) for its activities. It also acknowledges
the support of the Canada Council of the Arts for its
publishing program.

Canadian Cataloguing in Publication Data

Giussani, Luigi
    Why the church?
    Translation of: Perché la Chiesa?
    Includes bibliographical references and index.
    ISBN 0-7735-1654-9 (bound)
    ISBN 0-7735-1707-3 (pbk.)
    1. Church. I. Hewitt, Viviane II. Title.
    BR145.2G58 2001   262'.7   C00-900898-5

Typeset in 10/12 FFScala by Acappella

Contents

Preface

"Jesus Christ continues his presence and his work of salvation in the Church and through the Church, which is his Body." These words by Cardinal Ratzinger, contained in the latest document issued by the Congregation for the Doctrine of the Faith (*Dominus Iesus*), introduce us to the contents of this volume which, in an ideal sense, conclude the trilogy begun with *The Religious Sense* and continuing with *At the Origin of the Christian Claim.*

The logic of *Why the Church?* becomes clear when we understand the lengthy premise which places the problem within its true terms: The Church offers itself as the continuity of Christ. How can the Church be recognized as this continuity? The introduction presents, with basic clarity, the problem of how this recognition can come about: through historical texts (as maintained by *rationalism*), by inner enlightenment (as *Protestantism* maintains), or (according to the *Orthodox-Catholic formulation*) by the working of Christ's spirit: the mystery of the communion of believers. This third way – since we always begin with the present moment – provides, precisely through the present experience in which we participate, the solution to the question of the historical reading of texts and the movement of the Spirit which we need in order to understand who is standing before us.

Why is it so hard to admit this road, which seems to be the easiest? The difficulty lies in the triumph of rationalism, which maintains that the truth of reality is what can be measured by reason or observed by experience in the naturalistic sense of the term. This is reason understood as the measure of all things, a concept which limits its value because it deprives it of its capacity to be open to Mystery and to be fortified by the workings of Grace. The triumph of this rationalism is explained by adopting literally the formulation given by Henri Daniel-Rops in his induction speech to the Academie Française in 1955 (see pp. 58–9). This dominion of rationalism is described in its slow historical process of affirmation, beginning with the rupture of the unity of the conception of the self and the world which was ensured in the Middle Ages by a human reason open to faith.

This long introduction is not a dense cultural theorization. Rather, it describes the effort our soul makes in living the relationship with God and with Christ every day. The central idea is that only by starting from *present experience* can humans read any past with accuracy. This is an extremely important principle which is easily understood. Christ, knowing that the beginning for human beings is the present, became present – in order to be understood in his origin – in the mystery of Christian communion, in the mystery of the Mystical, that is to say mysterious, Body of Christ. Therefore, it is in an experience of companionship that human beings can penetrate the darkness of the past and discover the light that was already present in it.

This idea then is developed in three parts. The first part presents a concise, simple evaluation of the historical information contained in the Gospels, drawing from it the principal categories of the fact of the Church as such, and discussing the Christian event with certain characteristics that are so elementary as to be axiomatic. (The discovery some years ago of a fragment that in all probability belongs to the Gospel of Mark and can be dated around 50 AD makes us more aware of the contemporaneity with Christ of the historical data.)

What then, are the basic factors of the Christian event which emerge from the texts? They are

- a community,
- comprised of people who are aware that what brings them together is determined by the gift of the Spirit,
- from which derives a new kind of life, a new conception of existence, which is the fruit of a *metanoia*.

The second part describes the terms of development in history of this community's self-awareness, a self-awareness that the Church has of itself in all times in an explicit and mature form: the fact of being composed of the *human* and the *divine*. This part is extremely important from the dialectical point of view. No objections are possible, because everything that is deviant, in terms of human nature and actions, can be contained within the Church because it is made up of human beings.

However, at the same time, it is the bearer of a reality that is not human. And this divine reality is expressed both as knowledge (*Dogma*) and constructive energy (*Grace*). By this new self-awareness and this new capacity for action, in the Church things become possible which would otherwise be impossible either to understand or to do. "By human resources it is impossible, but not for God; because for God everything is possible" (Mark 10:27).

The third part answers this question: "How can we be sure that what the Church claims as the contents of its self-awareness and its capacity for human fulfillment is true?" We could answer immediately that there is *verification,* and that the verification of this is the holiness of life. More precisely, it is a different kind of life that is born in those who try to live the Church. The fundamental characteristic of this type of life is the occurrence of a *unity* (the category of unity is the supreme category of Being as such) which would otherwise be inconceivable. In human beings this becomes the unity of self-conception and self-fulfillment (*holiness*), the unity of a view of reality throughout all historical time (*apostolicity*) and in all human and cultural contexts (*catholicity*).

There is a premise to the development of these four points: certainty comes as the consequence of an experience lived within the Church as such. Lived *experience* means to be immersed in a *present* that involves our whole personality, engaging all the factors that make up a human being. It is the evidence of a living experience. And no proposal or experience exists that corresponds to the factors making up the self in a way that can be compared to the Christian experience.

Truth is beautiful; and in beauty we experience truth. What might be objected to as illusion ("Yes, it's beautiful, but it's an illusion") is refuted by the fact that this is a present experience. The method used by the text to describe these things may not be the best one, but certainly it is a way of pointing to what matters most: to realize what we have among us, Emmanuel, God with us.

Luigi Giussani
November 2000

BOOK ONE

The Claim Continues

PART ONE

1 How to Enter into an Understanding of the Church

1 A FUNDAMENTAL PRESUPPOSITION

The Church is not just an expression of life, something born from life. It *is* a life, a life which has come down to us through many centuries. Anyone seeking to verify a personal opinion of the Church must keep in mind that any real understanding of a life, which is the Church, requires that one share that life in a way that lets him or her know it. Although true understanding of a reality which is somehow bound to life demands time, it is difficult to calculate just how much. In a reality which arises from life, there are characteristics and aspects we never cease to discover and fathom.

The conditio sine qua non for understanding life is *living out a shared existence* with it. Normally, an individual is tempted to set a limit, either a pre-established one upon which, at a certain point, he decides. To avoid the limitations this implies requires a particular position of simplicity and loyalty. Otherwise, a person will restrict the possibility of making a critical judgment about this form of life and concomitantly, make even a minimum of objectivity impossible.

2 BEING IN TUNE WITH THE PHENOMENON

Whatever the position of an individual approaching the Church, it is a reality which can be categorized among religious phenomena. Some might judge it as a falsified, or falsifying religious phenomenon of little interest, while others might take its validity for granted. But in no case,

I believe, can we avoid categorizing it as a religious reality. It is precisely this point that I propose we consider first of all.

The Church is religious "life."

Johannes Lindworsky, a German psychologist and philosopher, in his book, *The Training School of the Will*,[1] argued that the primary condition for any education – the transmission of a certain ability to enter reality – is that the steps taken by the individual approaching reality be constantly motivated by something that somehow rests upon the experience that individual has already acquired. I use the term "somehow" for the precise reason that a person's contacts, encounters, the web of his relationships are all a beckoning to the individual's innermost self, to what is implicit in him; they are an invitation to a more open, a more evolved fulfillment. This web of relationships actuates and then gives us an even greater identity insofar as it calls upon a reality syntonically present within us.

If the Church is a religious reality, then the degree to which the religious aspect within me has not been sparked into life or is childishly retarded will make it more difficult for me to judge that religious fact objectively, with a critical eye. If, for example, we approach a great poet of the past, such as Dante Alighieri or William Shakespeare, we immediately begin to respond to the lines that express feelings alive in us today and, in this way, we find these lines easier to understand. But, on the other hand, when reading other passages where the poet refers to an attitude or a practice of the time in which he lived, which is unique in its own ephemeral circumstances, in its own purely momentary value, it is much more difficult for us to understand. There must be correspondence if there is to be understanding.

There is an explanation, then, for any possible difficulty in approaching a reality of the religious kind, and this can be found in the personal circumstances in which we live, in the sphere of contemporary attitudes. All too easily, the absence of education in the natural religious sense makes us feel that those realities, which are really rooted in our own flesh and our own spirit, are far removed from us, whereas on the contrary, the liveliness of the presence of the religious spirit makes the terms of a reality such as the Church more easily understood. Given this situation, the first difficulty in approaching the Church is a difficulty in understanding. It is a struggle due to the indisposition of the subject in relation to the object to be assessed. This is a problem of understanding caused by the fact that the religious sense has not evolved.

During a conversation I had with a leading university professor, he let slip this remark: "If I didn't have chemistry, I would kill myself." In the very way we take things in something like this is always at play, even if we are not aware of it. There is always something which makes our lives worth living in our own eyes, and while we might not reach the point of wishing to die, without it everything would be colourless and disappointing. Man offers all his devotion to that "something," whatever it may be. There is no need to theorize about it or express it as a mental system, for it could even be an aspect concerning the most banal matter in life. No one can evade being ultimately implicated in all one's actions and, whatever it may be, the moment the human conscience corresponds to it in life, a religiosity is expressed, a level of religiosity is attained.[2] The characteristic proper to the religious sense is that of being the ultimate, inevitable dimension of every gesture, of every action, of every type of relationship. It is a level of asking or an ultimate adherence that is an irremovable part of every instant of life because the depth of its need for meaning is echoed in every passion, initiative, and gesture.

Clearly, if anything were to remain outside of what we call the *ultimate* thing, what we call "god" (whatever our understanding of him may be), then it would no longer be the *ultimate*, the "god." It would mean that there was still something even deeper within in the way we behave, and we would be devoted to that instead. The proof that the religious sense is not adequately educated, as I mentioned earlier, can be found in this precise point: there exists a repugnance in us, a repugnance which has become instinctive, towards the idea that the religious sense might dominate, might consciously determine our every action. This is none other than a symptom of atrophy and merely the partial development of the religious sense in us. It is that widespread burdensome difficulty, that sense of extraneousness we feel when we hear it said that "god" is all-determining, the factor we cannot escape, the criterion by which we make choices, study, produce in our working lives, join a political party, carry out scientific research, look for a wife or a husband, govern a nation. On one hand, education of the religious sense should foster the awareness of the fact that an inevitable and total dependence exists between man and what gives meaning to man's life. On the other, it should help man, through time, to expunge that unrealistic sense of extraneousness he feels towards his original situation.

3 TRAINING THE FOCUS ON THE ORIGINALITY OF CHRISTIANITY

This theme of the religious sense is important for an understanding of the originality of Christianity, which is nothing more than the answer, through Christ and the Church, to our religious sense. Christianity is a solution to the religious problem, and while *not* the means of resolving political, social, and economic problems, the Church is the instrument of this solution.

The gravest errors along all of man's pathways have their origins rooted in the religious sense. And since we have reached the final volume of this trilogy[3] I want to return to the point of departure in our reflection, which, if left undeveloped, becomes a hindrance to every step of the way. If it is developed, however, it becomes the irreplaceable yeast needed for the reasonable progression of the human spirit.

Recalling the earlier quotation from Johannes Lindworsky, we have to say that living the solution that Christianity proposes to the religious problem implies a state of alertness. One must be ever ready to be surprised by the possible correspondence of mind and heart with the subject of the proposal. Without this, any adherence to Christianity is ideological. I would stress that this correspondence is revealed within a living religious sense and is only fostered by its continual education. This gives rise to the hypothesis that the mystery surrounding all things, the hypothesis of revelation in the strictest sense of the term, the hypothesis of the mystery turned into historical fact, manifested itself to man.

The Christian message is that this hypothesis came true. A man said he was God.

At this point, the problem that concerns us is beginning to emerge.

4 THE HEART OF THE CHURCH PROBLEM

How can those who encounter Jesus Christ a day, a month, a hundred, a thousand, or two thousand years after his disappearance from earthly horizons, be enabled to realize that he corresponds to the truth which he claims? In other words, how does one come to see whether Jesus of Nazareth is or is not in a strict sense that event that incarnates the hypothesis of revelation?

This problem is the heart of what history has always called Church.

The word "Church" indicates an historical phenomenon whose only meaning lies in the fact that it enables man to attain a certainty about Christ. It is, in short, the answer to this question: "How can I, who arrived the day after Christ left, know that this really is Something of supreme interest to me, and how can I know this with any reasonable degree of certainty?" We have already noted[4] that, whatever the answer may be, it is impossible to imagine a problem graver than this for a human being. For any person who comes into contact with the Christian message, it is imperative that he or she attempt to obtain a certainty about it, since this is such a decisive issue for his or her life and for the life of the world. The problem can obviously be censored, but considering the nature of the question, that would be like saying "no."

It is important, therefore, that he who comes after the event of Jesus of Nazareth – a long time after – may draw near to him today in such a way as to arrive at a reasonable and certain evaluation befitting the seriousness of the problem. The Church presents itself as the answer to this need for a sure evaluation. This is the theme we are about to deal with. Facing it head on presupposes the seriousness of the question: "In truth, who is Christ?" That is, not only does it presuppose that we make a moral commitment by putting our conscience to work in the face of the historical fact of the Christian message, ultimately, it also assumes a moral seriousness in the life of the religious sense as such.

If, on the contrary, we do not make a commitment to that inevitable and omnipresent aspect of life which is the religious sense, if we think that we have the option not to assume a personal position concerning the historical fact of Christ, then the interest that the Church has for our lives will only be reduced to the level of sociological or political problem or a problem of association to be fought for or defended according to these various points of view. But how degrading for reason to be stripped of an authentic and living religious sense, the one aspect that makes its connective capacity more human and fulfilled! However, it is a fact that, whether we like it or not, whether we resist or come to terms with it, the annunciation of God made man runs right through the entire course of history.

2 The First Premise: How to Attain Certainty about the Fact of Christ Today

In keeping with my constant concern for method, I must at this point formulate two premises, each of which is an answer to a fundamental question and which, as such, are still a means of approaching the problem at hand.

Although the first premise has already been formulated in our introductory reflections, it needs to be re-examined in detail in order to find a suitable answer to the question: "How is it possible today to arrive at an objective evaluation of Christ, that is equal to the importance of the adherence he claims from us?" This is just like saying: "By what method can I reasonably adhere to the Christian proposal?"

In answering this question, the cultural domain splits into camps, and man's attitude towards every aspect of reality is revealed. As old Simeon said when he met Mary and Joseph bringing their little son to the temple: "You see this child: he is destined for the fall and for the rising of many in Israel, destined to be a sign that is rejected ... so that the secret thoughts of many may be laid bare." (Luke 2:34–5). In other words, before him, the soul's most intimate motions, one's deepest moral fibres are destined to surface.

Three cultural attitudes give rise to different answers to this question: one view is rational – it sees Jesus as a fact of the past; the other judges the presence of Jesus through feelings, through enlightenment; while the third one is the Orthodox-Catholic view.

I would stress here, stepping back down from our discussion for a moment, that, within this context, when I say "three cultural attitudes," I do not mean to leaf through three chapters of the cultural history of the West. First and foremost, what I mean implies laying bare the hidden folds that the history of man's conscience has formed in the face of the problem we are tackling here. And what I intend to do is to indicate three ways, which we might adopt, not so much and not only to approach Holy Scripture as to approach the most disparate circumstances of our lives – from a desired encounter to the admiration of a starry sky. For in its most radical value as vision of self and the world, one's cultural attitude invests the very way one approaches one's relationship with all things, and every error in this sphere denotes a temptation to which we are all prey.

I THE RATIONALISTIC ATTITUDE

The first attitude of the three could be summarized as follows: Jesus Christ is a fact of the past, just like Napoleon and Julius Caesar. If this is the case, how can any reasonable man approach the lives of Napoleon and Julius Caesar in such a way as to be able to make an assessment of them? Perhaps the following will explain. Man's reason, in its search for a solution, feels pushed, first of all, to gather all possible information that has come down to us from the past through documents and "sources." Then, in classifying and evaluating these sources, a man's reason will also – and above all – attempt to determine how the fact under examination developed. This means analyzing the mark it left on history, because this element, too, is part of all the documentation that will be useful in forming an assessment. All the information is collated, compared, and weighed until an evaluation is arrived at that will be certain about some factors and uncertain about others.

This is the normal application of the method of reason to a fact of the past. At first glance, it is a system that would raise no objections. I remember that I, too, used this method in my first year of theological studies. However, let us look now at the effects of this attitude when applied to the fact of Christ.

The results of this method, which aims to attain greater certainty about the credibility of Christ's claim, instil in us an initial state of perplexity. What emerges when we have put all of these studies together is, hundreds of different interpretations, the ancient Latin proverb, *Tot capita, tot sententiae,* in action.

At the turn of this century, the great German theologian Albert Schweitzer, still in his youth, took it upon himself to sum up over two and a half centuries of scientific literature on the figure of Christ. In 1906, he published a book destined to become famous. It was called *The History of Research on the Life of Jesus.* I was twenty years old when I read it for the first time, and I can still recall the dramatic sensation that gripped me when, after finishing reading the analysis of its various authors, I began the epilogue of this great study. The author concluded that there were two trends at work in the research on the life of Christ: one dealing with the problems of limited sources and the other apocalyptic or eschatological.

Concerning the first trend, some of the authors argued that there were not enough sources to provide us with a certain image of the figure of Christ, and because of this, Christ would remain, in the final analysis, someone unknown to us. This conclusion cannot but remind us of Saint Paul as he stood in the Areopagus in Athens and praised the Athenians because they honoured their gods. By this, he meant to praise them for the religious sense expressed in their polytheism, and, in doing so, he manifested an openness of spirit still lacking today in those who are not at peace with their Christianity. But after his eulogy he added: "I noticed as I strolled around admiring your sacred monuments, that you had an altar inscribed: To an unknown God. Well, the God whom I proclaim is in fact the one whom you already worship without knowing it" (Acts 17:23). This was the way, then, that Saint Paul introduced himself to the people of Athens to reveal to them how that unknown god had let himself be known. According to this point of view, therefore, after centuries of study, that God has gone back to being *unknown territory*.

The other tendency that emerged from the young German theologian's remarkable study is the apocalyptic or eschatological one. This view argues that Jesus was one of many who, at the time, were waiting for the imminent end of the world, and it was in this sense that he understood the true meaning of his life. If this were the case, however, the figure of Christ would thus be *strange*, it would be extraneous to the men and women of today. According to Albert Schweitzer:

The study of the life of Jesus has had a curious history. It set out in quest of the historical Jesus, believing that when it had found Him it could bring Him straight into our time as a Teacher and Savior. It loosed the bands by which He had been riveted for centuries to the stony rocks of ecclesiastical doctrine, and rejoiced to see life and movement coming into the figure once more, and the historical Jesus advancing, as it seemed, to meet it. But He does not stay; He passes by our time and returns to His own. What surprised and dismayed the theology of the last forty years was that, despite all forced and arbitrary interpretations, it could not keep Him in our time, but had to let Him go. He returned to His own time, not owing to the application of any historical ingenuity, but by the same inevitable necessity by which the liberated pendulum returns to its original position. ...

It is not given to history to disengage that which is abiding and eternal in the being of Jesus from the historical forms in which it worked itself out, and to introduce it into our world as a living influence. It has toiled in vain at this undertaking. As a water-plant is beautiful so long as it is growing in the water, but once it is torn from its roots, withers and becomes unrecogniz- able, so it is with the historical Jesus when He is wrenched loose from the soil of eschatology, and the attempt is made to conceive Him "historically" as a Being not subject to temporal conditions. The abiding and eternal in Jesus is absolutely independent of historical knowledge and can only be understood by contact with His spirit which is still at work in the world. In proportion as we have the Spirit of Jesus we have the true knowledge of Jesus.[1]

This great theologian, who was also a talented musician, concluded that since his reason could only lead to "aimless wandering" as far as the historical figure of Jesus was concerned, and since he felt the vitality of this Jesus who had been proclaimed to him, he abandoned theology and went to Africa, striving to follow Jesus in his work as a doctor healing the sick. Albert Schweitzer founded a hospital at Lambaréné where he died after a life dedicated to the needy. In this way, as perfectly formed a Protestant as he was, he overcame the fragile incapacity of theoretical reason with the reason of the heart. In any event, the conclusion he reached as a young man remains acute because later exegetical studies, carried out by perhaps more expert methods and supported by new discoveries, all arrived, somehow, at one or the other of the two tendencies – the historical – and the apocalyptic – pointed out by him. Schweitzer was, therefore, ingeni- ous in pin-pointing the inevitable limitation or impossibility of the kind of solution that the application of this method must generate.

Let us call this first attitude the *rationalistic attitude.*

Remember, if you will, that rationalism, as a mental position is born of that concept of reason which sees reason as the measure of all things. If, as this position contends, reason is the measure of all things, then the ultimate reason for things is the one our reason gives them. This attitude, then, implies projecting dimensions – which reason has already fixed and recognizes – onto reality and whatever presumes to go beyond these measures *does not exist* by an a priori definition. However, this position contradicts the supreme law of realism which we have already had occasion to discuss in the first volume of this trilogy whereby the object dictates the method of knowledge.[2] This is only possible, however, if we affirm a concept of reason as awareness of reality in the totality of all of its factors.

If, indeed, reason is this total consciousness of reality, then there is the possibility of something new, that is, it is possible to discover the existence of something beyond the confines of our measure. Rationalism is the abolition of the realm of possibility: if, in fact, something is only possible if it is measurable – or dominable – by measures within our grasp, the real category of the possible is truly repudiated. Rationalism denies the possible existence of something whose nature goes beyond the bounds of the limited horizons man can reach, however flexible they may be.

It is crucial that we keep this observation in mind with regards to the Christian fact. If we were to approach the fact of Jesus as if it were a mere fact of the past, we would not be able to say anything certain about such an extraordinary message. But from an ethical-moral point of view, we are inclined to ask: if this message is so important for man, how can it possibly be reasonable (that is, befitting the gravity of the problem) for it to remain within the realm of the aimless wandering of his reason? This opens us up to an understanding of the real motive of the rationalistic attitude. In reality, the rationalistic attitude *diminishes the content of the Christian message even before taking it into consideration.* The Christian message is: Emmanuel, to use the Gospel word that appears in the Christmas liturgy, "God-with-us." The Christian message is that God has made himself a human, carnal presence in history.

For 2,000 years, the history of humanity has transmitted to us the voices of men, women, and children, undistinguished by sex, age, social position, or cultural formation; they are voices that ask, like the angels in Luke's account on the morning of the resurrection, "Why look among the dead for someone who is alive" (Luke 24:5)? Some of these voices reach us from far-off times.

Take the words of Origen, that great erudite of the third century eastern Church, for example: "In the outbreak at Smyrna, in the middle of the second century ... the sufferers were conspicuous for their serene calmness. 'They made it evident to us all,' says the Epistle of the Church of Smyrna, 'that in the midst of those sufferings ... the Lord stood by them and walked in the midst of them.'"[3] And with Origen, let us add: "So that which the prophet said is fulfilled in us: 'I will dwell in them and walk within them.'"[4] Other voices such as the voice of the great convert, John Henry Newman, are closer to us in time: "Christianity is a living truth which never can grow old. Some persons speak of it as if it were a thing of history, with only indirect bearing upon modern times; I cannot allow that it is a mere historical religion. Certainly it has its foundations in past and glorious memories, but its power is in the present."[5] It is as if the theologian Friedrich von Hügel were adding to this when he said: "For a Person came, and lived and loved, and did and taught, and died and rose again, and lives on by his Power and his Spirit forever within us and among us, so unspeakably rich and yet so simple, so sublime and yet, so homely, so divinely above us precisely in being so divinely near."[6] And let us conclude with the words of Karl Adam: "As the history of Christianity shows, it is a life, which manifesting its power first in the Person of Jesus, not merely laid hold of the restricted group of His disciples, but in an incredibly short space of time gripped the whole ancient world and brought into being new civilisations, new peoples, new men, and which still alive and effectual among us, attests itself to our own day as a perennial source of spiritual life".[7]

To approach such a message with what we have called a rationalistic attitude would mean emptying the Christian message of its content. It would be just like saying: "To verify if Jesus Christ really is God present with us, the method is to cast him back into the distance, as distant as the divine was before making himself man, to cast him back into a state of absence from the present." In this way, the terms in which the problem is posed fall away.

The Christian message tells us that God made himself a presence in history: "God is with us." To verify this, the rationalistic attitude places the question within terms antecedent to the message itself, reformulating the problem in the same way that all man's religious striving has formulated it in the attempt to build a bridge between one's ephemeral circumstance and the mystery.[8] If Christ is an entity 2,000 years away from us, we strive with every means of scientific research to overcome this remoteness. Even though the Christian message says, "God has made himself present," the rationalistic attitude works on the hypothesis of his absence.

The rationalistic attitude, as we have described it, may be the attitude of each one of us. It tends to lead the mind back to a concept which in any case is more familiar. It is a mystery to us that God made himself a human presence, and faced with the Christian message, we are always tempted to reduce God, ever present, to the level of the images we have of presence and absence. And, this is not new, that men have always tried to understand their relationship with God in this way – this is how the various religions were born. However, what is new in the hypothesis of Christian revelation is that God is not a distant fact towards which man strives with great effort. Rather he is Someone who has joined man on his path, who has become his companion. To assess whether this hypothesis is true, the rationalistic method eliminates it, emptying it of its specific content, which is the nature of his presence. And by casting the event of Christ back to the remote past, using the approach that considers him an historical fact in order to ascertain the truthfulness of that claim, prevents us from considering what makes up the very essence of that claim: God as a human presence along man's pathway.

We must obviously note here that while the rationalistic position wants to consider Christ as an historical fact, it calls "historical" only what it sees as historical, and, in conceiving of reason as the only measure of reality, this attitude finds itself the victim of the consequences of this, its own formulation, even as far as the historical fact is concerned. It excludes the possibility that a fact that does not have the characteristics it has predetermined might be historical. In this sense, the rationalistic attitude appears to be decidedly against anything new, against the realm of possibility. If the fact announced or described were a miracle, the mental position we are examining here would not consider it historical for that very reason. So, then we must ask: can a fact that is different from anything we can imagine happen at all? One amazing passage from the Bible in which God sets man face to face with his radical disproportion with respect to the possibility contained in the origin of all things, their reality and existence, can be found in the book of Job:

> Where were you when I laid the earth's foundations?
> Tell me, since you are so well informed!
> Can you guide the morning season by season
>   and show the Bear and its cubs which way to go? ...
> Have you grasped the celestial laws?
> Could you make their writ run on the earth?
> Can your voice carry as far as the clouds
>   and make the pent-up waters do your bidding? ...
> Do you know how mountain goats give birth,
>   or have you ever watched the hinds in labor?
> How many months do they carry their young?
> At what time do they give birth? ...
> Does the hawk take flight on your advice
>   when he spreads his wings to travel south?
> Does the eagle soar at your command
>   to make her eyrie in the heights?
> (Job 38:4,32–4; 39:1–2,26–7)

Job, won over by the long, almost interminably detailed description of God's power, his imagination, and his loving care for his creatures, answers: "I know that you are all-powerful: what you conceive, you can perform" (Job 42:2).

What is real is not what we, a priori, establish as such, and if what we have to evaluate is the content of the Christian message, it is logical to look at it straight in the eye, face to face, and not at what we already believe it to be. It may well be that having done this, we will judge it to be untrue. However, it should at least be considered for what it is: God become presence, a companion for men and women, whom he will never, ever leave.

This affirmation is precisely the only interesting one to verify – God who is present, is with us, is alive. This is the content of the message regarding Jesus Christ, and any other would be a serious contradiction of the method God chose in order to reveal himself to man. It is a question of freeing ourselves from giving first place to our effort to identify ourselves with or to formulate a mystical actualization of the past. For this is an imposing feat of interpretation for our reason and our feelings that God could not possibly ask us to perform, to pursue as if it were the usual pathway to him, He whose pedagogy has proved so rich in compassion for man.

2 AN INNER ENLIGHTENMENT

Let us now examine the second attitude. This is a profoundly religious position, and as such, has a clear perception of the interminable distance between man and God – God, the different, the Other, the Mystery. This position recognizes the "ultimate reason" as being much greater than man because the human mind cannot imagine its nature, the human imagination cannot define it as the source of a possibility.[9] This is why the religious man who lives the realm of possibility so intensely is like the angel who tells Mary when she is troubled at the annunciation of Jesus' conception: "For nothing will be impossible to God" (Luke 1.37).

This attitude we are now studying is well disposed, therefore, to understand that if everything is possible for God, then the content of the great message is also possible: God become presence, God made an experience in the here and now. But how can man become certain of this presence, the truth of this experience? Man is powerless to do this, since this presence is destined to remain a mystery. It is the spirit of God itself which enlightens the heart, and inspiring it, makes one "feel" the truth of the person of Jesus. It is recognition by means of an inner experience. This describes the fulcrum of the *Protestant* attitude. Through contact with the book – the Bible – which God wanted man to write as a reminder of his relationships with him, or through fragments generated by a history of faith, or spurred on by the accents of a certain tradition, or an evocation in the here and now, man's heart comes alive and understands what is right and what is not right with regard to Jesus. Therefore, to reach that distant Christ, that fact (which the great theologian Karl Barth called "contact by tangent": the quick, immeasurable, unimaginable entrance of God in man's history on earth), the Protestant method uses an interior, direct relationship with the Spirit, an interior encounter.

This is how C.F. Stäudlin, a nineteenth-century Protestant theologian, criticizing the historical method, describes the way in which the words of Jesus can come alive for us: "Jesus' teaching is not merely something historical, not merely a part of history, not simply of a historical nature; it also contains eternal, unchangeable, divine truths which one can fully explain to himself and make comprehensible to others, never on the ground of history and grammar alone, but rather by one's own spirit, by meditation, by elevation to ideas of the reason, and from [the truths] themselves."[10] The interior nature of the encounter defined by the words and teaching of Jesus takes on an even more evocative tone in these phrases of J.E. Weiss, a theologian writing in the first decade of our century:

A tempestuous enthusiasm, an overwhelming intensity of feeling, an immediate awareness of the presence of God, an incomparable sense of power, and an irresistible control over the will and inner spirit and even the physical condition of other men – these are the ineradicable features of the historical picture of early Christianity. ... Anyone who is accustomed to find fresh strength and uplift in prayer will recognize at once what early Christian belief in the Spirit implied, and no amount of scholarship is adequate to explain it away. Religious experience is an area which in the end resists analysis and rational explanation.[11]

Technically speaking, this was the experience of the prophets. The prophet was set apart from the rest of his people precisely because, as events transpired, he heard a message in them others did not hear. His conscience was enlightened by this message, and he was made the interpreter of God's own reality. Protestantism has always highlighted these Old Testament figures because it has seen its spirit expressed in them. However, we will see if this position is fully justified. It must be said, moreover, that this cultural attitude, which judges the presence of Jesus through feelings, is also the easiest and the most apparently comprehensible one for Catholics. If we cannot "feel" something, it leaves us cold and perplexed. On the other hand, if we can "feel" it, we are confident and trusting. And if this is assumed as a criterion, we are each our own judge, we are each our own prophet. Therefore, if from one point of view the Protestant attitude is the opposite of the rationalistic – because it is religious in the purest of ways, dominated as it is by the fact that Being is totally beyond any human measure, and everything is possible for Him – from another standpoint, to a certain extent, the danger exists of identifying one attitude with the other (it is not by chance that, in the Christian field, rationalism became widespread in the Protestant world). In fact, the common denominator of both positions is an ultimate subjectivism.

Protestant subjectivism provokes two questions. First, how can one determine whether what one "feels" is the result of the Spirit's influence or the idealization of one's own thoughts? How can this method be stripped of its ambiguity? Let us return to the example of the prophets of Israel. We must remember that these prophets were adept at shielding themselves from the danger of subjectivism. The prophet was a gift for the people, and it was precisely his relationship with them that verified everything he said: Time and the history of the people were the verification of his words. The prophet's challenge to the people lies in the passage of time: "Time will prove me right," declares the prophet. So the prophet, in the true sense of the word, has, by his very role, the people and time, the history of the people, as his own objective means of verification. But if every man were his own prophet, how could a distinction be drawn between an enlightenment by the Spirit and the codification of one's own concept, between an experience wrought from On High and the expression of a personal opinion, between the experience of God within me and the pretension of a passion of mine.

The second question provoked by Protestant subjectivism asks: How could it possibly be that in its intention to come into contact with man in order to help him, the Spirit itself decided to use a method that would heighten confusion – a feat, unfortunately, that man was already perfectly capable of performing himself? This question is similar to our first observation of the rationalistic attitude and in practice, gives rise to an infinite number of interpretations, different solutions, to an inevitable muddling of theories. However, this is certainly not the fundamental objection to Protestant subjectivism. If he had wanted to, the Lord could have used a purely individual relationship with the human spirit to convey his message, and we cannot say, a priori, that such an eventuality is or is not possible. On the contrary, the real objection to this attitude is that it does not respect the facts of the Christian message, its original connotations: one who is divine became man, a man who ate, drank, slept, a man one could meet on the street, a person one could encounter by stepping out the door of one's house, in the middle of a small group of others while talking – and his words struck one's soul. What he said changed people within, but they were words that came from without. This is to say, the Christian message is a *wholly* human fact according to all the factors of human reality, factors interior and exterior, subjective and objective. The Protestant attitude annuls this wholeness, reducing the Christian experience to a *merely interior* experience, and, in the process, assumes an a priori position to which it has no right.

3 THE ORTHODOX-CATHOLIC VIEW

The third attitude we will consider – that of the Christian tradition proper – is the most adequate, that is, the reasonable way to attain certainty about the message of Jesus Christ. I have called it the Orthodox-Catholic view because Orthodoxy and Catholicism share the same vision. This attitude is the realization of the whole tradition, to which, at a certain point in their itineraries, every other position had to oppose this already-consolidated tradition. The main characteristic of the Orthodox-Catholic attitude is that it is consistent with the structure of the Christian event as it presented itself in history.

How did it present itself in history? It presented itself as the news or the proclamation of God, the Mystery made "flesh," made a wholly human presence, in exactly the same way that friends are a completely human presence to each other when they meet in the street and a mother is a wholly human presence for the child with whom she shares her life. People could talk to Jesus, they could argue, react, or adhere to what he said in the town squares, and he could answer and correct them. Something distinctly objective educated man's subjectivity. The existence of this entirely human presence implies the method of *encounter*, of the chance meeting with a reality external to the self, an objective, eminently "encounterable" presence that, while "outside" of the self, moves the heart. (The word "encounter" has an exterior connotation just as decisive as the interior one.)

This is what must have happened to those who met him. But what of today, 2,000 years later? How can this wholly human presence be encountered by the man of today, 2,000 years later?

Let us look at the tenth chapter of Luke's Gospel account. In this narrative, many wanted to see Jesus, to be healed by him, to meet him. Unable to visit all the towns and villages, he began to send his closest followers to the places he could not reach. First, he sent the twelve he had chosen, and then about seventy other disciples, in two's so they could tell people what had happened with his coming. The disciples returned full of enthusiasm because people listened to them, miracles occurred, individuals believed, and were changed. So, what kind of face did the God made a human presence have for those who listened to – or put up with – the first two sent by Jesus to the first village? What did he look like to them? He had the face and appearance of those two disciples. For, as they set out, Jesus had told them: "Anyone who listens to you listens to me" (Luke 10:16).

So even when Jesus was at the height of his earthly activity, the event that he was assumed an identifiable form that was not merely his external, physical appearance, but also that of those who believed in him; so much so that they were sent by him to convey his words – his message – to reproduce his prodigious acts, to bring the salvation that *his* person was. The so-named Orthodox-Catholic approach shows us this method for reaching Jesus Christ even today, so that we can verify whether his great claim is real or not, whether he is God or not, whether the Christian message is true or not. This method is the chance encounter with a reality comprised of those who believe in him. For the presence of Christ in history – the visible appearance – visibly abides in the unity of believers, which is the encounterable form of his presence. Historically speaking, this reality is called "church," sociologically "the people of God," and ontologically, in the profound sense of the word, the "mysterious Body of Christ," an expression which, while touching the depths of the question, clarifies its method to a certain extent.

The energy with which Christ is destined to possess all history and the whole world – every single thing was placed into his hands by the Father – the energy with which he is destined to be the Lord of the world and of history is the means whereby he assimilates to himself the people the Father entrusts to him, the persons upon whom the Spirit bestows the gift of faith in Him. This assimilation is ontological and cannot be directly experienced by us. This energy takes hold of the believer in such a way as to assimilate him as a part of the mystery of Christ's own person. Saint Paul sensed this when, thrown from his horse, he heard a voice saying to him: "Saul, Saul, why are you persecuting me?" (Acts 9:4). He did not even know Christ, and yet he was persecuting people who believed in him. Paul would give form and clarity to this intuition of his when later he would say that the unity we have with Christ makes us members of the one body: "Though there are many of us we form a single body." (1 Cor. 10:17). It is in this very realistic way that we become members, one of the other (cf. Eph. 4:25).

To express this same reality, the Gospel cites the characteristic Mediterranean imagery of vines: "I am the vine, you are the branches. Whoever remains in me, with me in him, bears fruit in plenty; for cut off from me you can do nothing" (John 15:5). And when Saint John says in his first letter: "Something which has existed since the beginning, that we have heard, and we have seen with our own eyes, that we have watched and touched with our hands: the Word, who is life – this is our subject. That life was made visible: we saw it and we are giving our testimony, telling you of eternal life which was with the Father and has been made visible to us. What we have seen and heard we are telling you so that you too may be in union with us" (1 John 1:1–3), he is voicing a most beautiful expression of the method of the Christian message – it is the truth become flesh, a God made presence, who even after 70, 100, or 2,000 years reaches you through a reality that you can see, touch, and feel. This is the company of believers in him.

Sometimes these formulas are repeated in the Christian world as if they were metaphors incapable of touching the imagination and the heart's real interests, of constituting the expressiveness of a human fact – an expressiveness which even the term "word" itself also possesses, if it is not used in the diminishingly abstract way characteristic of western intellectual thinking. A word always indicates someone who expresses himself.

This then is a brief exposition of the conception with which all Christian tradition – conserved in Orthodoxy and Catholicism – defines the method by which the Christian event realizes itself, by which it endures in history. It is by encountering the unity of believers that we quite literally meet up with Christ, by encountering the Church as it emerges in the way it has been fixed by the Spirit. To encounter the Church, I must meet men and women in given surroundings. It is impossible to encounter the universal Church in its entirety, for this is an abstract image: we meet the Church as it emerges locally, in each environment. And in one's encounters with it, one has the chance to be serious in a critical way, so that any possible adherence to it – and this is, indeed, serious, because the whole meaning of life depends upon it – may be totally reasonable.

It cannot be denied that on one hand, this method challenges our reason in exactly the same way as Christ, the man, challenged the Pharisees's reason: it is the mystery of God that is present. On the other hand, neither can it be denied that, in terms of method, we find ourselves within the same dynamics that were verified 2,000 years ago.

The Orthodox-Catholic attitude conceives of the Christian message as the invitation to a present and wholly human experience – an objective encounter with an objective human reality. This reality is profoundly significant for man's innermost being, giving a meaning to and provoking a change in life, and therefore, penetrating the person in exactly the same way as it did 2,000 years ago. Even at that time, one could experience the Christian event by simply coming upon an objective reality: a man people could listen to, look at, touch with their hands, but a man who penetrated the person, deeply provoking him to a new experience, a new life.

The ways in which this encounter takes place obviously evolve through time, just as adulthood has developed from the state of childhood. But the structure of the phenomenon remains identical. More precisely, the reality of Christ becomes present. It becomes an existential encounter in all ages through the human form chosen by him, as if it flowed inexorably from him in history, as the tangible experience of his divine reality. As Karl Adam wrote:

> We Catholics acknowledge readily, without any shame, nay with pride, that Catholicism cannot be identified simply and wholly with primitive Christianity, nor even with the Gospel of Christ, in the same way that the great oak cannot be identified with the tiny acorn. There is no mechanical identity, but an organic identity ... and the continual emergence of new forms. The Gospel of Christ would have been no living gospel, and the seed which He scattered no living seed, if it had remained ever the tiny seed of A.D. 33, and had not struck root, and had not assimilated foreign matter, and had not by the help of this foreign matter grown up into a tree, so that the birds of the air dwell in its branches.[12]

We must conclude therefore that the original dynamism of the Christian fact tends to be diminished in the first and second positions, while it is undeniably analogous to or consistent with the third attitude we have described.

4 A GAZE THAT VALUES THE OTHER POSITIONS

In concluding this first premise, I would like to stress that the first two attitudes we have studied do highlight certain values, and that these values are recognized and recovered in what we have described as the third attitude.

a) Not only does this third attitude not eliminate or censor historical enquiry, it places a person in a condition to make a more adequate use of that enquiry. Let us recall the words of Henri de Lubac:

> God acts in history and reveals himself through history. Or rather, God inserts himself in history and so bestows on it a "religious consecration" which compels us to treat it with due respect. ... From the first creation to

the last end, through material opposition and the more serious opposition of created freedom, a divine plan is in operation, accomplishing its successive stages among which the Incarnation stands out as chief. So in close connection with the social character of dogma there is another character, equally essential, and that is the historic.[13]

Historical sources amount to words that express and document a type of experience of the past. What we need "today" is to possess the spirit and the consciousness proper of that experience which gave rise to the Gospels 2,000 years ago. Only in this way can the true message of those texts be grasped. The following example will illustrate my point.

Let us imagine that an Italian engages in a relationship with a Japanese girl during a visit to the United States, and that after a year they have to part because the girl has to return to Japan. Let us also suppose that she is very attached to the traditions of her country and she lives them with the heart of a poet. While separated, they exchange letters; the girl's are rich in references and imagery which sound strange to the western ear. However, during that time of intimacy, the boy had entered into the same spirit as hers. He had attuned himself to all of the aspects of her spirit, affection, mind, and imagination. Let us further suppose that one of these letters falls into the hands of the boy's mother. The mother is greatly disturbed by the girl's language, and her concern for her son grows because those words sound to her like the ramblings of a vaguely unbalanced mind. Patiently, the son tries to explain that what his mother finds so disconcerting is the fruit of a different logic, an imaginative structure distinct from what we Westerners are accustomed. However, his mother does not really understand him. The question is, then, "Which is more objective, the son's or the mother's reading of the Japanese girl's leters?" From a purely literal point of view, the mother's interpretation would seem to be more objective. However, from the perspective of understanding the contents of those letters, the son's is evidently much more objective. Indeed, his reading is the only objective one of the two, for the word expresses a spirit, a type of consciousness, and the boy, who had drawn so close to the spirit and mind of the girl, was able to grasp her mode of expression.

But how can one come to have the experience which dictates the words? To attain this, one needs an encounter, something *present*. One needs to meet that experience today. It is only by participating in the particular experience which dictated certain texts or produced a certain literary expression that they can be understood with the fullness that unveils their objective meaning, and that the unity underlying them and consistently expressed in them can be easily perceived. This is the great openness and peace to be found in the Catholic reading of the Bible and the texts of early Christianity. The indescribable interpretative confusion is avoided (the confusion generated by other approaches), the "ifs" and "buts" weighing on every attempt at reading are dispelled, and above all, a total interpreta tion emerges – one that overlooks nothing, an all-embracing, exhaustive point of view. The least that can be said is that, even in the framework of all the possible hypotheses, one cannot question the reasonableness of the Catholic interpretation, which above all, highlights the wholeness and the simplicity of the event.

The objective nature of historical knowledge, which is the value the rationalistic attitude seeks to affirm, is retained if one participates in the experience that dictated those historical texts. There is only one hypothesis: that the experience be present, that it have a place now. This place is the Church; it is the unity of believers within it.

This observation, however, is valid for any text. We need humanity to understand the human experience that became the *Iliad* and the *Odyssey*, the human factor that became *The Divine Comedy*. Humanity needs to be in me if I am to comprehend the humanity expressed in Leopardi's *Canti*. Those who are arid, whose humanity is not developed, do not understand. In order to penetrate any literary or historical fact, we must activate, in our historical inquiry, the human root within us, which is developed and asserted in the present experience, and which is, substantially, the same experience that gave birth to those events and those texts. But if the Event is divine, if the texts in question intend to report precisely this divine event, then our observation about method also remains valid – and evidently the only hypothesis for a truly adequate enquiry is a living participation in the presence of that same divine fact.

b) Let us now examine the underlying value of the Protestant attitude: the idea that the Absolute, independent of human deviations, can reveal itself directly to its creation. This is what is called mystical experience.

How can we describe this mystical experience? Perhaps the following will illustrate my point. Is a man's impetus to admire, to contemplate the woman he loves greater when he imagines her or when he is face to face with her? Mystical contemplation – let's call it that – is a thousand times more powerful in the presence of our object of love than when it relies upon our albeit intense affection from afar. That is why there have been so many Catholic mystics, and the greatest mystics as well! Love for the object is much more compelling when the object sets the tone of a scene by its presence than when our imagination sets it before us with its projection of sentiment, which is necessarily more vague.

If the divine is an existential encounter, an experience wholly human, then coexistence with it strengthens its decisive evidence and reinforces rational conviction. Evidence is the fundamental way by which man knows and his conviction grows as the object becomes familiar to his eyes. God has prized this natural dynamism. The divine in Christianity is communicated through a personal experience, and ingeniously the Protestant approach senses the novelty of Christianity as inspiration. What this attitude is unlikely to generate is an intimate, concrete, and respectful familiarity (like the familiarity of children with their mother) and a well-founded rationality, both of which derive from a belonging which is experienced and lived. The Hebrew notion of "body" clarifies this concept. In the Semitic languages, "body" has a broader meaning: it also indicates what man produces – the whole spectrum of the I's tangible expressions. A son is part of the body of his father and mother, as is the work of an artist one body with him and his personality. Similarly Christ – as we have already said – invests man so profoundly that man is part of him, one body with him. From this is born an experience to which the image of a body – even according to the above, broader meaning – is only a pale allusion. But in it we can catch glimpses of more intense human experiences, such as the artistic or affective ones. In these experiences, we can have the first fruits of that one experience of concrete unity, that more than concrete unity between Christ and "those who are his own," a unity exceeding the limits of our nature, yet inscribed within it. To continue with the analogy, when the experience of love, for example, is clear and powerful, unity becomes like a the prophetic jolt, a type of unity that for now is unimaginable. It is that obscure yet splendid adventure which, like art, leads to a greater reality, an all-surpassing reality.

I would like to conclude by noting that these observations of the three distinct attitudes constitute the keys to the Christian problem from spiritual and intellectual points of view. For the attitude – even if it is a practical one – that we apply so often to the Christian problem depends on the type of education imparted to us, a type not clearly based on the third attitude, but on a heterogenous and muddled profusion of references.

3 The Second Premise: The Contemporary Difficulty in Understanding the Meaning of Christian Words[1]

In the introduction, I mentioned the difficulties experienced by contemporary man in approaching a reality of the religious type. These difficulties pertain, first of all, to understanding and then only adhering. Fredrich Nietzsche was fully mindful of this when, in his *Beyond Good and Evil*, he commented on the insensibility of his contemporaries to the Christian paradox of the Incarnation and the Crucifixion in particular, and when he spoke of "men of modern times whose intelligence is so obtuse that it no longer grasps the meaning of Christian language."[2]

How is it that today's man is so hampered in becoming aware of the meaning of words directly linked to the Christian experience? And this lack of original attunement generates difficulty in understanding the very expression of the Christian message, in that it is conveyed in history by that form of a presence which is the unity of believers, or "Church."

In order to reply to this, I would like to return briefly to the formation, over the centuries, of the perplexity we feel today about recognizing a religious sense of *life* and, therefore, about a proposal that tends to base all of life under the Mastery of God.

I first became aware of this condition of ours as modern men when, years ago at Assisi, I had the opportunity to hear the silver trumpets of the town's brass band accompanying a medieval hymn. It was the hymn of the Assisi sentinels, and the words urged vigilance and alertness in defending the city from enemies and the soul from attacks of evil. The words of that hymn stirred an instinctive feeling of vexation in me. I felt as if a part of me were extraneous to that rallying call to defend the city and preserve the soul from mortal sin. This sense of extraneousness corresponds exactly to the difficulty one may experience in considering the religious factor the all-determining one. Perhaps an image may clarify this. In the past, an attack on a steep rocky escarpment, entailed a march towards it, and demanded much time and energy. Today, in contrast, we have the means, in a very short time, to reach a rock or an edifice we are to climb. In this way, the composers of the Assisi sentinels' hymn were like an Alpine regiment today – so easily did they discern the religious element as a link with life that they had cable cars that brought them up to the base of the mountain cliffs, while we are like the climbers of a century ago who first had to face a long march to the rock face. In the past, men were able to approach the words deriving from the Christian experience in a vigorous and undaunted way, while today, we arrive at the wall of those words tired before we have even begun to scale it.

2 THE MIDDLE AGES FROM THE POINT OF VIEW OF DISSEMINATING A MENTALITY

We have said that the composers – and probably the singers – of that Assisi sentinels' hymn did not arrive as we do, breathless and exhausted by the long march towards the attack on the wall of expressions born of the Christian life. No, they tackled those expressions with more serenity, and medieval culture should undoubtedly be considered the primary cause of this greater syntony in approach.

Medieval culture fostered the formation of an attitude whose distinguishing feature was an authentic religious sense – an authentic religious sense determined by an image of God as the totalizing horizon of every human action, and, therefore, a conception of God as pertinent to all aspects of life, underlying every human experience excluding none. In other words, a conception of God as the unifying ideal. The English historian Christopher Dawson, viewed this aspect of medieval civilization in this way:

One of the most remarkable features of mediaeval guild life was the way in which it combined secular and religious activities in the same social complex. The guild chantry, the provision of prayers and masses for deceased brethren, and the performance of pageants and mystery plays on the great feasts were no less a function of the guild than the common banquet, the regulation of work and wages, the giving of assistance to fellow guild-men in sickness or misfortune and the right to participate in the government of the city. For it was in the life of the Church and the extension of the liturgy into common life by art and pageantry that the community-life of the mediaeval city found its fullest expression."[3]

Anticipating today's bewilderment at the structural complexity of a society which, in terms of ways of life and ambits that form a mentality, could be called a Christian civilization, Dawson again points out:

But, it will be asked, is not the idea of a return to Christian civilisation irreconcilable with the conditions of the modern world which are accepted today by Christians as well as secularists? Certainly there can be no question of a return to the old regime of the alliance between Church and State or the ecclesiastical domination of society. But this does not mean that we can afford to reject the ideal of a Christian civilisation ... The kingdom of God is a universal kingdom: there is no aspect of human life that stands outside it or which is not in some way tributary to it. It is in the nature of Christianity to be a world-transforming movement."[4]

What can it mean to grow up within a culture in which the concept of God is an authentic one, in which the pondered, imagined, experienced God is truly God, or, as we have already stated, someone whom nothing escapes? A popular Italian proverb counsels: "Not a leaf falls without God willing." Evocatively and dramatically, the Gospel anticipates the meaning of this when it reports what Jesus taught: "Why, every hair on your head has been counted" (Matt. 10:30).

One particular encounter with a television director left a lasting impression on me. In the course of our conversation, I had quoted this phrase from the Gospel. The director, as if its meaning had come as a surprise to him, was reluctant to believe that the Gospel's concept of life could be so concrete, and almost thinking out loud, he kept repeating, "But that's impossible!" However – and this can never be emphasized enough – God's penetration of life to such an extent is the inevitable consequence of a God conceived in the right way. Only a God perceived for what he is – the ultimate substance of all life – is a credible God, because conviction comes when every aspect of existence is bonded with a universally determining value.

In this sense, then, the Middle Ages are not to be considered a more interesting epoch than others just because at that time everyone was more devout or capable of behaving in a less morally reproachable way. No, it was more interesting, because it was characterized by a unitary mentality. If we derive our personality from a living Reality, then its root in our consciousness is the criterion with which we see and by which we manage things.

Dawson warns us that "a Christian civilisation is certainly not a perfect civilisation. But it is a civilisation that accepts the Christian life-style as normal."[5] Now it might be said – although in a somewhat banal but concise way – that the Middle Ages witnessed a widespread religious culture, where men were helped to grasp the fact that the religious sense coincides with man's interest in the whole meaning of his life, that the reality of God is the origin of his human personality and the determining factor in his evolution.

This point explains some apparently contradictory phenomena whereby several dramatic antinomies have emerged throughout the ages: for example, religiosity as a declaration of peace (Franciscanism) and religion as a pretext for wars (the Crusades); the exaltation of one's fellow man as freedom in the face of the infinite and the attempt to bend man's will with violence (the Inquisition). If we highlight the negative aspect of these antinomies, as modern culture often does, we will never find the reasons for them. Rather, we must try to discern the source of each one.

Let me try to clarify this point by relating an imaginary – though not an altogether improbable – episode which has some rather paradoxical elements. (As Father de Lubac teaches us: "For paradox exists everywhere in reality, before existing in thought. It is everywhere in permanence. It is for ever reborn ... The synthesis of the world has not been made. As each truth becomes better known, it opens up a fresh area for paradox ... Paradox, in the best sense, is objectivity.")[6] Let us imagine, then, that we have travelled back to the height of the Middle Ages and we know that there are four thugs in the pay of a certain petty lord who has ordered them to kidnap a nun from a convent. It would not be unlikely if the narrator of this lamentable tale were to tell us that the four thugs said a "Hail Mary" before they set out, in the hope of pulling off the job successfully. Here we have one of those antinomies mentioned earlier. What elements does this imaginary episode present for our analysis? On one hand, there is a principle that is quite right – the sign of a truth the social framework recognizes – that God is Lord of everything. Evidently, however, this principle was wrongly applied, not because God could be appealed to at all times only on devout occasions, but because we cannot ask for God's help in carrying out an objectively evil act.

In the same way, proper to an age when fratricidal divisions bloodied lands and cities, there rose the incarnate symbol of fraternal unity among all men who were all equal in the sight of the infinite, ultimate ideal, to whose judgment they all felt subject, and for which they all ultimately yearned. This is the miracle of the medieval cathedral, the unsurpassed symbol of unity, fraternity, and equality in which all converged – friends and foes, those near and far – on "feast days," which were the anticipation, as Jacopone da Todi says, of that

> celestial kingdom
> which brings every fulfillment
> the heart ever desired.[7]

Something that really did happen to me a few years after the war made me think along the same lines. Near my home, I was crossing the road in the company of a young labourer, with whom I had become friends on the occasion of his conversion. Persuaded by the testimony of the Little Sisters who for months had tended to his sick wife and his home, he had changed, in fact, from being a rabid anticlericalist and nonbeliever into a regular churchgoer. We were on our way to have a coffee at the bar on the corner when a group of boys, standing about on the street, started to hurl insults at me because I was in clerical dress. Before I knew what was happening, my friend had knocked down one of the boys with a punch, and the others, seeing this, ran away. It occurred to me on that occasion that a certain type of onlooker watching from a window might have commented: "That's Catholicism for you: violence in the name of defending religion! Just like the Crusades." What would be wrong with this kind of reasoning? As we pointed out in relation to the episode of the four thugs recounted above, the onlooker should have acknowledged that my friend's reaction was more than justified. It was a sign of the right conviction taking form within him, but his way of applying it was still crude and inappropriate.

Now, to return to medieval culture, we must realize that the very existence of a widespread religious mentality provided individuals with the necessary education to interiorize a criterion. Once they had grasped and assimilated it, it might have been applied well or badly; it might have been the source of creativity and the root cause, too, of the type of behaviour that we twentieth-century men would easily judge iniquitous – such as wars or certain systems of violence. While the various applications might have been the fruit of either a certain level of civilization or the distortion of personal freedom, we are called to understand that the principle – however altered in its application – responded to that all-embracing demand for justice which only an ecclesial type of education developed. Therefore, it was a living, true idea of God that gave rise to cathedrals and the Franciscan movement; but, it was also an experience historically conditioned by this same idea that generated phenomena in life contradictory to it.

No type of formation can preserve man from these contradictions with respect to the just principles by which he is inspired. Rather, "there is always a considerable gap between the moral standards of a society and the moral practice of individuals and the higher the standards the wider the gap; so that we should naturally expect the contrast between moral principles and social behaviour to be much wider in the case of Christianity."[8] This becomes even more noticeable when "moral and spiritual values ... influence culture in all sort of ways – through institutions and symbols and literature and art, as well as through personal behaviour."[9]

It was precisely this authentic religious mentality that made adherence to religious tradition and religious conviction itself easier in mediaeval life. God was treated and conceived of for what he really is – the source of all things and, therefore, the supreme presence in any aspect of life. The most difficult thing for medieval man to imagine – in contrast to our modern culture, which unfortunately sees it as obvious – was God as something *beside* real life with all its worries and commitments. Remember what Saint Paul said when speaking of the divine plan: "he would bring everything together under Christ." (Eph. 1:10). It is in Christ that the substance of things, their meaning is to be found, and as the meaning of all things, Christ is what is most intimately deep and present in anything.

By focusing on the existence of this attitude in mediaeval life, we are able to see the reasons for the contrasts in the age. This perspective takes into account both antinominal elements: the education of the soul that the Church provided, and the greater crudity of the historical times, when the values of that education might well have remained unevolved.

The aim of this digression is to underline the powerful unity of the conception of life which familiarity with the notion of the living God (whose meaning the Church sought to impart) transmitted to the Christian. The ease with which religiosity or adherence to religious tradition came was due precisely to the authenticity of this experience. This is why the historian of the time, Giovanni Villani, observed in his *Chronicon*: "There are very few atheists, and all condemn them." The reason for this religiosity was not that medieval man was more ingenuous, but rather he possessed a deeper and more exact perception of the presence of the "Ultimate Meaning."

3 HUMANISM FROM THE POINT OF VIEW OF THE DISARTICULATION OF A MENTALITY

a) A Problem Posited Adequately

To simplify, it might be said that our attitude as modern men towards the religious fact is nonproblematic. In other words, it is not normally a truly problematic attitude. As I have said on a previous occasion: "Life is a web of events and encounters which provoke the conscience, producing all different kinds of problems. But a problem is nothing other than the dynamic expression of a reaction in the face of these encounters. Life, then, is a series of problems, its fabric made up of reactions to encounters that are provocative to a greater or lesser extent. Discovering the meaning of life – or the most pertinent and important things in life – is a goal which is possible only for the individual who is involved with life seriously, its events, encounters, and problems."[10] When a problem arises, then, it implies that an interest has been sparked. Intellectual curiosity is thus aroused, which, unlike doubt, whose existential dynamic tends to corrode the active dynamism of interest, renders us more and more extraneous to the object.

So far, we have been discussing a medieval mentality capable of transmitting a true, living idea of God, a mentality which aims to express its global importance in all aspects of life, of the individual, and his surroundings. The environment, in fact, represents the fabric of influences we experience, as a reaction between our originality and the web of various circumstances. What we have called the problematic attitude or allowing ourselves to be provoked by the problem, is none other than the moment in time determined by the content of circumstance plus our personal and critical revision of that content.

It is evident that if a certain sphere or mentality provides an adequate springboard for posing a problem, then the problem and all its essential components will concomitantly assume a clear form and lend itself more easily to a solution. In the Middle Ages, then, for a certain period of time, there existed the right conditions that tended to foster an adequately problematic attitude to Christianity: the mentality and the environment helped individuals perceive God as the root of all things. If, however, in contrast, the mentality and the environment do not provide the elements for setting in motion the dynamics of a given problem in the right way – if they activate the dynamics factiously or unilaterally – then the problem will appear in unclear terms and a human subject will easily feel impaired.

b) The Beginnings of a Process of Disarticulation

This impairment is the source of our modern difficulty in understanding the language of Christianity. Since the only concept of God which is not self-contradictory is one that "has to do with" all things in life, an attitude of mind which does not recognize this totality of God's presence will be unable to prevent the problem from arising because man thirsts for this presence. However, it will make him pose the problem in terms that are harder to decode and that give the wrong perspective.

We can date the beginning of the process of the disarticulation of the unitary religious mentality (which was able to posit the religious problem adequately) during the course of the fourteenth century. This is not the place for a thorough analysis of the factors contributing to this process, for they were many and varied and we will mention them only briefly as examples. However, it is more important to recognize that the origin of this weakening of an organic mentality towards the religious problem is an option permanently open to the human soul. It occurs when there is a sad lack of committed interest and an absence of curiosity towards all reality.

Let us ask ourselves, then, why it was that, in G.K. Chesterson's words, something "lost or impatiently snapped the long, thin, delicate thread that had descended from distant antiquity; the thread of that unusual human hobby, the habit of thinking."[11] Chesterton's vivid expression refers precisely to the end of Medieval times: and here, the word "thinking" has all the weight of that problematic and thus critical attitude greatly favoured by a unitary mentality. Undoubtedly an important factor in the snapping of the "delicate thread" was, as communal society evolved, the greater and more widespread well-being, "one of the greatest social creations of the Middle Ages."[12] Obviously, no human achievement can be attributed to mere outside circumstances alone, since man's freedom, albeit made fragile, remains as the indelible mark of God's creature. As Henri Daniel-Rops comments: "The destiny of the world is shaped in the secret recesses of the mind, through the hidden dialectic of ideals and passions, and the new forces which made old empires crumble are the selfsame forces which each individual confronts in the depths of his own soul."[13] If this is the case, then one should say that in a climate of greater affluence, where *otium* (idle time, leisure) is more enjoyable, human instinct makes advances and gradually turns itself into ideology until it reaches the point where it fosters an atmosphere of disengagement in the midst of the universality and incarnation of those ideal values, which, theoretically, remain. Such disengagement contributed all the more to an unhinging of the social climate of the time, making the contrasts within the life of the civil community more unsettling. The dawn of the year 1300 saw Europe bearing not only the scars of famines and plagues but also of man's struggles. Again Rops comments, "Its violence notwithstanding, medieval humanity had been a brotherly society; that too was no more. In the face of mortal danger, charity and friendship and such deeper sentiments as family love lost their hold."[14] This situation persisted, so that about a century later it would be possible to observe that "few periods in human history have known such a scandalous gulf between the insolent ostentation of the wealthy and the misery of the poor ... Such a contrast had nothing remotely Christian about it."[15]

Within this set of social circumstances, then, falls the shadow of the dismantlement of this unity, to which Humanism would lend cultural support. Certainly, "they were a long way from the century of St. Thomas! The great syntheses there once were had come undone. New catastrophes: the schism of the West, the fall of Constantinople ... accelerated the changes. New sources of knowledge had sprung forth. New divisions were manifest. If the moral wretchedness and civil wars that were tormenting Christianity were to be remedied, the unity of spirits would have to be re-built on new foundations; 'concord' would have to be forged ... what Pico called ... a Pythagorean friendship."[16] These are the opening lines of a crucial chapter in Henri de Lubac's book on Pico della Mirandola. And this was not an isolated view. Other literary passages of the period document the degree to which this dream of concord was alive, not only at the social and political level, but also in terms of personal unity.

One author in whom we truly find emblematic signs of this is Francesco Petrarch. From his verses transpire the marks and counter-blows that, compared with the past cultural and social climate, the on-going dismemberment of society was leaving on the human personality, as the following lines illustrate:

> What grace, what love, or what destiny
> will give me wings like a dove
> That I may rest and lift myself up from earth?[17]

All Petrarch's verses document a "soul wounded by discordant life," a soul torn between the still clear, pure but theoretical recognition of a certain vision of man, and therefore, a certain moral sense, and a general sensation of life that appears to waver of its own accord, detached from the theory. The final part of Petrarch's "Rhymes," the last stanza of the "Hymn to the Virgin," is a moving testimony to the state of mind divided at this moment of transition:

> The day draws near and cannot be far,
> time so runs and flies,
> single, sole Virgin;
> and now conscience, now death pierces my heart:
> commend me to your Son, true man and true God,
> that He may receive my last breath in peace.[18]

One interesting historical reflection shows that "the more one studies the origins of Humanism, the more one is brought to recognise the existence of an element which is not only spiritual but definitely Christian ... Humanism was, it is true, a return to nature, a rediscovery of man and the natural world. But the author of the discovery, the active principle in the change was not the natural man; it was the Christian man – the human type that had been produced by ten centuries of spiritual discipline and intensive cultivation of the innner life."[19] I also would like to point out that the verses cited above certainly unveil man as the doctrinal fruit of Christian history. However, it is precisely this "human type" who, by this time, suffers a laceration: his personality is divided, broken, and the tension this breach provokes is the last sigh of his poetry. The seal of Petrarch's work can only be a sigh of the restless, anguished soul, desiring something precious, aspiring towards it even as we feel it slipping from our grasp and drawing away.

c) Man Fragmented Into a Myriad of Ideals

No longer able to live his life in a relationship with something greater than himself, something capable of unifying all life, conveying all energy to it, man, in the historical circumstances we are discussing, begins to cut the bonds – to simplify, in a way – the all encompassing risk of his existential thrust. He begins to separate and distinguish. But it is striking to see how the punishment fits the crime. Every time man manipulates the radical nature of his reference to God, he diminishes it. Man divides himself: he crumbles into his own interests, falling back within his own ambit and, in the process, becomes prey to his own measure, for "by the very fact that a man lives, he poses this question, because this question is at the root of his consciousness of what is real, and not only does he pose the question, he also responds to it, affirming the reality of an "ultimate." For by the very fact that he lives five minutes he affirms the existence of a "something" which deep down makes living those five minutes worthwhile."[20] In other words, if God is not the reference for his whole life, excluding nothing, some other specific thing will occupy God's place because it is a place that will never be empty in man's heart.

When man cuts himself off in this way, the one ideal becomes fragmented into a myriad of ideals – aesthetic, political, cultural, and so on – each of which despotically seizes human energy. In fact, man, whatever his main field of interest, feels that if he is dedicated to one of the fragments, he is bound to realize something excellent so that his life may be worth living. Humanism cancels familiarity with that synthesis of life characterizing the medieval mind: the ideal type is no longer the "saint" (the man unified by the ideal of God), but the man who could be powerful in one or another aspect of existence and human activity. This means that partiality moves in to take the place of synthesis.

Humanism, therefore, does not attack or detach itself from religious doctrine. The humanist is not against God. However, since his desires and opinions are no longer unified by God, the interest which makes his life worthwhile no longer has anything to do with God. Quite simply, God is removed from man's existence. This is clearly exemplified by certain humanists who, on the discovery of ancient manuscripts (which Benedictine monks had faithfully transcribed over the centuries), gave several points of reference more befitting the new flavour of life to the new sentiment of humanity that freely existed alongside Christian dogmatics. Thus, in the new-found memory of the ancient Pantheon, it is man himself who is the new, ideal reference: man committed in the world with all his energies.

Let us compare this situation as does Charles Moeller's famed comment, with that of humanity of old, as described in the literature of antiquity: "The gods are wicked or arbitrary in their designs, ... fatality ... is the well of tears not only because it sends misadventures but also because it induces men to commit crimes. And in any case ... men are better than the gods ... If, then, heaven is weighted and charged with maledictions, swollen with tears and sadness, men as men are noble and right: they strive in this dark chaos so that a little beauty and greatness may reign through heroism and glory."[21] And he adds:

The ancients ... wanted to save something beautiful: failing to find it in the gods, or in the world, or in events, they trained their desire for light onto the face of "wretched mortals" ... In this night of the world, men's faces appeared strangely beautiful to them. But, the ancients felt that there was something mysteriously abnormal in this. They felt disillusioned, fearful that such a lofty desire for good could turn into a hope so swamped in tears. Even then, human wickedness was the unhappy reality. The Greeks did not want to admit it because that would have been hateful in a world whose gods were wicked.[22]

The humanist Coluccio Salutati echoed this light of glory reflected on the face of man as the only alternative to the bleak obscurity of destiny when he said: "The man who has fulfilled great works on this earth is worthy of Paradise." But like all echoes, it drowns out something of the original voice.

The humanist is one who resurrects the ideal of the "star" – of the Greek hero who will count on his own strength to prevent fate from crushing him, who, even though his sadness is indestructible, will take action (but in the knowledge that all he can do is die a death that is at least noble) and trust in his own strength. However, unlike the Greek hero, the humanists's sense of man's tremendous powerlessness is diminished or softened. It no longer has the same breadth of the ancients. In its place stands an ultimate uneasiness at the inevitability of time, of death, a nostalgia for the last flush of beauty or strength. This melancholy resounds in the famous verses of Lorenzo de' Medici: "How beautiful youth is, yet it flees. Let him be glad who would be, for nothing of tomorrow is certain."

The dominant factors of Humanism – and this is the formula that best defines how Humanism values life – remain the zest for glory, the quest for Fame and Fortune: the fundamental interest in living as "achieving." Humanism replaces the anthropological ideal of saint – of the ideal of unity wrought by the continuous search for the bond with God – with the ideal of a type of new man, who is made worthy of history's admiration by accomplishing any kind of feat, made possible by chance, by "Fortune," but conceived of and fulfilled by forces springing from and determined by man's skill and capabilities.

d) The Exaltation of Man in the Christian Tradition

Yet, Church tradition has always affirmed the value of the person, the singular man, the individual. In almost wondrous admiration, Henri de Lubac reminds us of this: "Let us remember St. Bernard's cry of admiration for man: '*Celsa creatura, in capacitate majestatis!*' which summarizes a long tradition as old as Christianity itself."[23] He also stresses that: "all the great Mediaeval works dedicate a part to the greatness of the rational creature made in the image of God. Like our humanists of the fifteenth century, the Christians before them had no fear of diminishing God by exalting man."[24] And it is true that the more adequate the concept of God, the only source of an adequate concept of man, the more unjustified such a fear would be.

Church tradition, which values the person, is expressed in the Catholic idea of *merit*, the idea that it is enough to live the ultimate relations that determine our time – consciousness of destiny and affection for the world in the circumstances in which God calls – with intensity for just a few seconds. In proportion to this, man has *worth*, as tradition says, man goes to "Heaven," which means he lives adhering to his own destiny, he runs towards his own fulfilment. Such an idea locates man's utility in the consciousness that generates action. Nothing else is needed. Such an idea means locating this consciousness in a human recognition of, and in a love for, truth. We would find it remarkable if we reflected on this exaltation of the moment (which is totally Christian), pure and free, in terms of its value, from conditioning, chance, and the misfortune of circumstance. Nothing else corresponds to man so totally and in such an all-encompassing way. Nothing else safeguards the freedom and divine mark of the "I" like this possibility which, however apparently hidden or fortuitous is harboured in every moment.

In this way, Christian tradition sweeps away the notion of the useless man, of time without meaning, of the purely banal act. In the Christian perspective, each of man's actions is for the whole world. Each act assumes a cosmic dignity because each one collaborates consciously with the heart and will to the design in which the mystery is revealed and fulfils its plan: from washing dishes to guiding the Church, from caring for a child to governing a country. In this perspective, man is free from circumstance. Chance does not determine his value. He can be great, he can journey to perfection, even under the worst or the most humble of conditions.

Humanism is a historical and cultural circumstance which galvanized the dissolution of a unitary mentality. Let us conclude our reflection by stressing that no element of the new climate, in itself, can be assessed in opposition to the previous vision of things. The real difference lies in having separated true Destiny from life. With this imperceptible cutting of bonds, then each particular element can take the place of that ideal point of reference whose wholeness faded and slipped away.

4 THE RENAISSANCE: A VIEW OF NATURE AS THE ULTIMATE SOURCE OF HUMAN ENERGY

a) An Unreasonable Hope

Let us now note how the ideal points of reference for the humanistic mind we have just examined have remained the psychological hinge of our culture. To begin with, an *extreme optimism* regarding man's energies was introduced to historical social reality, and was destined to characterize the whole modern age, including our own. This hope, resting entirely on human measure and enterprise, pinpointed the word "success" as the new ideal reference. It was, however, primarily an unreasonably placed hope, unreasonable because it did not take into account the whole human situation, apart from a vein of ultimate gloom at the conditioning we inevitably encounter, such as that subtle, humiliating one of old age, and the unavoidable one of death. Apart from this veil of sadness, the meaning of life is played out by highlighting a detail, in the partial exaltation of the field in which one excels. And, it does not really matter at all which field it is. This splintering of the ideal as our reference point has remained a part of our modern thinking and has had its consequences. The first is precisely that man's acts are no longer based on moral judgment, but are made on the grounds of success. If someone is successful, if he has gained power and fame, the means no longer matter – and it no longer matters in which particular of life he has distinguished himself: it might be in sports, entertainment, politics, or a criminal organization. In the end, the individual's judgment becomes grotesquely preoccupied with detail, and this tends to compromise his unitary equilibrium.

At first glance, an aspect of this "tipping our hat" to the name of one who is "successful" might seem understandable in human terms. After all, being successful means being incisive in some way in the life of society. It also means to realize something for humanity. This is the supreme criterion of John Dewey's educational project – the most influential American pedagogue of our times – the idea of "social efficiency," which was also exported to Europe. This concept is an obvious one in any culture which does not have God as its real point of reference. It can be understood as the answer to the need not to confine the idea of success totally to individualistic usefulness and consumption, but rather for others to make use of the success of a great man, since his success is also useful to society. However, in the process of evaluating men, this formula of judgment introduces a formula of permanent inequality, a radical discrimination which, to the modern mind, sanctions another consequence of the humanistic climate: the veneration of Fame and Fortune as divinities. What would happen to the person who did not have the necessary talent to make a name for himself, or to the person who did have it but whose circumstances were unfavourable? Such a person would be doomed to be underestimated. In this way, an injustice becomes a fundamental principle for assessing a person's value, and this differs little from the situation in Roman society two thousand years ago when man was considered fulfilled only if he were a "Civis Romanus," one who, therefore, hinged his own value on the condition of belonging to Rome.

How different the vision offered by Church tradition which teaches us that the value of the individual is totally derived from his freedom. The equality of human beings depends on this fact. In this way, the absolute irrationality of exalting a strength one may or may not possess is replaced by the exaltation of an instant that the "I" can live in the fullest freedom, in the awareness of being "made in the image of God" (and, therefore, of destiny), and in *any* situation. So if we should reject such extreme optimism in the forces of man-turned-the-measure-of-things, then "there is certainly no paradox in Etienne Gilson's title for one of the chapters of his classic work, *L'esprit de la philosophie médié-*

vale: 'Christian Optimism.' That was the legacy of the Fathers of the Church."[25]

b) The Search for a Source of Human Energy

It is at this point that the second factor emerges. This factor, destined to be a mainstay of modern, contemporary culture, also explains the motions of our minds. The humanistic mind fostered and nurtured a certain sense of limitation in men's understanding. It believed that the energy that could make men famous, renowned, and fortunate was not an energy they generated themselves, but one given to them, one they found bestowed on them, like a gift. However, given that the God in their heaven had become a distant cloud, it obviously seemed to them more realistic to look to the earth as the source of the energy responsible for man's greatness, and it was during the Renaissance that this found its systematic basis, its cultural translation in pinpointing nature as this energy source – nature, soon to be understood in pantheistic terms.

With the loss of the socially widespread sense of a concrete relationship with God – man's mysterious origin – the divinity, the wealth of man's origins, nevertheless acknowledged as something independent of man, was identified in *nature*, then understood as the source of being, energy, life, which gave all individuals their zest for living and their capacity for action. Nature, then, was no longer a sign of God. Rather nature began to take the place of his presence, since he – although still not denied – was nevertheless so remote from life's concerns that the need was felt to trust in something more concrete and easier to define. Thus, to the Renaissance mind, nature was nothing more than the pantheistic notion of God rendered immanent.

Now, if nature is divine and expresses the wealth of its resources in man, then the assessment of what is good and what is bad should also fit in with this image for it seems obvious to conceive of nature's dictates as good, and all that contradicts the life-giving energy of natural impulses (one's instincts) as bad. As Nicolò Machiavelli observed: "We are the most impious and most immoral men conceivable." This observation does not seem to be a denunciation but the cynical registration of a fact which responds to an apparently cogent logic: if nature is at the origin of all things, then all that comes from nature must ultimately be good, even though it might not fit in with morally codified norms. In this perspective, then a revealing quote from Rabelais, one of the most expressive figures of the French Renaissance, springs to mind: "Do as you will, because by nature man is spurred to virtuous acts."

What man feels corresponds to the impetus of nature and, therefore, inevitably represents man's greatest good. Giving vent to instinct, then, becomes an ethical ideal, made legitimate by the supposed tuning in of the instinct with the natural ideal. Here morality is identified with spontaneity, and it becomes increasingly difficult for the common mentality to grasp the idea that whatever is dictated by impulse could also be bad for man. In this context, then, a God who dares go into detail by saying, "You can't do that," is perceived as an impediment to man's free expansion, an unacceptable intrusion obstructing human achievement. This is the first evidence of a step that would soon become the road to hostility towards the Christian God proposed to us by tradition .

c) To Forget a Factor in Reality

This hostility towards God is the offspring of a persistent forgetfulness and, therefore, of a diminishing of reality. The mechanisms of its genesis are similar to those to which G.K. Chesterton alludes when he observed that all errors are truths gone mad. And there is nothing like madness for disconnecting certain shades of expressiveness from a context able to represent reality in its totality, nothing like a reduced vision of what is real for generating disconnection and the risk of committing oneself to "truths gone mad."

We will hit upon the truth of these points by returning to the quotation from Rabelais: "Do what you will because by nature man is spurred to virtuous acts." For 1500 years, Christianity had been teaching that the law of God, the spur to virtue, is written in man's heart, and that man can be receptive to it because it is natural, because it is a constituent element of his original dynamics. In his letter to the Romans, Saint Paul expressed it this way: "When Gentiles, who have not the law, do by nature what the law requires, they are a law to themselves, even though they do not have the law. They show that what the law requires is written on their hearts." (cf. Rom. 2:14–15). In this sense then, Rabelais's phrase would seem to be a perfectly Christian one in that it expresses the idea that man, by his very nature, is orientated towards God and, therefore, towards good. Paul himself says this when, at the Areopagus in Athens he speaks of men's ceaseless seeking, spurred on by God himself:

From one single stock he not only created the whole human race so that they could occupy the entire earth, but he decreed how long each nation should flourish and what boundaries of its territory should be. And he did this so that all nations might seek the deity and by feeling their way toward him, succeed in finding him. Yet he is not far from any of us, since it is in him that we live, and move, and exist, as indeed some of your own writers have said: "We are all his children" (Acts 17:26–28).

However, Rabelais is forgetting something that the Church (through which the person of Jesus, and therefore, ever-present Christianity has come down to us) does remember: what always tends to be forgotten is reality in the *totality* of its factors. It was for this reason that in the first volume of this trilogy[26] I devoted the first chapter to realism, and demonstrated how, when faced with reality, man's primary need is to compare himself with the totality of its factors, whatever the problem he might have to face. And this is all the more true if that problem is his destiny.

To return to our point, the Church, as stated above, does not forget. We hear its realistic warning, for example, resounding, once again, in the words of Saint Paul:

The fact is, I know nothing of good living in me – living, that is, in my unspiritual self – for though the will to do what is good is in me, the performance is not, with the result that instead of doing the good thing I want to do, I carry out the sinful things I do not want ... Wretched man I am! Who will rescue me from this body doomed to death? Thanks be to God through Jesus Christ our Lord (Rom. 7:18–19,24–5a).

There is an ideal law written in man's heart, but we also need to recognize, with Saint Paul, the existence of another law which contradicts the first one. Viewed in this way, man in his completeness takes on a face. This is why the Church does not deny, but rather affirms, that man is by nature spurred on to virtuous acts. However, the Church also considers man's existential situation: although man's very nature is orientated towards good, he finds himself, through time and in the circumstances of his earthly life, unable to maintain his adherence to those "virtuous acts," to which, however, he remains originally inclined. I remember a dogmatic text of the seventeenth century which was written with the intention of responding to open questions on Jansenism. It said that without grace, man cannot resist "for long" committing mortal sin. What does the phrase "mortal sin" say to our minds as modern men, far removed as we are from the terminology of classical Christian moral theology? The whole catechetical turn of phrase could sound antiquated, even irritatingly incomprehensible. But we must remember that an easy way to register intelligent things as stupidities is to turn a stupid eye on them.

Karl Adam recalled the opinion of Adolf Harnack, that great Protestant scholar and historian of dogma, on this point. "I am convinced from constant experience of the fact that the students who leave our schools have the most disconnected and absurd ideas about ecclesiastical history. Some of them know something about Gnosticism, or about other curious and for them worthless details. But of the Catholic

Church, the greatest religious and political creation known to history, they know absolutely nothing, and they indulge in its regard in wholly trivial, vague and often directly nonsensical notions." According to Adam this type of ignorance, which was "the cause of the worst kind of prejudice, produces indifference and dislike, nay, even contempt."[27]

"Mortal sin" means that man goes against himself, against the truth of himself and, therefore, against his destiny. Now, in a very realistic way, that seventeenth-century ecclesiastical text warned that man, without the gratuitous help of Christ, cannot live for long without harming himself, without seriously acting against himself. Look at the words carefully: I refer to man on his own, man as man – man who holds the stimulus of the ideal in his heart, but who also harbours within his personal reality a contradictory force at work, which tries to drag him away. In another work, I observed that Ovid had also affirmed this: "I see and approve better things, but follow worse." That is, as I commented:

While the soul, across the centuries, is by nature a web of ideal pointers, in the concrete it is suffocated by a great weakness. If man by nature possesses a strength of his own, existentially he is wounded, ambiguous, equivocal. It is as if man suffered vertigo, as if his heartbeat were racing. Suppose, for example, we were to draw a line on the ground, and were to challenge those present to walk along it, placing one foot in front of the other; no one would have any difficulty. But were we able to take the same line, and elevate it a hundred yards above the earth, the situation would change radically. The line, and the challenge, would be the very same as before, but the conditions would have been altered considerably, such that the identical task would have been made impossible for most of us. There are certain things man is structurally able to do, which historically and existentially he cannot do.[28]

The Renaissance tends to censor this evidence of human experience, which is ambiguous and contradictory at its very root. Such censorship, represented, as we have seen in Rabelais's phrase, has, in some way, formed the mind of modern man, and Christian realism would complete the phrase in this way: "Man is by nature spurred on to virtuous acts, but he cannot do what he wants because the existential situation in which he finds himself makes him incapable of realizing the ideal impulse of nature." Man is one, but divided. This is what Christian tradition calls original sin. This does not mean that he is evil by nature; rather, his nature, destined towards good, is placed in an existential condition which makes it impossible for him to maintain that orientation.

Henri de Lubac, in his book dedicated to Proudhon, offers us the testimony of this socialist theorist on original sin:

He had wanted to eliminate the mystery of original sin; he had wanted to replace every idea of grace with the sole idea of justice. Now here was a case which had ended in Justice being revealed as "insufficient and ineffective"; it had had to "call on other strength, a higher grace". The institutions and the laws could not be taxed with this check; it would seem that it is the soul itself which labours under some innate disorder. ... What witchery besets us, and makes us continually find, on analysis, evil and death where the instincts of our heart told us life and virtue should be?[29]

Thus, just as the "efficiency" that prizes the instant as expressed in the Church's concept of merit has proven to be much more human than John Dewey's "social efficiency," so, too, is the Church's position infinitely more realistic and, therefore more complete than the Renaissance forgetfulness we have mentioned because it recognizes the ideal impetus inside man and the fragility that makes him incapable of realizing it.

d) An Example

This forgetfulness, characteristic of and related to the cultural climate of the Renaissance, grew into blatant naturalism, and became evident to me as I read some Elizabethan plays. Coming as they did about a century and a half after the Italian movement, they are a perfect expression of some characteristics of the Renaissance on English soil.

Packed with references to Italian princely courts, sprinkled throughout with maxims of a tone that would not have been displeasing to Machiavelli (whose ideas "were fervently welcomed at Cambridge toward the 1570s"),[30] these theatrical works stand out for the general attitude to human nature they denounce. The dynamics driving the dramatic mechanisms of these plays all bear the mark of an impassioned, fatal involvement with the impetuses of nature, as if they were a perpetually overflowing river, from which it is almost impossible to escape. The nineteenth-century critic A. De Bosis described this group of English authors as "a chorus of giants ... formidable, violent, inexhaustible in their horror, in tenderness, in passion, disarrayed and many-souled, lords of life and of its laws."[31] And it is precisely this supposed "lordliness," partly unmindful and challenging, partly abandoned to suffer the more uncontrollable aspect of passions, which has come down to us and which makes us say even today in justification: "It's only natural," or "The heart rules the head."

On the one hand, it is a characteristic of the Elizabethan text that in the face of passion (the protagonist), a voice is raised (that of a counsellor or a friend) which expresses the need and inevitability, already acquired as an attitude of mind, to follow the instinct. On the other hand, the voice express the instinct's confrontation with moral rules believed to be social conventions. This is a dual counterposition: morality, rather than being the renewing, collective root of human affairs and passions, is represented as the token paid to officialdom, to a series of ecclesiastical and formally accepted social laws, like some kind of judgment superimposed on human affairs and passions already triggered, accepted, and affirmed.

Mario Praz, the editor of this theatrical anthology comments: "In practice, the Protestant morality of the English public could not but be reflected in the theatre, and many plays are but the explications of a morbid Manichaeanism, which believed that in the Italy of the Popes it had plumbed the depths of the evil that held it in its charm."[32] Significant for our reflection is the epilogue of *Dr Faustus* by Christopher Marlowe, in which the chorus takes its leave of the public by referring to the tragic death of the protagonist:

Cut is the branch that might have grown full straight,
And burnèd is Apollo's laurel-bough,
That sometime grew within this learnèd man.
Faustus is gone! Regard his hellish fall,
Whose fiendful fortune may exhort the wise
Only to wonder at unlawful things:

Whose deepness doth entide such forward wits,
To practice more than heavenly power permits.[33]

Here is the obstructing veto by a God felt to be opposed to the fascination by which man is captured in relation to all things which stimulate his existence, the double register of the Law, and the mysterious "unlawful things" made for "forward wits." Yet, there remains a vague uneasiness, an irresolute spark, which is a sign of the censorship. Another Elizabethan author, John Webster, defines this spark well when he has one of his characters in his tragedy, *The White Devil*, say:

I have lived
Riotously ill, like some that lived in court,
and sometimes when my face was full of smiles,
Have felt the maze of conscience in my breast.[34]

So here we no longer have a clear root judgment of one's limitations, a recognized incapacity for "virtuous acts." Rather, there is an uneasiness and dismay that, thank God, cannot be totally eliminated. In this sense, then, de Lubac reminds us: "*Fecisti nos ad Te, Deus* – no acid will ever be corrosive enough to cancel these words engraved by Augustine to express the deepest human reality."[35]

5 RATIONALISM: THE DIFFICULTY OF MAN CONCEIVED IN THE ABSTRACT

a) Reason Which Allows No Interference

We have arrived at the third historical epoch which has influenced, in a profound way, not only our modern attitude, but also has unsettled our understanding of Christian judgments on human reality.

Naturalism continued its influence, and we have seen how it is recognizable as a chief factor in our way of perceiving existence. If we are to detect the emergence of this third factor, then it might be said, somewhat simplistically, that the exaltation of nature we mentioned, which is at the origin of naturalism, worked to some degree to facilitate in man the discovery of a correspondence between the workings and dynamics of nature and the workings and dynamics of thought. In this way, an abundant evolution in the discovery of natural laws seemed to man to mark the age in which reason – man's own energy – would dominate and be lord of reality and, from a certain point onward, when the Renaissance had matured, the age of rationalism emerges with well-defined concepts of reason and conscience which permit neither outside interference nor integration.

The results of this development are far-reaching. If conscience is the place and the original subject of truth – if man is the "measure of things" – and if reason is the one tool of conscience, we cannot, on any occasion, go beyond reason. Anything that presumes to do so is considered an illicit intrusion, abuse, or enslavement of the spirit. All things are locked within the limits of reason, the world's true god, manipulator, and creator. Reason will be required to solve unresolved enigmas, and concomitantly, enable man to utilize these solutions. Man, then, places his hopes in reason. Nothing outside of the realms of reason is conceivable or feasible, unless it is seen only as worthy of the inferior aspects of man.

This is the ultimate outcome of the process we have described. The true lord of nature is not remote from man, for the true lord is man's reason. If there is a God, then rationalistic culture sees his all-embracing way of acting in the world as through man's reason. Once again, ratonalism does not necessarily abolish a God. Rather it totally eradicates any possibility of liberation of the present through God's intervention that goes beyond the horizon of rational creativity.

Now we must highlight two points concerning this concept of reason, which, on one hand, is the end of a parabola, and, on the other, marks the beginning of a series of consequences which have come down to us through the ages.

1. First, it must be stressed that the Catholic Church proposes exactly what this conception of reason considers as arbitrary intrusion. That is to say, its message is that the divine has become man's companion on his journey. Through the Church, this companionship of God presents itself as something which surpasses the strength of individual awareness, reason, and will, surpassing them not to annul them, but to render the individual capable of self-realization. In this way, if man has such a companion, the companionship of Christ, he sees clearly what he is and with certainty. He begins to be what he really is, journeying as a person because Christ, the Redeemer, God-made-man, knows what is in humans. This is the focal point of the wonderful encyclical, *Redemptor hominis*. But, a proposal such as this – this supreme annunciation of the divine who becomes an individual's companion on his journey so as to enable him to be more himself and journey more as a person – is, to a mentality formed by rationalism, viewed as the imprisonment of the spirit and the intellect, for if truth is whatever an individual can demonstrate, the first thing to be excluded *a priori* as nonsense is that God has the power to intervene in human history.

But, we may ask, is not the mind that is open to the possibility of any announcement and ready to verify it a freer mind? And is not a vision of man which recognizes the paradoxical combination of limitation and potential more realistic? Henri Daniel-Rops wrote, quoting Cardinal de Bérulle: "Two centuries of effort are summed up in some words ... which give the answer to many errors: 'What is man? A nothing capable of God.'"[36]

11. The fragmentation of a mentality, which we have seen appear at its inception as the breaking up of a unity, continues, even in its conclusive aspect, its course of theoretical positions and social incisiveness in rationalism. According to Louis Cognet, the success of Cartesianism, for example, which was destined to influence modern man's way of thinking: "was extraordinary. To be sure, its success was most prevalent in the social salons, but even the best of minds were affected by it. ... In Port-Royal as well as in secular circles Cartesianism was of great interest for the sciences, especially mathematics and physics. This interest spread to the intellectuals among the clergy."[37]

And Daniel-Rops would add the following: "As soon as the system of Descartes became known to the intelligentsia it was welcomed with open arms. Patronized by Condé and many noblemen, this 'bold and attractive' philosophy was quickly adopted in the *salons*. ... Cartesianism was victorious in England, Italy, Belgium and, of course, despite fierce resistance, in Holland; ten years after his death Descartes was read and admired by everyone in Europe who claimed to be educated and intelligent."[38]

Let me repeat: this fervour for the "ratio" which discovered its correspondence with the dynamism of nature, which built systems designed to bestow reason on its own mechanisms, is not in itself hostile to the Christian God. But, by becoming a "partnership", in which "the great personalities [and] the multiplicators, who had a profound effect on the broad segment of the educated, including those people who, while they could not read, had themselves read to," took the mentality of people a step further from this God, "the absolutely regular course of the world in accordance with theoretical principles [was] without the need for the continued presence of God once it was set in motion."[39] Yet theoretically, "the laws of mathematics and physics could be conceived as the work of the *factor coeli et terrae*, the master builder of the world." It helps to repeat that this further step found a clear path in the wide diffusion of an attitude of mind which was now no longer being applied in its social context to the integral nature of the bonds between man and God, and so, to the global vision of the image of the Christian God. Thus, in a progressive exaltation of particular aspects of human reality, not considered in all its factors, "the Augustinian 'illumination' of God within man was now conceived to mean man's self-illumination in the light of autonomous reason. This authorization of the human intellect which had its prehistory in the power asserted by Thomism that enables man in the knowledge of creation to rise to an analogous knowledge of God, except that rationality (according to Scholastic philosophy) is to be combined with the belief in revealed religion, now sought its reason within itself."[40] And the man who offered the most systematic formula for this concept of man's reason – *norma sui* and *norma universi* – was Spinoza, from whom western thought still draws much inspiration.

These attitudes persisted and grew throughout the centuries. For example, in reference to the eighteenth century, Henri Daniel-Rops once again observes: "The 'philosophical' spirit was not so much a system of thought as a general attitude to life. ... What then were the most widely accepted beliefs? The primacy of man, regarded as the focus of the universe; the omnipotence of human reason, considered as the arbiter of all thought and of all conduct. Hence the cult of science on the one hand, and on the other a declaration that natural morality suffices, having no need of divine instruction or of rewards and punishments beyond the grave."[41]

b) Two Effects of Rationalism on an Understanding of the Church

In the previous chapter, we examined the effect of rationalism on historical criticism of the figure of Christ, and we emphasized how the rationalist, or those who have grown up within this cultural sphere, reduces (or tends to reduce) the proposed problem to notions already formulated within the self, to categories of possibility which he himself, the sovereign of self, establishes. In this way, a problem is appraised within a predetermined framework, and not on its own real terms, leaving one doomed to incomprehension and emptying of its content the very way the problem presents itself.

We have also seen how the Protestant attitude to the same theme is nothing more than a different version of the same subjectivism whose root lies in sentiment. The man who makes his decisions exclusively by means of his *ratio* or his capacity for feeling condemns himself to losing his objectivity, and ultimately, paradoxically, this will culminate in damage to both his *ratio* and his capacity for sentiment. As G.K. Chesterton observes:

The object *is* an object. It can and does exist outside the mind, or in the absence of the mind. And *therefore*, it enlarges the mind of which it becomes a part. The mind conquers a new province like an emperor; but only because the mind has answered the bell like a servant. The mind has opened the doors and windows, because it is the natural activity of what is inside the house to find out what is outside the house. If the mind is sufficient to itself, it is insufficient for itself. For this feeding upon fact *is* itself; as an organ it has an object which is objective; this eating of the strange strong meat of reality.

For, as the English author adds, with a touch of irony: "No sceptics work sceptically; no fatalists work fatalistically; all without exception work on the principle that it is possible to assume what it is not possible to believe. No materialist who thinks his mind was made up for him, by mud and blood and heredity, has any hesitation in making up his mind. No sceptic who believes that truth is subjective, has any hesitation in treating it as objective."[42]

And again, it is Chesterton who compassionately describes the man who entrusts himself exclusively to feeling. This individual he sees in the figure of Luther:

Man could say nothing to God, nothing from God, nothing about God, except an almost inarticulate cry for mercy and for the supernatural help of Christ; in a world where all natural things were useless. Reason was useless. Will was useless. Man could not move himself an inch any more than a stone. Man could not trust what was in his head any more than a turnip. Nothing remained in earth or heaven, but the name of Christ lifted in that lonely imprecation; awful as the cry of a beast in pain." Thus, spasmodically, Luther inaugurates the other face of the "modern mood of depending on things not merely intellectual. ... He did in a very real sense make the modern world. He destroyed Reason; and substituted Suggestion."[43]

This is how the Protestant attitude completes the picture: with a religious impulse that finds itself joined to rationalist subjectivism.

6 THE COMMON DENOMINATOR OF THE THREE FACTORS

a) Man at the Centre?

The extreme exaltation of man is the common denominator recognizable in the three factors we have identified as responsible for our difficulty in understanding Christian reality: Humanism in its efficiency-orientated way and in its capacity to destructure a unitary mentality, the Renaissance with its naturalism, and rationalism, in its exaltation of man as the measure of all things.[44] And it is imporant to recognize that the whole modern age has been determined by this exaltation, which subsequently became a presumptuous detachment from God: Man at the centre of all things, nothing less.

The following two highly interesting corollaries derive from this position:

1. The first shows us that this "man," placed at the centre of all things, is seen in an abstract way, because the "man" conceived in this way will be different according to the concept that proclaims him. In this sense, the "man-in-general" does not exist. "You" exist, and you are not proclaimed as the centre, even though in practice, you may very well live as if you were. However, this proclamation of the centrality of the concrete "I" of an individual to this degree is intolerable! It is so false that it is theoretically repugnant, although, in practice, because of our capacity for deception, it is possible to live this way. In this position, humanity as a whole is acclaimed at the centre of all things. However, this is not the real-life, here-and-now man being hailed, for, after all, what is humanity as a whole? Humanity is something abstract, because the identifiable human subject is the one who says "I." And even when "we" is used, it does nothing to diminish the fact that "I" am and "you" are the manifestation of what is human, for humanity's "we" is a condition to which each of us contributes to create a climate for the relationship of the individual man with other men. In this sense, then,

structurally, the human phenomenon is the phenomenon of the "I," a phenomenon so powerful that it can become what polarizes the universe, because if I love reality all existing reality can be my brother. I use the word "I" here because beyond the "I," the human does not exist except by participating in it. All other conceptions will inevitably be standardizing, depersonalizing, because, in the vigorous words of Hans Urs von Balthasar, it "is not an abstract humanity which exists unassailed throughout the centuries, but rather the concrete number of human beings, thousands of whom die at every moment."[45]

And so, from the springboard of rationalist culture, we have arrived and continue to arrive at this abstraction. Father Teilhard de Chardin's warning is significant, as Henri de Lubac reminds us in a work dedicated to this theologian: "In 1936, when he was considering the state of our human world, he wrote: 'Society will inevitably become mechanical unless its successive aggrandisements are not gradually crowned by Some One.' ... 'God is Person! ... we think of him as a Person: A God who was not personal would not be a God.'" But, let us add, that if we are to do this, then we must think *as* a person. We must risk the "I." If we do not do this, we cannot participate in any type of personal reality, either that of man or God. Teilhard de Chardin sees precisely the danger of this vague abstractedness in modern man: "As he pointed out himself, 'God...is almost inevitably conceived by the modern positivist as a shoreless ocean', as a 'diffuse immensity'; 'unlike the primitives who gave a face to every moving thing, or the early Greeks, who deified all the aspects and forces of nature, modern man is obsessed by the need to depersonalize (or impersonalize) all that he most admires."[46] This is truly a flight from everything that man lives, a flight to which Henri de Lubac alludes in another of his works, when he quotes one of Fyodor Dostoyevsky's letters: "This is the result of the 'absurd enterprise of self-deification; the individual, increasingly lost, increasingly unhinged by a desire that nothing can satisfy, ends up seeking the divine essence in ... the inanimate.'"[47]

Certainly, it is possible to exalt man in the abstract, just as it is impossible to escape concrete man. Elsewhere, I recalled a passage of a letter Karl Marx wrote to his wife on 21 June 1856 which exemplifies precisely this: "I feel like a man again, because I experience a great passion; and the multiplicity of things in which study and modern culture entangle us, and the skepticism by which we must be brought to criticize all impressions, subjective and objective, are deliberately made to leave us small and weak and mournful and indecisive. But love, not for the man of Feuerbach, not for the metabolism of Moleschott, not for the proletariat, but love for the beloved, for you, this is what makes a man to be a man once again."[48] Man conceived in an abstract way, then, proves to be a great illusion, because we must live with ourselves and our needs. Proudhon's testimony is also interesting on this point, as again de Lubac reports:

Whereas, for Marx, "humanity lays down for itself only problems that it can resolve," Proudhon, on the contrary, was of opinion that "our thoughts go further than it is given us to reach." Therein he saw the greatness as well as the destitution of our intelligence, in that powerlessness which kept it ever open and prevented it from being satisfied with any solution in which it would be imprisoned. ... Let others fancy they have reached the goal. Let the Positivists think they have banished metaphysics for evermore. Let the Humanists think that they have rid themselves of the great Phantom for evermore, Proudhon, who was their victim, shared in their negations, but he shows them that the pendulum has swung the other way. No, "the antinomy cannot be resolved." "The fight against God is never-ending."[49]

11. The second corollary concerns the structure of the phenomenon of man. If it is not seen as having to do with the "I," then one could easily speak of man and humanity in connection with a power logic. We have seen that if man is identified with the collective, then the word "God" becomes indistinguishable and, in the final analysis, lost. This faceless collective would then be guided by someone who, although presuming to be outside of this anonymity, yet retains his own definite face. Olivier Clément makes an interesting comment about Lenin's personality as it is presented in Solzhenitsyn's *Lenin in Zurich*:

There is nothing beyond the movement of the masses, beyond the history of generic man. It is the certainty of being the holder of absolute knowledge – the only knowledge capable of establishing absolute power – which always led Lenin to multiply factions and surround himself with only those who unreservedly shared his point of view ... "And even if only the most mediocre remain, the non-entities, there is no limit to what one can do, providing they are unanimous in their obedience," and so anything goes. "Anything goes if God does not exist," Dostoyevsky would say. Anything goes for him who becomes – and Lenin believed himself to be such – the absolute conscience of a humanity called to self-deification. Knowledge of the laws that govern the coming into being – and given that nothing else exists, being the master of such laws – must mean having access, sooner or later, to the power which will model that coming into being. "Parties, the masses, continents ... continue to clash and turn in different, aimless ways. They don't know where they're going – you, and you alone, know:" this is how Lenin thought.[50]

No one can say that they have an experience of "humanity-in-general," for such an experience and consciousness do not exist. A woman exists who gives birth to a man, and all experience and consciousness are bound to the dignity and emotion of the fact that this man exists, to the event of the subject in the "here-and-now." And reference to any other category that eludes the "I" in the name of humanity will be a reason – the strongest and most terrible one in history – for man's destruction.

We must conclude then that the extreme exaltation of man is the common denominator emerging from the three factors we have isolated as determinants of modern mentality. This does not, however, mean man as a concrete person. Rather, it refers to man forgetful, first of all, of the essential factors of his own reality, man seen as the subject matter of an abstract conception, the designated victim of human power games.

b) The Intensification of an Attitude to Contemporary Scientism

Reason's exaltation of man grew to become the cultural norm, an increasingly influential current of thought in the European sphere. In the centuries to follow those first rationalist positions, this attitude was to be pursued, intensified, and then applied everywhere. After discovering that its dynamism corresponded to the dynamism of nature, reason witnessed periods of brilliant advances in the scientific fields, and it was precisely to science that man's mind turned for the meaning of things. "Men were looking more and more to science rather than to the intellect for true 'enlightenment'; what science could not explain must be rejected without discussion."[51] This attitude is called scientism. It is a conception whereby scientific progress is promoted as the only true form of human enhancement, and used therefore, as the yardstick for all forms of development. According to Henri Daniel-Rops:

Scientism, born in the sixteenth century and developed in the seventeenth won very large numbers of recruits during the eighteenth because science appeared to lend it support. ... There was at that time no scientific or technical discipline which did not achieve some notable success. Geometers and astronomers, confirming the theories of Newton, calculated the distance between Earth and Moon, discovered new planets through the genius of Herschel, and measured the terrestrial meridian. Physics and chemistry, which were all the rage, made important advances. ... Properly scientific methods were introduced in the field of natural history by Linnaeus and Buffon (1707-88), who systematized the world of living beings. There was much progress in the practical sphere. The steam engine, used in the early eighteenth century for pumping water from mines and adapted by James Watt for other industrial purposes, ... Montgolfier, a paper manufacturer of Annonay in Vivarais, sought to realize the ancient dream of Icarus by flying through the air, and succeeded in 1783. It was almost inevitable, in face of such achievements, that the human mind should believe itself endowed with unlimited powers. ... The presence of such vast achievements, how could man have resisted the lure of pride? There were indeed eminent scientists, among them Newton and Leibniz, who felt their faith strengthened by all those wonderful discoveries, and declared that so marvelous a world could not have been devised except by an intelligence far transcending that of man. Others, however, saw in these things nothing but grounds for exalting human reason.[52]

It is interesting to note that historically it has always been individuals who, amidst the conformity of an accepted culture, have introduced the new into an established society. And this type of innovation generates a context which will then use political struggle to introduce a new kind of stability, a different type of conformity. The French Revolution did just this. Using politics as a tool, it assumed rationalism as its own ideology and made the rationalist culture the dominant one. In the centuries to come, rationalism as the expression of scientism, travelled through time in the form of the official culture, and like a bacterial cloud, it slipped into the minds of people almost as if by osmosis. In this way, a new mass culture was born.

This climate persisted throughout the nineteenth century and settled in at various levels, increasingly becoming the approved norm. In the second half of the nineteenth century, for example, a disconcerting optimism, declaring that the world's destiny of happiness was just around the corner, appeared in a certain type of American philosophical and theological literature. A passage in Ralph Waldo Emerson's essay, *Self-Reliance*, is symptomatic of "man's profound self-confidence" which is due to

a conception of radical intimacy between the divine and the natural, which ... increasingly proves to be pantheistic immanence. "We lie in the lap of the immense intelligence which makes us receivers of its truth and organs of activity." Optimism without quarter permeates this conception ... in a vision of man in which ... sin is interpreted as mere difficulty inherent in the inevitable mechanism of evolution, and regeneration is made to coincide with natural immanent development ... Consequently, optimism determines all philosophy in history by which evil is destined to be out-classed, and with reforming impetus, social progress is assured through the realisation of the divine potential man possesses.[53]

This optimism also surfaced in Washington Gladden's 1895 book, *Ruling Ideas of the Present Age.* Gladden, the founder of the thought and action Protestant movement known as the Social Gospel, wrote the following: "The thought of this world is gradually being freed from superstition and prejudice; the social sentiments are being purified; the customs are slowly changing for the better; the laws are gradually shaped by finer conceptions of justice."[54] Nor did the outbreak of the First World War totally eradicate this optimism, although there appeared to be "more caution in maintaining the optimism they inherited." John W. Buckham was one of those individuals, although he did confess in a 1919 book that "it seemed to many of us who were studying theology and beginning our ministry in the eighties and nineties as if humanity were on the eve of the golden age."[55] Others, like Shailer Matthews, for whom "history in practice is a sure pathway to the moralization of the human personality and of society" wrote that this was confirmed once more even in 1916, and the world situation did not lessen the conviction." Indeed, "there seems to be justification for saying 'war is a survival we shall yet outgrow.'"[56]

In his last work, *A Theology for the Social Gospel,* published in 1918, Walter Rauschenbush (who was considered the most brilliant, persuasive exponent of the Social Gospel) offered an "enthusiastic assertion of the potential result of human perfectability: 'And sometimes the hot hope surges up that perhaps the long and slow climb may be ending. ... Since the Reformation began to free the mind and to direct the force of religion toward morality, there has been a perceptible increase of speed. Humanity is gaining in elasticity and capacity for change, ... The swiftness of evolution in our own country proves the immense latent perfectibility in human nature.' "[57] This book "reproduced the Taylor Lectures at Yale that April 1917, just when America was being involved in the War, an event which would deal a mortal blow to the philosophy of liberal history. But, the certainty of a more proper fulfillment of things human remained as if it were untouched, still exuberant, still trusting 'of the fraternal ethics of democracy' and totally resting on the event of 'social common sense.' "[58]

But "the idealism of the Social Gospel was necessarily defeated by history itself. The First World War had begun as an indictment to its illusory, utopian character. The great economic crisis of about a decade later betrayed the incurable state of anguish thrust upon optimism by the force of circumstance. The Second World War marked the definitive decline of utopia, and as R. Niebuhr remarked: "Since 1914 one tragic experience has followed another, as if history had been designed to refute the vain delusions of modern man."[59]

Yet, the tendency to trust in science has come down to us as a general attitude of mind, despite great cultural dismay and hardened criticism of the hope man places in applying reason, to science and technology to create a good, truly human world. This general attitude leaves the conscious man without any pillar of support whatever. Karl Adam's description is to the point:

It is the mark of modern man that he is torn from his roots ... The sixteenth century revolt from the Church led inevitably to the revolt from Christ of the eighteenth century, and thence to the revolt from God of the nineteenth. And thus the modern spirit has been torn loose from the deepest and strongest supports of its life, from its foundation in the Absolute, in the self-existent Being, in the Value of all values ... Instead of the man who is rooted in the Absolute, hidden in God, .. we have the man who rests upon himself, the autonomous man. Moreover, this man, because he has renounced the fellow-ship of the Church, ... has severed the second root of his life, that is to say, his fellowship with other men ... And so the rupture of Church unity has ... loosened the bonds of social fellowship and thereby destroyed the deep source and basis of a healthy, strong humanity, of a complete humanity. The autono-mous man has become a solitary man, an individual.[60]

We have said that the conscious or anguished denunciation of this state of rootlessness does reach the deepest levels of human reflection. However, scientism, to the common mind and according to a more widespread, superficially obvious opinion, becomes the transmitter of the last signal rationalism launches: this is the concept of *progress* – the illusion of being able to project into the future accomplishments of which contemporary humanity is incapable. This is not to decry all the achievements or potential achievements of science and technology. Rather it is simply to emphasize that this potential is not the measure of reality.

Once again Henri de Lubac cites Teilhard de Chardin, this time to bring home to us the limits of science:

Analysis, that marvelous instrument of scientific research, to which we owe all our advances, but which, breaking down synthesis after synthesis, allows one soul after another to escape, leaving us confronted with a pile of dismantled machinery and evanescent particles. It builds up the edifice of science ... but it does so only by pulling down the great edifice of reality. To say this is not to condemn analysis, but simply to admit that it is not everything. ... The scientist who is not only content to use the "marvelous instrument" of analysis but has no desire to know anything that analysis does not tell him, thinks that he is being rigorous, but in reality he is slipping into one of those tendencies of the human intelligence which is to 'break nature up into pieces'. He is then liable, through a sort of inside-out metaphysics or mysticism, to accept a materialist or nihilist dogma. ... Such, according to Père Teilhard, was the mistake or the inevitable fate of nineteenth-century science.[61]

And such an error, as we have seen, is no longer just the error of the scholar. It permeates our entire approach to everything.

The notion of progress rebuked the religious spirit for attesting to a world that cannot be seen and for postponing, at will, the hope of humanity to some time in the future. However this progress, which attacks reality, sectioning it then turning it into the alleged achievement of human well-being, is the last-ditch formula for the rationally gratuitous, totally make-believe substitution of that future. The all-encompassing meaning of man and history is said to be reason indefinitely applied to dominate things. This is not an anti-science observation; it is an indictment of science's presumption that it can resolve the human problem. De Lubac comments on scientific conquests in the following way:

We have often been told – and in tones of finality – that all the paltry ideas of our Christian forebears about human history have been swept away by modern discoveries, which have shown to us the vastness and the complexity of this history. Even today theologians are to be found who perpetuate the objection by their timorous attitude to these discoveries ... We realise that the men of each generation could possess no more than the science of the time, that revelation makes no difference here: its light is of another order. Neither the biblical writers nor the Fathers nor the medieval theologians could have known, obviously, about Neanderthal man or *Sinanthropus*. ... But the material narrowness of their view was no hindrance to its formal breadth. And it is this latter which is proper to Catholicism; however remote the horizons which modern science discovers, Catholicism spontaneously incorporates them."[62]

However, if we are to form a new mentality able to draw on the strength of a religious spirit, and in order to make full use of this "enlightenment of another order" or of the full vision de Lubac cited, we must fully define the mentality which prevents us from doing so.

And yet, this myth of progress is also crumbling. In his address to the Academie française quoted above, Daniel-Rops spoke of progress. He also cited a passage from Plato's *Timaeus*, a tale of the happy isle where a perfect, self-satisfied humanity decides it can do without the gods. But, in punishment, a flash of Jupiter's lightning plunges the island into the ocean, and the great whirlpool of water which swallowed

Atlantis formed "an enormous mushroom as high as the sky."[63] And since humanity had already experienced the horror of the atomic mushroom of Hiroshima when Daniel-Rops made this speech, he had no hesitation in proclaiming Plato as a prophet and in charging that the tragic contemporary event was the outcome of man's claim to be an end unto himself. Today, several decades after that destruction, the ecological tragedy looms large with its ruinous, growing chain of consequences: man, by applying his reason as the sole measure and in his striving to dominate nature, destroys nature, and, in doing so, destroys himself – he can no longer live. Years ago, when I read that they had found traces of DDT in the penguins of the South Pole, I shivered at such a terrifying confirmation of my fear. And how is it unimaginable that the day will never come when men will use the thousands and thousands of bombs and weapons they build? Man-without-God no longer has a measure!

This is the consequence of the corruption which has tormented us in all ages, that temptation of old (as the Bible tells us with such supreme ingeniousness) the origin of evil in man. And, although the serpent tells man, "You will be like God," it does not say, "there is no God." Nevertheless it does insinuate that God is of no use to man, for since man can be like God, man can do everything.

This claim – to be able to do everything – hems in the horizons of human reason so that it will eventually say, "only whatever *I* can do exists." And it is precisely this reduction of the horizon that leads us to the conclusive point of our journey, into the realm of the contemporary difficulty in understanding a religious argument.

7 CONCLUSION

God, as we have said, is not denied. He was not denied in the seventeenth, eighteenth, or in the nineteenth centuries, just as he was not denied when the world was first tempted. On the contrary, the past few centuries of our western history have been governed by Theism.

Deism, born in England and spread abroad partly by the anglomania of that age, retained a God, but a God remote, pale and shadowy, never intervening in human affairs and demanding no act of faith. His existence was arrived at by a simple process of reasoning: no watch without a watchmaker. But this unknown God, who was beginning to be called 'the Supreme Being', was not credited with any attribute apart from existence. If he imposed a religion at all, it was natural religion, as old as the world, embracing all creeds without distinction.[64]

Even today, acknowledgment of God, the Supreme Entity, comes easily – providing it is clear that he has nothing do with human reality. God is certainly not denied – as long as it is accepted that man can do without him. And, if someone insists that he cannot do without God, religion will find its own forum in a place set apart from the normal life of society, in a place foreign to it. This principle of "policing religion," is the expression of today's genius. Self-sufficient man who makes himself his ultimate criterion and separates himself from God commits an error which men of all ages are liable to make. But our age has made this same error resound so that it has been able to influence all minds. The same old temptation holds court in modern man; but our times are dominated by such concerns as criteria and issues, which censor authentic religious sensibility.

This mentality is called *secularism.* It is derived from rationalism and is the fruit of disaggregation. It is so advanced that it inspires society as a whole, society in all its forms, especially in the area of education.

But, as we have said at the beginning of our discourse, a God whom something might escape is not God, but someone we can easily replace. A God who agrees to remain apart from human affairs *is not the God of the Christian message* who came into the world so that he could be man's companion. This is why secularism is, at least implicitly, *atheism*, it is life without God. More precisely, atheism is the most theoretically and practically consequential attitude derived from secularism.

If the world and man's existence are a field in which man is wholly master of himself, able to draw on himself for all the solutions to his problems and needs, then man reduces, in a peremptory fashion, the meaning of life and reality to whatever he creates or thinks he creates. And this reduction is complete if man applies even partially the principle of separating religious experience from the experience of life in any of its aspects, For then he comes to ignore a bond of life with the one who is the maker of life. A God confined to the place of worship or to the sacristy is that useless God, the God of ancient temptation, and the man who yields to it is the man whose possibilities are tragically limited.

God, in order to be God, is inside life, is life. Here is another testimony from Teilhard de Chardin, once again reported by Henri de Lubac:

Everything in this world, things and events, and human relationships, had for Père Teilhard a sacramental character. ... For the Christian whose eyes are open, there is nothing in the world that does not make God manifest. Everything in the world can lead to God, the "ultimate point" upon which everything converges: everything and, more particularly in the first place, what constitutes our constant daily portion – work. And this does not mean only the (humanly speaking) specially privileged work that makes a man feel that he is "making history," ... or, again, makes him feel that he is helping to raise higher the continually growing structure of science. It means all human work without distinction, from the humblest household task to the most spiritual activity. In this order, no instrument is specially favoured: God "is at the tip of my pen, my pick, my brush, my needle, of my heart and of my thought."[65]

Stepping beyond a world reduced to the space the human mind can measure towards the panoramic vision that provides man with the companionship of a God disdaining nothing in order to be with man, his creation, means to have the simplicity and the courage to ask a question. It is the question asked of Jesus by Nicodemus, an important man, and Jewish leader, who was spurred by the desire to know something more about him and who resolved to meet him by night. And, in response to the enigmatic words of Jesus, who said: "You must be born from above," (cf. John 3.3), Nicodemus asked: "How can that be possible?" (Jn 3.9) If this is not an expression of premeditated skepticism, it is the question of passionate human searching, capable of uncovering the answer and understanding the meaning of a Word.

The Constituent Factors of the Christian Phenomenon in History

4 The Continuity of Jesus Christ: Root of the Church's Self-Awareness

I THE PATH WE WILL FOLLOW

We are now about to enter into an analytical explication of our theme. However, it should be said that we will only be able to outline it here as my present concern is to indicate an adequate structure of categories through which to tackle the problem of the Church. Within the context of a brief historical résumé, we will first try to pinpoint the structural factors of the Church phenomenon as they appear at its inception. The Church is an historical phenomenon: it emerged or "came to the surface," we might say, in the flow of history, at a certain point. With this in mind, we will ask ourselves what were the recognizable decisive factors of this phenomenon at its origins? In other words, I would like, in this first series of reflections, to draw attention to a certain number of high points, immediately obvious on even a cursory reading of primitive texts.

In the second part, we will examine the outcome of the awareness-building process that Christian life has wrought throughout the centuries with regard to the value of these factors to be identified in our historical résumé. Throughout its history, the life of the Church has become ever more conscious of the specific weight of these factors which constitute it. We will see, in this second part, how the Church presents itself in history and what it claims to be. We will, therefore, make a summary mention of the doctrinal, dogmatic vision that the Church has acquired of itself.

Thirdly – and in my view the most interesting part of this inquiry – we will attempt to verify the Church's affirmations, asking ourselves: "How can we know that what the Church claims to be can, in all reason, be proven true?"

2 THE LINK WITH JESUS CHRIST

In pinpointing these original constituent factors I have just introduced to the argument, I would like once again to emphasize a premise: Primarily, the Church presents itself in history as a relationship with the living Christ. All other reflections, all other considerations are a consequence of this position. In the Acts of the Apostles, Luke depicts a group of people who, from the time of Jesus' earthly life, continued to live as a community after the Easter event, even though every reason in the world existed for dissolving their association, born of the advent of an exceptional man. Once he was dead, the definitive dispersion of disciples would have been understandable, if the presence around whom their companionship revolved had been destroyed.

In the year 29 or 30 of our era and in a period coinciding with the Jewish Passover, three crosses were erected outside Jerusalem. On two of them common criminals died. The third, in contrast, was reserved for a political agitator, at least according to the plaque bearing the name of the condemned man and the reason for his excruciating execution: "Jesus of Nazareth, King of the Jews." Executions of this kind were frequent at the time and did not attract the public's attention. Historians and chroniclers had too much else to do and did not feel it their duty to record the deeds and misdeeds of poor souls who were condemned to die on the cross, often for paltry reasons. The execution of Jesus, then, would have gone unnoticed if two days later, some of his friends and disciples had not seen him appear to them full of life – the same man whose body they had respectfully placed in a new tomb.[1]

It is this fullness of life, mentioned in Gustave Bardy's vivid version of the event, which is the key to the enigmatic period following Christ's death. It explains why the demise of this man, who had been their reason for living for three years, so shocked the disciples – disorientating and confusing them – just as Jesus himself had predicted shortly before his death. "You will all lose faith, for the scripture says: I *shall strike the shepherd and the sheep will be scattered,*" (Mark 14:27). But his death did not make them fall away; it did not scatter them, leaving them without the possibility of coming together again. On the contrary, after their initial sensation of being lost, they started to meet, perhaps more often than before. They even began to rally others. Even in their pain, in their fear of the consequences of the execution of Jesus, we can gather from the texts that the group grew stronger, became more established. Their confused perception of that life, which came to them when the risen Jesus appeared before them, had been hidden on the horizon of their convictions all the time. It was something that must have made some of them wonder: "Has his death really put an end to everything?" But a devout remembrance of an individual would not have been enough to keep that group together under such difficult, hostile circumstances, even if it had been supported by the desire to spread the Master's teaching. In the eyes of those men, the only teaching that could not be doubted was the presence of their Master, Jesus alive. And this is exactly what they transmitted: the testimony of a Man, present and alive. The birth of the Church is none other than this company of disciples, this small group of friends who stayed together even after Christ's death. And why did they stay together? Because the risen Christ made himself present in their midst.

Together the disciples bear witness to us that this man is alive and present, this man whose divine mystery his followers, as we have seen, gradually, slowly learned to acknowledge as they followed a path of progressive certainty along which he himself led them.[2] They tell us that God did not come into the world, that he did not take his place as a man in history at some random time only to be remembered vaguely in some abstract recollection of the past: no, Christ remains in history, with his person and his reality, in the life of man. He has the historical, living face of the Christian community, of the Church. Through their lives and their testimony, those first disciples, that small group of friends, communicate to us that God did not come down to earth for just one instant to be some kind of point in history elusive to those who would be born after the time when he was in Galilee and Judaea. On the contrary, God came into the world to stay in the world: Christ is *Emmanuel*, "God-with-us."

This is certainly the conviction, the conviction of the reality of this presence on reading the opening lines of the Acts of the Apostles, where we are immediately told that "he had shown himself alive to them after his Passion by many demonstrations: for forty days he had continued to appear to them and tell them about the kingdom of God" (Acts 1:3). Moreover, the texts specify that these appearances were not the fruit of the imagination, but that actual conversations took place – for example, "while at table with them ...". Other accounts of these appearances contain the same tone. Matthew refers to the understandable fear of two women who had followed Jesus to the entrance of the empty tomb, to their fear at the sight of the apparition of an angel. He also notes that Jesus walks towards them and greets them with "Hail" in a familiar way (cf. Mt 28:1–10). Mark's Gospel observes that after appearing to various people, Jesus presents himself to all eleven disciples as they eat together, and he rebukes them for not believing those who had seen him risen (cf. Mark 16:14). In a similar vein, John describes (cf. John 21) an incident on the shore of Lake Tiberias, where Jesus is preparing the fire to cook the fish which had just been miraculously caught, while Luke reports Jesus' appearance at a meeting of the disciples (cf. Luke 24:36–43). On seeing their terror, he simply reassures them by inviting them to touch him and prove for themselves that it is really he and to convince them, he then asks for something to eat. These are all untheatrical undramatic observations simply testifying to a familiar presence still with them. They are the translation into facts of the phrase "God-with-us."

There is, then, truly a physiological continuity between Christ and this first nucleus of the Church. And this is how that small group of people begin their journey in the world: permanence of the life of the man Christ, present and at work among them. And the reality of this presence contained in the conviction those first men tried to transmit to us is even more evident later on in the first chapter of the Acts of the Apostles, in following way:

All those joined in continuous prayer, together with several women, including Mary the mother of Jesus, and with his brothers.

One day Peter stood up to speak to the brothers – there were about a hundred and twenty persons in the congregation: "Brothers, the passage of scripture had to be fulfilled in which the Holy Spirit, speaking through David, foretells the fate of Judas, who offered himself as a guide to the men who arrested Jesus – after having been one of our number and actually sharing this ministry of ours. As you know, he bought a field with the money he was paid for his crime. He fell headlong and burst open, and all his entrails poured out. Everybody in Jerusalem heard about it and the field came to be called the Bloody Acre, in their language Hakeldama. Now in the Book of Psalms it says: *Let his camp be reduced to ruin, /Let there be no one to live in it.* And again: *Let someone else take his office.*

"We must therefore choose someone who has been with us the whole time that the Lord Jesus was traveling around with us, someone who was with us right from the time when John was baptizing until the day when he was taken up from us – and he can act with us as a witness to his resurrection."

Having nominated two candidates, Joseph known as Barsabbas, whose surname was Justus, and Matthias, they prayed, "Lord, you can read everyone's heart; show us therefore which of these two you have chosen to take over this ministry and apostolate which Judas abandoned to go to his proper place." They then drew lots for them, and as the lot fell to Matthias, he was listed as one of the twelve apostles (Acts 1: 14–26).

In this passage we can clearly see that the first community wanted to communicate to us the awareness of being the continuation of Christ. Could it be that their praying was constant and with one heart because their foundation was the overwhelming drama of all that had just happened? It would have been more logical for the Lord's passion to have led to skepticism and division, as happens in history every time the leader of a group, the founder of a given reality, dies. However, the fact that they were constant and prayed with one heart was rooted in their trust and the experience of the Master who was present. And their concern at replacing Judas in order to re-form the little group of twelve Jesus had chosen revealed their conviction that they were the bearers of a mandate, the testimonies of an event without comparison, the harbourers of the expectation of a fact that, according to Jesus' promise, would have given them strength, "not many days from now" (cf. Acts 1:1–8).

This is not the picture of a group that had merely been able to re-organize after the blows of adverse fortune. No, here is a group which had never broken up, because the reason for their union never abandoned them. To them, Jesus is not someone to be remembered, in an effort, perhaps, to keep faith with his words. Rather, he is someone still present and still at work to whom they bear witness. This, again according to the Acts of the Apostles, is what Peter said: "Yet three days afterward God raised him to life and allowed him to be seen, not by the whole people but only by certain witnesses God had chosen beforehand. Now we are those witnesses – we have eaten and drunk with him after his resurrection from the dead – and he has ordered us to proclaim this to his people and to tell them that God has appointed him to judge everyone, alive or dead" (Acts 10: 40–3).

In a way then, nothing has changed since he walked the streets of Galilee, working miracles and remitting sins, scandalizing the doctors of the law. He is at work as before. But a problem arises here and it involves the nature of his continuity in history. This is how the problem of the Church arises and it is linked by the very problem of Christ itself. Yet, before this problem can be tackled in a critical way so as to assess the proposal it contains, the problem of the Church must be viewed in terms of its root, which is the continuity of Christ. This is how it revealed itself to those first men who lived it first hand and how Jesus himself presented it, given that his whole mission in this world was to render the Father present through himself. And having appeared as man, how could he then detach himself from man – man who had sought him throughout the centuries and in all ages and who still seeks him – and entrust his name and his work to a mere apparatus, to something other than him, than himself? According to Jacques Leclercq: "Reading the Gospel it appears that Christ was extremely concerned about discarding whatever could have marred the personal nature of his relationship with his disciples. He manifests his dislike of formulas for long prayer (*in multiloquio*), of formality (he reacts against the excesses of the Sabbath day of rest and the Pharisean interpretation of the Law); his religion is love and the giving of self; he comes with his Father into the soul of those who give of themselves; he makes his dwelling place within them."[3] So, it might be said that we normally "only, or mainly, ask history to tell us what happened at a given time; but, for the primitive Christian tradition, Jesus, principally, is not a figure of the past but the Lord present in the community with his will and his words; he is, of course, the Master of Nazareth, of Galilee and of that death in Jerusalem, but at the same time, he is the risen one, the bringer of salvation."[4]

It is, therefore, the Lord, present as he is, who even today defines the problem of the Church. And before approaching this problem in a more detailed way in terms of its constituent factors, it would be opportune to stress our awareness of the fact that presents itself to us by means of its first emergence in history. The Church feels itself to be the community of Jesus, the Messiah; this, not just because the disciples adhered to the ideals he preached (which they certainly did not grasp fully at the time), but because they abandoned themselves to him, alive and present among them, as he had promised to be: "And know that, I am with you always; yes, to the end of time" (Matt 28:20). In this they were truly adhering to all he had taught – that his work was not a doctrine, not an inspiration of some kind for a more just life, but that he in person was sent by the Father to be a companion to man along his pathway.

To conclude, we could say that the Church's self-awareness of its origins consists in the fact that it is the continuity of Christ in history so that every analytical detail, every step we take towards the heart of this problem must lead us to the verification of this same root. Jacques Leclercq has affirmed this certainty in the following quote: "Primarily, a Christian is one who believes in the resurrection of Christ, in what it means that Christ is the living victor, that we can join with him who lives now, and that this union is the aim of our lives. The resurrection of Christ also means that Jesus Christ is not only the founder of the Church, but that he is always the invisible, but actively present, head."[5]

And the first communities expressed it in formulas which conveyed the content of this consistency and unity which experts call confessions of faith.

Faith here is always faith in Jesus Christ. This is why faith in the New Testament ... is not an abstract formula or some anonymous depths of reality. ... This God is the God who spoke and acted in the history of Jesus Christ. The content of New Testament faith is therefore a person, his work and his fate.

This connection is clearly expressed in the earliest confessions of faith made by the Christian community. The early nominal confessions have the form: "Jesus is the Kyrios" (Rom. 10:9, 1 Cor. 12:3) or "Jesus is the Christ" (1 Jn 2: 22; 5.1; 2 Jn 7). The most important formula, however, which later almost completely replaced all the others, was: "Jesus is the Son of God" (1 Jn 4:15; 5:5, etc.).

There are also several verbal formulas (*pistis formulae*) alongside these nominal formulae or homologies in the New Testament. This [sic] verbal confessions speak of God's action in Jesus Christ. ... The confession "that God raised him from the dead" (Rom. 10:9; see also Acts 2:24, 32; 3:15, etc.; 1 Pet. 1:21, etc.) is a verbal confession. The best known and most important of these verbal confessions of faith is found in 1 Cor. 15:3–5: "Christ died for our sins in accordance with the scriptures; he was buried; he was raised on the third day in accordance with the scriptures and he appeared to Cephas, then to the twelve." Paul introduced this strophically structured formula as traditional and made it the basis of his own theology.[6]

5 The Three Constituent Factors

The first nucleus of the Church demonstrated that it "not only carries on his work (Christ's), but she is his very continuation, in a sense far more real than that in which it can be said that any human institution is its founder's continuation." The Church then, even at the beginning, showed us that in its bond with Jesus, "she represents him, in the full and ancient meaning of the term; she really makes him present."[1]

Let us now examine the three constituent factors of the Christian fact as it appears as a phenomenon on the screen of history. This means asking ourselves the following questions: If a contemporary of those first days, an outsider, had observed the fact as it emerged, what elements would he have indicated in describing it? With what inevitable characteristics would he have been confronted?

I THE REALITY OF A SOCIOLOGICALLY IDENTIFIABLE COMMUNITY

Primarily, the Christian fact presents itself in history – the Church presents itself to the observer – as *community*. This is the first feature which strikes one approaching the Christian event. And, on reading the Acts of the Apostles, the first historical document describing primitive Christian life, in the second chapter we immediately encounter an unexpected image of this communital characteristic of the early Christians. "They devoted themselves to the Apostles' teaching and fellowship to the breaking of bread and the prayers. And fear came upon every soul; and many wonders and signs were done through the Apostles and all who believed were together. ... Day by day, attending the temple together and breaking bread in their homes they partook of food with glad and generous hearts, praising God and having favour with all the people. And the Lord added to their number day by day those who were being saved" (Acts 2:42–44; 46–48).

This communital nature appears not only in the fourth chapter of the Acts of the Apostles, where one expression describes it in a synthetic, touching way: "The company of those who believed were of one heart and soul" (Acts 4:32), but also in the fifth chapter. Many signs and miracles were done among the people by the hands of the Apostles. And they were all together in Solomon's Portico (Acts 5:12). It is interesting how this later passage tells us first of all that the Christians also met in the temple, like all Jews, but adds that they would also meet up "in Solomon's Portico."

Try then to imagine the scene: it is around the Paschal season, when Jews throughout the world would be intent, as far as possible, on travelling to Jerusalem as pilgrims. Try also to imagine the reactions of one of these pilgrims, who, on going to the temple for a few days in a row, would have noticed, each time, a little group of people under the portico. The first day he would have proceeded on his way, without wondering why, and on the second day, he might have done the same. But at some point, he certainly would have asked someone: "Who are those people I always see together here?" And they would have replied: "They are the followers of Jesus of Nazareth." And so we can see how the Church began: it literally allowed itself to "be seen" under Solomon's Portico, it proposed itself through the mere sight of it, through a first perception which can only be described as community.

And so the first factor with which the Church evidently presented itself as a reality was as an identifiable group, a sociologically identifiable phenomenon, a company of people bound to one another. And even as the years passed, Christian writers took pains to forcefully stress this communital factor, this first characteristic. "Justin relates: 'On the day called the day of the sun, everyone in the city and the countryside meets in one place. They read the memorials of the apostles and the writings of the prophets, as they are allowed to do these days.'"[2]

On the basis then of the first Christian texts, it certainly cannot be argued that Christianity was lived exclusively as an interior, personal, and intimate interpretation of God, with individualism as its primary feature. On the contrary, the communital connotation is foremost. It reveals a certain logic to the eye, attentive to the reality in which this phenomenon emerged, a reality and tradition by which God's actions in history point to the communital dimension as the fundamental one.

This first factor turns our thoughts, in fact, to the basic Old Testament concept of Israel as the people of Yahweh. As Henri de Lubac notes: "The national character of the kingdom of God, in apparent contradiction with its world-wide character, was an antidote to all attempts at interpretation in an individualistic sense. Made spiritual and world- wide, as the prophets had indeed foretold, Judaism passed on to Christianity its concept of salvation as essentially social. If, having regard to the greater number of the faithful, the Church derives more particularly from the Gentiles – *Ecclesia ex gentibus* – the idea of the Church, nonetheless, comes from the Jews."[3]

Jesus himself lived as a man within this tradition, and it is he – as Mircea Eliade acutely observes – who proposes that his disciples draw from the depths of this method brought to light by tradition. It is the method by which God forges a relationship with man: "Jesus sought the radical transformation of the Jewish people, in other words, the emergence of a New Israel, a new people of God. The Lord's Prayer (Luke 11:2–4, Matt. 6:9–13) admirably summarizes the "method" for achieving this end. An expression of Hebrew piety, the prayer does not use the first person in the singular but only in the plural: *our* Father, give *us* this day *our* daily bread, forgive us *our* trespasses, deliver *us* from evil."[4] Father de Lubac makes a similar observation: "To believe in this one God was, therefore, to believe at the same time in a common Father of all: *unus Deus et Pater omnium.* The prayer taught us by Christ makes clear in its very first phrase that monotheism postulates the brotherhood of all men," also using Ciprius's splendid phrase in his commentary : "Since He who dwells in us is one only, everywhere he joins and binds together those who are in the bond of unity."[5]

That visible "we" was the first feature of the Church's face that an observer could have photographed. We must be aware of this even though it is easier for us today to develop a certain wariness concerning this aspect of the Church: this "we," this being a group, a sociologically identifiable reality, could become an enclosure, a ghetto. But, if a Christian communital identity is lived according to a ghetto mentality, it is only because of ignorance, or the total betrayal of its origin and its real content.

a) Old and New Consciousness: God's Choice

Let us move on now to compare ancient Judaean self-awareness with self-perception of the group of Jews who had become followers of Christ.

Fitting examples of this awareness appear throughout the Bible. In reporting God's communication to Moses, Exodus tells us: "If you obey my voice and hold fast to my covenant, you of all the nations shall be my very own, for all the earth is mine. I will count you a kingdom of priests, a consecrated nation" (Exod. 19:5–6) This concept of holiness illustrates man's relationship with God – man is placed in God's service. But it also indicates what primarily and fundamentally scandalizes man about God's action: the preference, the choice God makes of a particular aspect of his creation *specially* placed in his service. This analogy is also remarkable in Paul's letter to Titus where, referring to Jesus, he writes: "He sacrificed himself in order to set us free from all wickedness and to purify people so that it could be his very own ..." (Titus 2:14). Likewise, in Leviticus God promises: "I will set my dwelling among you, and I will not cast you off. I will live in your midst; I will be your God, and you shall be my people" (Lev. 26:11–12). And God repeats in the book of Ezekiel: "I shall make my home above them; I will be their God, they shall be my people" (Ezek. 37:27). In the same way, Paul, in one of his letters, combines the two previous quotations, in addition to other passages from the prophets and the Psalms, when he has God say: "I will make my home among them and live with them; I will be their God and they shall be my people. Then come away from them and keep aloof, says the Lord. Touch nothing that is unclean, and I will welcome you and be your father, and you shall be my sons and daughters" (2 Cor. 6:16–18).

The idea of belonging, of possession by God, defined the self-awareness of the Hebrew people. It constitutes the self-awareness of this little group of people who, initially, did not give at all the impression of being a people, for there might have been 50 of them under Solomon's Portico, then 100, then 1,000. However, they were all fully aware that like the Hebrew people, they too defined themselves as God's possession; and so they were too, to the extent that they appropriated the very same words of the original consciousness. In Paul and other New Testament writers who represent the first mature expressions of the Christian experience, the certainty emerges that they are the fulfillment of the Hebrew people phenomenon – they were certain that they were prolonging that reality by making it come definitively true, bringing to fulfillment the true people of Yahweh. Those who would gather under Solomon's Portico were the first sign. That emergent group of people presented themselves as people who, having the living presence of Christ among them, were the almost physiological continuity of that reality, bonded as they were to that living presence in the concreteness of daily, family life. That newly emergent group was aware that it was prolonging or rather communicating and actually realizing the truth of all that had constituted the history of Israel in the Old Testament – in short, they were aware that they were building the true, definitive people of God in the world. James, who was the first leader of the community in Jerusalem, says as much in one of his discourses, where he cites the prophet Amos: "My brothers," he said, "listen to me."

Simeon has described how God first arranged to enlist a people for his name out of the pagans. This is entirely in harmony with the words of the prophets, since the scriptures say:

> After that I shall return
> and rebuild the fallen House of David;
> I shall rebuild it from its ruins,
> and restore it.
> Then the rest of mankind,
> all the pagans who are consecrated to my name,
> will look for the Lord
> says the Lord, who made this known so long ago (Acts 15:14–18).

It is difficult for us to imagine the mental upheaval which a Jew like James would have suffered by announcing that the people of God is to be created from among pagans. And what of the repulsion of the Jews at the voice of another Jew telling them that God had taken pains to raise up his people from among those pagans – a people, that is, like the people of Israel?

Paul displayed a similar awareness. This becomes obvious when he goes for the first time to Corinth – that great port city in the Aegean Sea and a Roman province famed for its trade and for the dissolution of its society – and God encourages him in a nocturnal vision: "Do not be afraid to speak out, nor allow yourself to be silenced: I have so many people on my side in this city that no one will even attempt to hurt you" (Acts 18:9–10). We cannot help thinking here that in Corinth, in what could have been considered a metropolis, there must have been all of 100 Christians or sympathizers! Yet, the Acts tell us that the awareness, albeit intermingled with many understandable difficulties, was impressed on Paul's conscience, impressed by an initiative of God himself, that his "people" was indeed there and that it was a numerous people. (Incidentally, all this serves to highlight the fact that there has never been a time in history like that of the beginning of the Church, which has the right to be discussed in terms of cultural revolution, a perfect description of the particular moment in human time that concerns us here. And as much as we are now living the consequences of that revolution, we can never be aware enough of its origins.) And it is then, as we have seen, this new phenomenon, that was being born, that drew with confidence on its tradition because it sprang directly from it, at the same time constituted a fundamental upheaval because it possessed a different concept of its identity. In this sense, it led to a relationship with God utilizing the categories that he himself had taught man through the history of Israel – and this is a pedagogical clue to what an individual is and what God wants to be for him. With the compact simplicity that only an assimilated tradition can bestow, here was the materialization of one of Hans Urs von Balthasar's observations: "Seen alongside the path chosen by God, every other possibility, devised by the cleverest human speculation and fancy, will always turn out to be yet another superficial banality."[6] At the same time, however, the Christian fact made the awareness of its burning newness manifest to the world from its very beginnings: "The eternal day has dawned at last and no night shall ever follow it. The necessary preparations were of long duration, wisely spaced out in stages; but the bright light of the Word made flesh shone forth all at once, for it was the sudden beginning of a stupendous revolution."[7]

I now would like to cite three New Testament passages to explain the impact of this revolution on the idea of belonging to a people set apart for Yahweh. To do so, I will establish the stark difference between the awareness of this new and numerically small people that they were the possession of God and the Hebrew people.

In the first passage, Paul, writing to Christians in Galatia, expressed the new concept in this way: "and you are, all of you, sons of God through faith in Jesus Christ. All baptized in Christ, you have all clothed yourself in Christ, and there are no more distinctions between Jew and Greek, slave and free, male and female, but all of you are one in Christ Jesus. Merely by belonging to Christ, you are the posterity of Abraham, the heirs he was promised" (Gal. 3:26–9). Paul reiterates this same concept in a second passage, in his letter to the Colossians: "and in that image there is no room for distinction between Greek and Jew, between the circumcised or the uncircumcised, or between barbarian and Scythian, slave and free man. There is only Christ: he is everything and he is in everything" (Col. 3:11).

And again, in this third passage, he told the Christians of Corinth: "In the one Spirit we were all baptized, Jews as well as Greeks, slaves as well as citizens, and one Spirit – was given to us all to drink" (1 Cor. 12:13).

The most profound cultural revolution experienced by the early Christians regarding their consciousness of being a people, as expressed in the first Christian texts is this: that group, while seeing itself as a people (and, according to the tradition of their fathers, as the people of God), that group, growing day by day, affirmed that it had not been moulded from an ethnic root or from some sociological unity wrought by historical events. And this is the stark difference: for the Hebrew people, the very fact of being born into that people made a person part of an ethnic nucleus chosen by God, a unity established in the course of history in which God intervened and defined frontiers. On the contrary, from the very first instant that the Christian existence is recorded, for them, the ethnic nature of God's preference is totally eliminated. This new people, in fact, is formed of those that God united in the name of their acceptance of his Son's coming: they could well be of different races, even each other's traditional enemies (as Jesus and the Samaritan woman were); they may have vastly different ideas and backgrounds; they even may have been strangers in the world prior to this time. But as they are a people united by God through faith in Jesus Christ, any type of native or "carnal" qualification liable to keep human beings apart is radically overcome.

Immediately then, the Christian phenomenon picks up on the "chosen by God" idea that Israel formulated, and, in its turn, it is moulded by this idea, without any carnal limits, because God's choice coincides with adherence to faith in Christ.

b) The Cultural Value of a New Concept of Truth

This first factor of the life of the Church also has another precise cultural value. The new phenomenon, which was gradually being verified, had a surprising correspondence with its roots, with respect to the image of the Hebrew-Semitic tradition of truth. Here the newness was mainly apparent to those whose point of reference was the Greek-Latin world, and so to us, too, since we are the heirs of that world.

How then, do we perceive truth – for the western world, which metaphor most easily indicates the truth? For us, light – the brightness of what is true, coincides with truth, where certainty depends on the evidence of what we see. In this way we emphasize the persuasive aspect of the truth: where there is light, we can see – we cannot help but see. Therefore, it is evidence that engages our eyes; our faculty of vision and the truth is the object of this potential evidence.

None of this can be denied, and, in fact, John the Evangelist himself would use this same metaphor, since the scenario of Christianity in the world had reached such a point in its evolution that it had already penetrated the Graeco-Roman reality and was ready to embrace as many of its categories as was possible.

However, according to Biblical tradition, the most frequently used definition of truth and allusion to it is found in another metaphor: the "rock" or "crag." Originally nomadic desert-dwellers, the Semites were particularly sensitive to the point of reference provided by great rock formations, fixed as they are, compared with sand and dust which can be blown away and scattered by the wind. In the history of Semitic consciousness, therefore, human aspiration for a safe place – for something solid that would mean stability, and therefore water, food, shelter, the possibility to build – turned to the image of the rock to identify the divine, to clarify what the divine was for man – something on which he could lean and build and in which he could find meaning.

The use of this metaphor demonstrates how seeing with one's own eyes is not the supreme method in the Semitic mind for developing an awareness of the truth. What is more important is reference to something secure, something stable. Indeed, the word "amen" in Hebrew has the same root as the word "truth," and this root means, precisely, "stability, permanence." And the word "amen" is an affirmation of security: this remains, and so it is true, it is like that.

This stability we are discussing here is not eroded by time. Duration proves truth. Something that challenges time, that is certain and permanent, presents itself as the expression of what is true. Again in Hebrew, the word describing man as a changeable, ephemeral creature and the concept of "lie" have the same root. And if one views the notion of lie in the strictly gnoseological as opposed to the ethical sense, the ephemeral is a lie; the truth is permanence.

This Hebrew notion of stability also appears in the Psalms, which run through the centuries of Hebrew tradition, are used by the Church, in its official prayers today, and expressions such as these:

> I love you, Yahweh, my strength
> (My saviour, you rescue me from violence).
> Yahweh is my rock and my bastion,
> my deliverer is my God (Ps. 18: 1–2).

Or:

> May the words of my mouth always find favor,
> and the whispering meditation of my heart,
> in your presence, Yahweh,
> my Rock, my Redeemer! (Ps. 19:14).

Or again:

> In God alone there is rest for my soul,
>   from him comes my safety;
> with him alone for my rock, my safety,
>   my fortress, I can never fall (Ps. 62:1–2).

And finally, let us remember this awesome expression:

> My flesh and my heart are pining with love,
> my heart's Rock, my own, God for ever! (Ps. 73:26).

Now, I would like to stress how this Biblical tradition of the rock image as the metaphor of truth is rooted in a greater human completeness than the metaphor of light. It is, quite simply, a more adequate way to communicate, discover, and accept the truth. Moreover, I would also like to emphasize that this is not a mere peculiarity of Biblical interpretation: it is what God wanted to reveal. If God has chosen, as the instrument of his communication with the world, a certain type of human structure, corresponding to a certain type of mentality, this means that it must contain something that is pedagogically important for the knowledge he wanted to convey to man.

What, then, is the method emerging from this metaphor of the rock? Perhaps the following will explain. With great psychological intuition, Saint Thomas wrote that man is much more persuaded by what he hears than by what he sees. If we reflect a while on our own attitudes and behavior, we will realize just how acute this observation is. An individual lives the experience of a deeper conviction when he finds himself adhering to the message of another rather than when he sees for himself. In adhering to someone he is listening to, man, in fact, must rest the *totality* of his person on the "you" of another. And, while it is very easy for all of us to doubt ourselves, it is much harder to cast the shadow of our "ifs" and our "buts" on a presence we admire and love. In any person-to-person relationship, the totality of our "I" is put into play so that knowledge and love form a oneness, and the act of adherence to the truth concerns the *totality* of the factors constituting life.

This is not irrationalism, for an encounter with a person in whom we experience the truth he communicates to us does not mean we exclude a critical attitude. Rather, it ensures the immanence of a critical attitude in that whole living context from which the attitude cannot be separated. It is from this total context, therefore, that the person's attitude assumes the authenticity of its dynamism. Nothing is more fragile then depending upon ourselves. Everything we can see as self-evident, that which we can verify by ourselves is burdened by ultimate fragility. This frustrates our self-confidence, which might very well be strong in an emphatic moment of self-affirmation, but is liable to wane. Nothing is more fragile than leaning only on ourselves in the search for truth.

The methodological lesson which definitively emerges from the rock as the image of truth is the solidity of the witness. In contrast to seeing with our own eyes, which engages only a part of our person, the figure of authentic testimony engages the adherence of our whole person. The witness is an entire personality at play, and for this reason, the entire personality of the listener is summoned to an engagement with it – the light shed by a piece of evidence represents only one aspect of the personality. The testimony is a living oneness, an existential whole. And let me insist on this point: if it is true, then these two methods are not contradictory, it is just that one is more complete than the other.

The Lord, who made the world and man, so as to facilitate the bond between man and truth (which is Himself) chose as his instrument not the terms of a vision, but those of an abandonment, of a love, the process by which man follows the testimony of truth. Moreover, this is the very same process by which nature, the expression of the Creator, makes a child grow. A child grows through the testimony of his mother and father as they continually propose solid ground for him to walk on.

Primarily then, the first experience of the Church referred to just such a solid image by bonding itself in an intimate way with the Biblical conception of truth. If, according to this conception, the human condition is to arrive at conviction, especially to the degree that the object of inquiry concerns life and destiny, it does not depend so much on the solitary emergence of a piece of evidence – like a light penetrating the mist – as on a sure co-existence. And by its nature, testimony implies an involvement, a companionship, which as we have seen, was the point of departure for that newly-formed reality that would be called Church.

The living God is born witness to by a living reality; God-made-man in the world is first of all witnessed. He is not made the object of research, of a critical enquiry. Naturally, as we have said, acknowledgment of a testimony does not exclude the possibility of evidence, when it may be given. The evidence factor is only excluded when the "seeing" is extrapolated – interpreted in such a way that is separated from a living context, from an organism as a whole.

Thus, the Christian community at its birth saw itself as the place where testimony was at the fore, the place where the solidity of the Biblical rock was seen to be the site of human reconstruction.

c) The Term Used: Ecclesia Dei[8]

Let us now examine a few observations concerning the language used to depict this communal reality, the initial notable and documented characteristic of the first Christian reality that emerged.

We have seen how the Christian phenomenon presented itself in history as a group, as a community – a community expressing its awareness that the term represented the definitive fulfillment of the people of Israel. How did the Hebrew language describe these people of Israel?

The Hebrew word for the reality of Israel as God's people was *qahal*. This word indicates a reality made of many individuals who were united and who gave expression to their unity by gathering together in a type of assembly. Now, this group, which first gathered under Solomon's Portico, gradually grew in number and spread, and, according to the Hellinistic trends which had, by then, taken root, called its own reality an assembly, *ekklesia*. *Ecclesia* in Greek means, literally, "assembly," a meeting of people. At a time when the imparting of the message of the Christian newness reached a world that did not strictly terminate at Judaism, this word was deliberately taken from the Greek language, which used it to describe all kinds of assemblies, to indicate routine realities in the life of society, a call to meet that might not only have referred to Christians but could, in any city, have concerned totally different ends and reasons.

An example, from the Acts of the Apostles, should illustrate this point. When Paul, who was preaching, encounters problems in Ephesus, caused by the silversmiths appointed to the temple of Artemis because they feared that his message would damage their trade, the tumultuous scenario is described in the following manner: "The whole town was in an uproar and the mob rushed the theatre dragging along two of Paul's Macedonian travelling companions, Gaius and Aristarchus. Paul wanted to make an appeal to the people, but the disciples refused to let him. ... By now everyone was shouting different things till the assembly itself had no idea what was going on." (Acts 19:29–30; 32). For this impromptu and turbulent rally, even the author of the Acts of the Apostles uses the word *ecclesia*" to describe it, the same term as was used for Christian assemblies. This proves that it referred to the normal practice in civil life of meeting together for some reason or other.

However, there was more to it than this. The Christian assembly, like the Hebrew idea *Qahal Yahweh*, is described using the genitive *Dei*, *Ecclesia Dei*, the community of God. In what sense is this genitive added to the word of common usage? In both the objective and subjective sense: that is, in one respect (the more obvious) this "of God" means that the subject matter of the assembly is God; while in the other, whereby the formula's origin is identified, it means that it is God himself who is calling the community together, it is God who unites those people who are "his own," to use the expression often featured in the New Testament. So, *Ecclesia Dei* means those gathered together by God.

Which categories are used in this highly original formula of the primitive Christian community? We have already mentioned the primary one, election, God's choice. And here, we again find this category applied to this people taking form, this people so easily identified, although they had no ethnic boundaries. And in his plan for the whole world, offered to the whole world because he is Lord of all, the Lord God presents himself to all by choosing a particular human reality. We remarked previously that this method is scandalous, and it is even more so for us today, beset as we are with difficulty in grasping the authentic Christian language. The concept of election, of God's choosing, is *the* one case that demonstrates the most startling proof of our extreme incapacity to understand, for nothing so contradicts the rationalism within which we have been formed, and the equality and democracy-oriented climate which are its consequences. And yet, the initiative which God takes and has taken within history in man's regard has precisely this characteristic: he began to allow himself be known directly through the Hebrew people and, using this same method, he continued his work. In fact, Jesus Christ, sent by the Father to save the world, communicates himself through chosen individuals who are the conveyors of the new and thus of the life that springs from it. Nothing affirms and teaches man about the absolute nature of God than the fact that he develops his work in the world through those he chooses through election. God is bound by nothing, and it is precisely in this phenomenon, this elective preference, that he manifests himself.

At this point, let us recall that famous passage from the gospel of Matthew in which Jesus asks his disciples what people think of him and who they think he is. Peter answers: "You are the Christ, ... the Son of the living God." Jesus replied, "Simon son of Jonah you are a happy man! Because it was not flesh and blood that revealed this to you but my Father in heaven. So I now say to you: You are Peter, and on this rock I will build my Church. And the gates of the underworld can never hold out against it" (Matt. 16: 16–18). It is clear in this context that this was an initiative taken in Peter's regard, and not one taken by the disciples: it was suggested by the Father. The Church is described as being built by Christ and *his own*. It is the fruit of a choice, a choice which becomes part of the great history of God's preference, and uses the method to which God has always remained faithful.

In the last chapters of the Gospel of John, which report Jesus' last words to his disciples and his testament – his final prayer – we ourselves can almost sense his anxiety for the perceptible unity of "his own," those of whom he speaks when he addresses the Father: "They were yours and you gave them to me." (John 17:6). And so too, the dynamic law of Jesus' moral conception is based on a uniting force, the result of a preference, a choice: "I am in my Father and you in me and I in you" (John 14.20); "You did not choose me, no I chose you; and I have commissioned you" (John 15:16).

All of this corresponds to the method which God has always used, and because of Jesus' almost sorrowful insistence, we cannot but think that man's problem is that he resists this logic.

The word itself, then, which the first communities used to describe their coming together and which expressed their awareness that, by the very fact that they were living as an assembly called by God in Jesus Christ suggests that they were the fulfillment of the *Qahal Yahweh*. This is the mark of a choice that they did not make.

It was a serious error to suppose ... that Jesus had no intention of forming a community and that this was far from his mind. ... Such an interpretation completely misunderstands the Messianic and eschatological thought of Israel, in which eschatological salvation can never be dissociated from the people of God and the community of God belongs necessarily to the kingdom of God. ... This reality was never denied or ignored in the prophecies, and both the pattern and development of God's salvific plan demand also the ultimate existence of a community of salvation and even the fulfilment of the special promises made to Israel.[9]

Thus, in these early Christian times, the Hebrew idea of *Qahal Yahweh* was succeeded by the definitive notion of *Ecclesia Dei*, the community of God – those gathered together by him. However, it should be noted that *Ecclesia Dei* is not a meeting of people only deserving to be called an assembly if many people participate. What constitutes the Christian community as church is not the number of individuals, any more than it is based upon the pure and simple fact of being together. Rather, it is the reality of being called together by God, a God who gathers together those he wants and who bestows on each person the gifts and responsibilities he wishes. Saint Paul stresses in his writings that: "God has appointed in the Church first apostles, second prophets, third teachers" (1 Cor. 12:28). This means that it is God who is at work in the Church, with the Church. God has always chosen and gathered his people together. The community only has value as a community because of the action of God, who by "appointing" and drawing his elected close, he thereby unites them.

d) The Church and the "Churches"

I would now like to discuss the word "ecclesia," which is used many times in the singular in the early Christian texts. For example: "News of this came to the ears of the Church in Jerusalem" (Acts 11:22); or, "he brought him to Antioch. For a whole year they met with the Church" (Acts 11:26); or again, "he went up and greeted the Church" (Acts 18:22). On the other hand, the word "ecclesia" also appears in the plural as the following citation illustrates: "The church throughout all Judaea, Galilee and Samaria had peace" (Acts 9:31). However, in one passage the singular word appears in a different way from the other examples, and this is not simply because it is used in a list or as part of a sum.

Rather, the passage recounts Paul's last days in Asia Minor, just before he leaves for Rome, where he would be killed and it reports his greetings to the leaders of the community in this way: "Take heed to yourselves and to all the flock in which the Holy Spirit has made you guardians, to feed the Church of the Lord which he obtained with his own blood" (Acts 20:8). (Here, this verse of the messianic psalm springs to mind: "Remember thy congregation, which thou has gotten of old" (Ps. 74 [73]:2). Now the price of the Messiah's blood was the redemption of God's people, of the whole people of God, and since this was the only act of redemption, one Church, therefore, emerges in all the places it was to be found.

In its fullest sense, then, the expression *Ecclesia Dei* represents the people of God in their totality precisely because they were inevitably brought together by God's initiative, his free and total choice.

For the redeeming act and the foundation of this religious society have an extremely close connection. These two works of Christ are in truth but one ... any attempt at separation will in this case run counter to the facts of history. No more to St. Paul than to the other witnesses to the early faith is the Church a sort of "aeon," a transcendent hypostasis which really existed before the work of Christ in the world. But neither is she a mere federation of local assemblies. Still less is she the simple gathering together of those who as individuals have accepted the Gospel and henceforward have shared their religious life. ... Neither is she an external organism brought into being or adopted after the event by the community of believers. It is impossible to maintain either of these two extreme theses, as it is impossible to keep them entirely separate. ... The *Ecclesia* that neither Paul nor any other of the first disciples ever imagined as an entirely invisible reality, but which they always understood as a Mystery surpassing its outward manifestations, this *Ecclesia* ... is *convocatio* before being a *congregatio*.[10]

It is not by adding communities that we arrive at the total Church, as is the case with the Protestant movement, whose conception is that each community is autonomous and constitutes itself: I am referring here to congregationalism, a temptation which can be perceived today in the Catholic Church, too. But, if each community is perceived to be a function of the total Church, every community, however small, represents the total Church, incarnating the Mystery of that call which was so present in the consciousness of the first Christians.

In this sense then, it is moving to read the final chapter of Paul's letter to the Romans, virtually dedicated exclusively to greeting, almost one by one, those who belonged to the community of Rome. At a certain point in this letter, Paul writes: "Greet Prisca and Aquila, my fellow-workers in Christ Jesus, who risked their necks for my life, to whom not only I but also all the Churches of the Gentiles give thanks; greet also the church in their house" (Rom. 16:3–5a). This same title, clearly indicated in this other passage from one of Paul's letters, also refers to the great communities of Asia Minor as well as the little group meeting in the home of friends: "The churches of Asia send greetings. Aquila and Prisca, together with the church in their house send you heartly greetings in the Lord" (1 Cor. 16:19). Clearly, then, the small group has the same significance as the whole Church. The individual group is remembered with affection in this passage, and is the mark of the Mystery for whom the apostle lives. And this is why a simple family assembly can be as much a point of reference as the large communities, as we read in this letter to the Colossians: "Give my greetings to the brethren at La-odice'a, and to Nympha and the church in her house. And when this letter has been read among you, have it read also in the church of the La-odice'ans; and see that you read also the letter from La-odice'a," (Col. 4:15–16). Here, too, the community of Laodicean believers was assimilated with a group that must surely not have been numerous and was accustomed to meeting in the home of someone called Nympha. How can it be explained, the dignity of the company of those people who met in the home of Aquila and Prisca, and at Nympha's house, for whom the whole mystery of the Church became operational and alive within it? Perhaps the following will explain: What the Church is for all men is Jesus Christ's self-communication to the world. In this sense, what do five or six Christians meeting in a house represent? They connote the same thing: Jesus Christ, who communicates himself to the world through that ambit. And in this sense then the value attributed by the first Christian texts to the individual and varied experiences of community – community in that the individuals were united with the apostles – is the same value attributed to the total Church, precisely because they express the Church's profound, united reality made to emerge by the Lord in different experiences.

Christians are often far from aware of this authentic source of their value, for we frequently find people who are either seeking clarity and security or a motive for their actions, and in so doing, they interpret their own community, or movement, or special association in a re-ductive way, depriving themselves of the source of unity that gives them life – the mystery of the Church as Church. Or, there are those who in referring to the Church, mean a mechanical super-organism unrelated to their daily reality, the concrete community close to them. In this way, then, they incorrectly separate themselves from the living Church. This is why one must learn what the total Church is, and this is why we must explore the depths of the ecclesiastical experience one has encountered, providing that it has all the characteristics of a true ecclesiastical experience. This means obedience to the total Church, depending on it, organizing one's life according to its rhythms, seeing oneself reflected in the other factors within the sphere of the Christian life. These are aspects which define the validity of gathering together. Otherwise, what gives value to our coming together is not the mystery of Jesus Christ who communicates himself to history and the world, but something that has diminished its import. Realistically, too, the local Church may only arise in a given place, a certain environment that is, in provisional circumstances. How can Jesus Christ be communicated in such an environment except through a group of Christians conscious of their true belonging to the Church proper? Without them, it would be as if the total Church in that environment did not exist. As Henri de Lubac wrote: "If God had willed to save us without our own cooperation, Christ's sacrifice by itself would have sufficed. But does not the very existence of our Savior presuppose a lengthy period of collaboration on man's part? ... God did not desire to save mankind as a wreck is salvaged; he meant to raise up within it a life, his own life."[11]

We have thus demonstrated how reflection on the word "ecclesia" has helped us to understand the type of consciousness of the first Christians of the value of their community, a value which derived totally, entirely from participation in the one Church, the Church governed by the apostles.

2 THE COMMUNITY INVESTED BY A "STRENGTH FROM ON HIGH"

We have seen that what remains to us of the first Christians' life as relayed to us in their texts is the firm conviction that the reality of the living Christ took hold of their lives, redeeming them, assuming them as its own, and rendering them the mystery of a united body. This does not mean that they were merely together physically, although that, too, had an ineliminable value. Rather, we have discovered here that the conviction of the first Christian communities was that one could not prescind from the community, especially and primarily in relation to the way they conceived of themselves. This brings us to the second constituent factor of the phenomenon of the Church we come across in the original texts, and marks an exceptional dimension of the awareness those first Christians lived.

We have already pointed out that the first Christians possessed an awareness of themselves as the real materialization, the definitive fulfillment of everything of which the people of Israel, as an historical entity, were the prophecy. Although they were a small circle, they were conscious that with the creation of their company, a new world was dawning, a new age that would have witnessed the existence of the people of Israel (which they represented) in its completed form – as the carriers of salvation for all humanity. However, these elements of the primitive Christian consciousness can be better explained in relation to another, more concise and decisive fact. From the interior point of view – from the self-awareness of the people who gathered together – the dominant idea was that their life had been jolted and transformed by a supernal action described as the "gift of the Spirit." This phenomenon is described in the following way: "When the day of Pentecost had come, they were all together in one place. And suddenly a sound came from heaven like the rush of a mighty wind, and it filled all the house where they were sitting. And there appeared to them tongues as of fire, distributed and resting on each one of them. And they were all filled with the Holy Spirit and began to speak in other tongues, as the Spirit gave them utterance"(Acts 2:1–4).

This, as related in the Acts of the Apostles, is a record of a fundamental fact of the primitive Church. However, this does not mean that the community of Jesus Christ was coming into being for the first time because, as we have seen, the community of Christ already existed. Rather, the origin of the essence of this community is, clarified as being permeated with "a strength from on high." And indeed, had not Jesus at the very moment of his return to the Father promised to give his people an energy, a new strength in understanding and consolation? "I will pray the Father, and He will give you another Counsellor" (John 14:16). Or, if you prefer, "I have yet many things to say to you, but you cannot bear them now. When the Spirit of truth comes, he will guide you into all the truth" (John 16:12–13). "And behold, I send the promise of my Father upon you; but stay in the city until you are clothed with power from on high" (Luke 24:49).

Let us now examine what it meant for the early Christians to be constituted by the "gift of the Spirit" or by "strength from on high."

a) Awareness of a Fact Which Has the Power to Change the Personality

Romano Guardini has described the experience of the early Christians in this manner: "What does the event of Pentecost mean for the Christian life? Before it happened, Christ presented himself – in person – 'to the eyes' of men; there was an abyss between them and Him. They did not understand Him; He did not come to be something of 'theirs.' ... Pentecost makes Christ, his Person, his Life and his redeeming action part of 'their' reality. ... Pentecost is the hour the Christian faith was born, the moment of being in Christ; not because of a mere 'religious experience,' but by the hand of the Holy Spirit."[12] The first Christians were well aware that everything happening in them and among them – the new and exceptional compared with the lives they had led before, the revolutionary compared with the lives so many others around them were leading – was not the fruit of their adherence, of their intelligence, or of their will, but a gift of the Spirit, a gift from on high, a mysterious energy with which they were invested.

We might say then that these were the formulas used to describe the first Christians' determination to clarify the origin of a new personality in which they felt they had been vested. And, it should be remembered that "from on high" is not to be understood as a mechanical, extraneous investiture; for, in Latin, *altus* also means "profound." If we say, then, that they were invested with an energy from on high, it is the same as maintaining that it was an energy lying at the root of being, an energy which communicates being. And so, it is right to say that the content of the new self-awareness that those people believed in was wrought by an energy from on high, it coincided with the form of a new personality. A personality was born in them, in the heart of them, a personality which was intimately different.

However we must ask: what forms a personality? A personality is moulded both by self-awareness and the creative impulse, by fecundity. And, this is precisely what that first group who led the way is testifying to us: they felt they were personalities in the world, in society, personalities who were different – different because of their conception of self and their ability to communicate. In his second letter to the Christians of Corinth, Paul used two highly effective images to describe the materialization of this new personality: "It is God who establishes us with you in Christ, and has commissioned us; he has put his seal upon us and given us his Spirit in our hearts as a guarantee" (2 Cor. 1:21–22). In this passage, the image of the seal and the image of anointing or consecration – which in Hebrew tradition means chosen to serve God – emerge. On one hand, then, what is emphasized is the mark, a stamp on the surface of an object. It creates something new, even from the formal point of view: the face of the object is changed. The same is true of the man clothed by the gift of the Spirit: his face changes, he is the expression of a new ontology. This is an alteration which later in the history of the Church would be translated by theology and catechism into that splendid phrase "supernatural grace." However, the image Paul uses indicates an ontological change because the seal is a physical reality. Wherever it is impressed, it transforms the appearance. What comes to the fore, on the other hand, is the image of anointing, that is of God's choice of the one whose task is to channel the meaning of history, as it is in Israel's case. And Paul concludes his train of thought by citing the pledge of the Spirit or the launch of the beginnings of the Spirit's effective action, of that same Energy by which the risen Jesus Christ, who holds all things in his hands and is steering all reality towards the ultimate manifestation of his truth. For as Paul says in that moving Christological hymn in his letter to the Colossians, "all things were created through him and for him ... and in him all things hold together," (Col. 1:16–17).

We should note from the testimony of those first groups of Christians that this action of the Spirit, felt as power and as a gift, is not just for the eminent figures in the community or for those who play a special role: it is for all those who believe and are baptized. As Peter himself taught: "Repent and be baptized every one of you in the name of Jesus Christ for the forgiveness of your sins; and you shall receive the gift of the Holy Spirit. For the promise is to you and to your children, and to all that are far off, everyone whom the Lord our God calls to him'" (Acts 2:38–39). Paul, too, would be insistent about this gift bestowed on all those who, freed by Jesus, are made strong in a new dignity: "But when the time had fully come, God sent forth his Son, born of woman, born under the Law, to redeem those who were under the Law, so that we might receive adoption as sons. And because you are sons, God has sent the Spirit of his Son into our hearts, crying, 'Abba! Father!'" (Gal. 4:4–6), because "God's love has been poured into our hearts through the Holy Spirit who has been given to us" (Rom. 5:5). And John the Evangelist seems to be adding to this idea in his first letter: "All who keep his commandments abide in him, and he in them. And by this we know that he abides in us, by the Spirit which he has given us" (1 John 3:24).

These expressions, referring to the Spirit given to all, would seem then to be the set formulas of the primitive Christian catechism.

b) The Beginnings of Experienceable Change

That expression of Paul's we have just highlighted, "the Spirit ... as a guarantee" – or the beginning, the token, the first fruits, we might say – indicates what the Christian is expected to experience and manifest: the dawn of a new world. This is reminiscent of one of Jesus' own expressions, promising that whoever devoted his whole life to following him would receive "manifold more in this time and, in the age to come, eternal life" (Luke 18:30).

An adult Christian, reasonable in his adherence to Christianity, is called to sense the whole existential weight of this phrase, to experience the stirrings of its importance. If the challenge this Gospel phrase transmits is not absorbed, then those who doubt that we could be talking about Christianity and faith in an abstract way are quite justified.

Christians who have the gift of the Spirit are given the possibility of a new experience of reality, in a way that is rich in truth and charged with love. For it is day-to-day reality that becomes transformed, and it is in the here-and-now that we receive "more." The routine connotations of human existence are changed: love between a man and a woman, friendship, the tension of our seeking, our studies, our work. If we were not to live this experience of the Spirit, it would prove very difficult – if not impossible – to acquire a conviction capable of building anything. And, if we leave the value of this dawning of the Spirit in the realms of the implicit – if we do not become conscious of it – we will never realize just how culturally powerful our faith is. Its critical, operational dynamism will not be fuelled.

The gift of the Spirit makes it evident that we are immersed in that new flow of energy generated by Jesus; it shows us that we are part of that new phenomenon. For the gift of the Spirit is a force which is bestowed upon the men whom Christ has called to his *ecclesia*. It confers a new consistence upon them, contributes to the immediate aim of the call – the edification of the community, the pledge of the new world.

In conclusion, I would like to point out that only our contemporary mentality, weakened by centuries of displaced emphases in regard to the human phenomenon, feels that the solidity of an individual personality is in opposition to the solidity of a living community. As Guardini acutely observes:

The Catholic conception of society and of individual personality starts on the contrary ... not from isolated axioms or one-sided psychological presuppositions, but from the integrity of real life apprehended without prejudice. In virtue of his nature man is both an individual person and a member of a society. Nor do these two aspects of his being simply co-exist. On the contrary, society exists already as a living seed in man's individuality, and the latter in turn is necessarily presupposed by society as its foundation, though without prejudice to the relative independence of both these two primary forms of human life.

The Church then is a society essentially bound up with individual personality; and the individual life of the Christian is of its very nature related to the community. Both together are required for the perfect realization of the Kingdom of God.[13]

c) The Capacity to Take a Stand in the Eyes of the World –
The Strength of Witness and Mission

The gift of the Spirit transmits an impetus to these new personalities which enables their lives to take on a fruitful capacity for communication, for communicating the newness Jesus brought to the world. Thus, both the individual and the community feel they can take their stand in the eyes of the world. In religious language, the expression most descriptive of this capacity for manifestation is to be found in the word "prophecy," a word exemplified in the following passage from the Acts of the Apostles which reports what Peter said after the event of Pentecost: "But this is what was spoken by the prophet Joel: "And in the last days it shall be, God declares, that I will pour out my Spirit upon all flesh, and your sons and your daughters shall prophesy" (Acts 2:16–17a).

A prophet is one who announces the significance of the world and the value of life. And this is the root of the most common meaning of the word "prophecy": the prediction of what the future holds – in other words, human life is made up of objective conditions which, if not recognized for what they are, carry certain consequences with them. The power of prophecy is the power to know what is real. Prophecy is not of man. It comes from on high, as the Old Testament so forcefully testifies when it narrates the prophetic vocation of Jeremiah:

> The word of the Lord came to me, saying:
> "Before I formed you in the womb I knew you,
> And before you were born I consecrated you;
> I appointed you a prophet to the nations."
> Then I said, "Ah, Lord God! Behold,
> I do not know how to speak for I am only a youth."
> But the Lord said to me,
> "Do not say, I am only a youth;"
> for to all to whom I send you
> you shall go,
> and whatever I command you,
> you shall speak.
> Be not afraid of them,
> for I am with you to deliver you" (Jer. 1:4–8).

This capacity to adhere to and confess a new, unfolding reality begins to form among the early Christians on the day of Pentecost. Later, with the maturity of time, Jesus' more explicit words of comfort are an apparent echo of this Old Testament passage, particularly when he refers to the times to come – times his disciples did not yet know –

times of difficulty and suffering: "When they bring you before the synagogues and the rulers and the authorities, do not be anxious how or what you are to answer or what you are to say, for the Holy Spirit will teach you in that very hour what you ought to say" (Luke 12:11–12).

Thus, this new impetus transmitted by the gift of the Holy Spirit – the consistency of one's personality and of the community as a whole, brought about so as to manifest to the world the newness Christ conveyed to each person – extracts its vital lymph from a force which is not just strength of language, which does not merely terminate at mere discourses, but which invests and changes the cardinal factors of life. And it does so to the extent that Paul was able to say to the Thessalonians, "For we know, brethren beloved by God, that he has chosen you; for our gospel came to you not only in words, but also in power and in the Holy Spirit" (1 Thess. 1:4–5), ending the same letter with this appeal: "Do not quench the Spirit, do not despise prophesying, but test everything; hold fast to what is good" (1 Thess. 5:19–21).

d) Miracles: Proof of the Presence of the Energy with which Christ Demonstrates His Dominion Over History

We cannot even begin to imagine how radical the combat was – the struggle, the totally different phenomenon that Jesus Christ had to bring about in terms of mentality, sensibility, in established ways of life – when he began to make his presence felt in the world. Christ's history among us chose to impose itself with an extraordinary capacity, through exceptional facts which, in the Gospel, are called miracles or signs – signs of the newness which had made its entrance in the world. But the normality of the existence of these signs is more marked in the chronology of Jesus' earthly life than in the centuries to come, even though this characteristic remains throughout the history of the Church, emerging in a special way in the glory of the lives of the saints.

So in the primitive Christian community, an experience perceptible to the senses was often the sign of divine power. Often, this Spirit, given in Baptism, was the literal generator of miraculous acts: people spoke unknown languages, comprehended the incomprehensible. This was just the beginning, and as time passed, the gift of the Spirit expressed itself in many exceptional and frequent phenomena, rendering so many extraordinary changes in people who received baptism that such manifestations became the sign of recognition of a divine election. The Acts of the Apostles describe this reality for us as a demonstrative element. This was precisely Paul's reaction in Ephesus: "There he found some disciples, and he said to them, 'Did you receive the Holy Spirit when you believed?' and they said, 'No, we have never even heard that there is a Holy Spirit.' And he said, 'Into what then were you baptised?' They said, 'Into John's baptism.' And Paul said, 'John baptised with the baptism of repentance, telling the people to believe in the one who was to come after him, that is, Jesus.' On hearing this, they were baptised in the name of the Lord Jesus. And when Paul had laid his hands upon them, the Holy Spirit came on them; and they spoke with tongues and prophesied" (Acts 19:1–6).

However, as one century followed another, as time went by, those first "miraculous" experiences became less frequent. But with the passing of time, an even greater miracle begins. It grows throughout the centuries: and what more exceptional, more wondrous miracle can there be than all of the people who would come later and who would perpetuate the recognition of Jesus in the event of his Church! When Jesus said to Thomas, "Have you believed because you have seen me? Blessed are those who have not seen and yet believe" (John 20:29), his precise intention was to indicate the exceptional, miraculous nature of an event of which each one of us is called to be a subject.

Man now stands before Jesus Christ in the same way today as he did 2,000 years ago. No sign will ever be enough to force man's freedom to look to the proposal of Christ in a way that is wide open, like the face of a child, or even with the wary, suspicious eyes of so many adults. The truth has a particular accent and if the soul is in the original position in which God placed it when he created it, it is unmistakable. The opposite of this is what the Gospel calls hardness of heart. Pierre Rousselot commented: "It is because of hardness of heart that miracles cannot be understood. 'Even if one were to rise from the dead,' – we read in Luke – 'they would not be persuaded.' And in John, 'Although he worked many signs for them, they did not believe in him.'"[14]

Today, only one great prodigy has taken the place of the original routine miracles and signs. Nevertheless, it is a miracle which, in order to be recognized, requires the same open soul, the same impetus of freedom that existed then. It is the miracle of our adherence as men to the reality of that Man of 2000 years ago, recognized as truly present in the face of the Church. It is the miracle by which Christ's Spirit conquers history. It is that fascinating event conveying the power of the Spirit to every corner of human affairs, the event by which Christ makes himself present, in the weakness, fear, timidity, and confusion of our persons in unity.

Consequently, man can experience the dawning of this new world being built with the power with which Christ has invested history. And the dawning of such an experience is the miracle of man asking for the gift of the Spirit, invoking it, begging for it, which means asking for the light and strength which enable us to experience the Mystery, whose nature we cannot see. And Jesus said of this asking: "If you then, who are evil, know how to give good gifts to your children, how much more will the heavenly Father give the Holy Spirit to those who ask him" (Luke 11:13). And even though we may feel incapable of taking the initiative to ask for the Spirit or express our plea, Paul's words are a comfort to us: "Likewise the Spirit helps us in our weakness; for we do not know how to pray as we ought, but the Spirit himself intercedes for us with sighs too deep for words. And he who searches the hearts of men knows what is the mind of the Spirit, because the Spirit intercedes for the saints according to the will of God" (Rom. 8:26–27).

The dawn of Christ's victory, the sign that the miracle continues is humble, grateful acknowledgment, the invocation of the gift of the Spirit, and the strength from on high.

3 A NEW TYPE OF LIFE

A third factor – a new tpe of life – is part of the initial framework of the essential elements of the Christian phenomenon as it presents itself on the stage of history and according to the testimonies which have come down to us from primitive documents.

One word is used to define *the type of life* to which that community, so animated by the Spirit, awoke, for it is not the community phenomenon as such that distinguishes the Christian fact, but the phenomenon of community in the particular way it was assumed and lived. The word which described this particular way of life is *koinonia* in Greek and *communio* in Latin; it defines the structure of relationships making up the group. It is the term which, in the New Testament, specifies a way of being and acting, a way of life proper to the Christian collective, a way of entering into relationship with God and with individuals.

Note, first of all, that these expressions, translatable by "communion," did not have the same meaning as "communion." This is because, as we saw with the word "ecclesia," this word is taken from common vocabulary, from the day-to-day spoken Greek language and, as such, it is not a word which alludes to special spiritual or psychological experiences but to something routine in people's everyday lives. The ordinary meaning of the word is also reflected in the Gospel. When Luke speaks of some Galilean fishermen, joint owners of a fleet of fishing boats, he remarks: "James and John, sons of Zebedee, who were partners with Simon" (Luke 5:10). Here he uses the word *koinonoi*, *communicantes*, in Latin meaning what we would call partners in a cooperative, indicating reciprocal relationships between people who, for one reason or another, have something in common and pursue a common interest.

This word then reveals two pieces of information: the first is that *koinonia* implied joint ownership; the second underlines that, as a result of this sharing of a possession, there was solidarity among these individuals. And, in the case of Luke's Gospel, the partners shared fishing boats, with the result that there was solidarity of effort among them to make the boats bring in a profit.

It is clear, then, that those Galilean fishermen, who were the joint owners of a fleet of fishing boats, could refer to themselves as *koinonoi, communicantes* and we would say that they had shared interests in a joint venture, in a cooperative. However, why did that same group of Christians who used to meet under Solomon's Portico use the same word later to refer to their community? What did they share that made them conscious of joint ownership? The answer is obvious: they jointly possessed a single reason for living, *the* reason for living – Jesus Christ. He was the communion of which the primitive Christians were conscious. John states this aptly in his first letter: "That which we have seen and heard we proclaim also to you so that you may have fellowship with us; and our fellowship is with the Father and with his Son Jesus Christ ... if we say we have fellowship with him while we walk in darkness, we lie and do not live according to the truth; but if we walk in the light as he is in the light, we have fellowship with one another" (1 John 1:3; 6–7).

The property the first Christians shared is the mystery of Christ. It was announced to them and was recognized as the truth regarding man's pathway and his destiny. In this way, man enters into direct communication with the very presence of God who intervened in history. This was an intervention which changes man's very being, a presence which, in turn, freely involves and transforms man. That is why those who are called are in constant communication with each other. Each possesses the other because they possess Christ and life, and they are possessed by him.

This word *koinonia*, then, first of all describes an existing reality (Christ) possessed jointly by the individuals who recognize him. Over and above all other values, it has an ontological one, which means that it is something that interests and involves man's being, which becomes a new being, a being possessed by the revealed Mystery and, therefore, in a unity of being with all those who are called, who are chosen by the divine hand. And this new being subsequently tends to coincide with a new attitude, an all-embracing solidarity, which we will see emerging in the lives of the first Christians. For them, a new reason for living came to the fore; and, throughout their entire lives, it would inspire solidarity in those who recognized it. If we share the meaning of life, we share all things in life.

And so, *koinonia*, the New Testament word, indicates a way of being and of life that derives from simultaneous recognition of a bond with the Presence constituting the meaning and destiny of the lives of every one of them. This is why they conceived of themselves as being essentially bound one with the other. The word *koinonia* then is the precise expression of the reciprocal state of being of each of those Christians in their common, ontological dependence on Jesus Christ and on the Spirit with which he began to manifest his possession of the world.

In detail, the ethical, practical aspects of this reciprocal state of being are the fruit of an awareness of a living reality at work in and among Christians. The profound awareness of this reality, the recognition of a structural unity binding them, in that each one is part of the mystery of Jesus Christ, constitutes the only exhaustive motivation for their attitude of solidarity, for the way they looked at one another, treated one another, for their acceptance – even if it meant sacrifice – of those who would otherwise have been strangers to them. In his letter to the Corinthians, Paul says: "I speak as to sensible men; judge for yourselves what I say. The cup of blessing which we bless, is it not a participation with the blood of Christ? The bread which we break, is it not a participation in the body of Christ? Because there is one bread, we who are many are one body, for we all partake of the one bread"(1 Cor. 10:15–17). Paul had said this as an introduction to his discourse aimed at settling the serious discord which was becoming evident in the community. Extraneousness, in terms of a door open to hostility, is not abolished with some generic call to love one another. Rather, Paul tentatively redimensions the problem in the form of an appeal to a fact: *we are* one single body.

In discussing a passage of Claudel, Henri de Lubac observes:

In the end it is an ever more real and more widespread spiritual society that must be rediscovered in the deepest, most abandoned interior silence. Claudel extolled it in his *Cantique de Palmyre*, where we hear the perfect echo of the ancient Fathers: "No one of our brethren, even should he desire it, can separate himself from us, and in the meanest miser, in the heart of the prostitute or the most squalid drunkard there is an immortal soul with holy aspirations which, deprived of daylight, worship in the night. ... I take and understand them all; there is not one of them I do not need, not one that I can do without! ... there are many souls, but there is not one of them whom I am not in communion in that sacred apex where it utters its *Pater Noster*."[15]

If we share Christ, then how much more do we share the things of life, both material and spiritual? As we have already said, this sharing is the guideline of the concrete relationships among the first Christians.

From an ontological reality, discovered and recognized, is born the need for a new behavior.

I would like to outline now the principal connotations of this word *koinonia*, or "communion," because although there are few, they are full of the meaning of an image of the Church which took form from the beginnings, becoming deeper and broader as the centuries passed.

a) An Ethical Ideal

It is precisely because they share the foundation and the meaning of life – Jesus Christ – that the first Christians feel their tendency to share everything, and in a more profound sense, to conceive of their own common material and spiritual resources as a rule of their co-existence. The important word in this first analytical element is the word "tendency," or tension. The word tendency implies freedom at work, freedom fired by an ideal value, as the generator of a dynamism conditioned by one's history, by temperament, by capacity, by the willingness of the spirit, an impetus, and, therefore, a dynamism that only God and no other can judge because each one stands before his Lord and is responsible before him. He knows the state of the soul.

Some exceptional passages from Saint Paul's letters indicate the type of human climate that was beginning to set in among the first communities of Christians. They illustrate the radicality, and yet the discretion and freedom with which this fundamental tension of Christian living was conceived.

In the first passage, Paul is writing to the faithful of Corinth, who were raising funds for the community of Jerusalem, where there had been a devastating famine. After a brief period of time, the initial burst of generosity ran out, and Paul took the initiative: he launched an appeal to the Corinthian Christians, telling them of the great commitment undertaken by the Macedonian communities which were much poorer than the prosperous Corinthians:

See you that you excel in this gracious work also. I say this not as a command, but to prove by the earnestness of others that your love also is genuine. For you know the grace of our Lord Jesus Christ, that though he was rich, yet for your sake he became poor, so that by his poverty you might become rich. And in this matter I give my advice; it is best for you now to complete what a year ago you began not only to do but to desire, so that your readiness in desiring it may be matched by your completing it out of what you have. For if the readiness is there, it is acceptable according to what a man has, not according to what he has not.

In concluding his plea, he defines the great test of human freedom in the following way: "Each one must do as he has made up in his mind, not reluctantly or under compulsion, for God loves a cheerful giver" (2 Cor. 8:7–12;9:7).

I cite this famous case of fund-raising for the Jerusalem community not so much because it was a great organizational effort on the part of Paul and early Christianity, but above all, because the enterprise was, in truth, not just of a material nature; it is a clear definition of the characteristics of tension towards life-sharing in all its aspects within the early community. Adalbert Hamman notes on this point:

Paul considered this initiative to be of maximum importance ... the material sum "raised" was believed to be something of lesser importance than its ecclesial meaning: by this act, the churches of the Gentiles not only manifested their gratitude to the church in Jerusalem but also the unity that existed among all the churches independently of their different origins and the different backgrounds to their formation. ... Its nature was at once that of a religion and a community because of its dual bond of service to God by which it was inspired and service to others of which it was the expression. ... Fund-raising is grace and service. God is the beginning and the end of it. He inspires it and does much more besides: not for nothing do all things belong to him. ... He is generous with men because he wants to make them participants in his bountiful giving. ... Moreover, this act of fraternal solidarity expresses and fosters *koinonia*.[16]

The first Christian communities' exalted vision of hospitality is also representative of its striving to engage its entire energy. Hospitality is sharing at its utmost – it means that a person's whole life is placed at the disposal of another. Listen again, then, to Paul in this exhortation to the Hebrews: "Let brotherly love continue. Do not neglect to show hospitality to strangers, for thereby some have entertained angels unawares. Remember those who are in prison, as though in prison with them; and those who are illtreated, since you also are in the body ... do not neglect to do good and to share what you have, for such sacrifices are pleasing to God" (Heb. 13:1–3,16). And Saint Paul was not alone in his concern for this issue. In his third letter, John too would insist on mutual care and hospitality among brethren: "Beloved, it is a loyal thing you do when you render any service to the brethren, especially to strangers who have testified to your love before the Church. You will do well to send them on their journey as befits God's service. For they have set out for his sake and have accepted nothing from the heathen. So we ought to support such men, that we may be fellow workers in the truth" (3 John 5:8).

In concluding this brief description of the first Christians, ethical attitude towards each other in their daily lives, I think it would be helpful to reiterate how that attitude and the wonderful expression of their sharing of all things were motivated not only by the fact that they were one, but also by the reality that they possessed freedom as its condition. This is one of the great criteria of Christian mortification which we have just recalled in Paul's citation of a line from Proverbs in his letter to the Christians of Corinth: "God loves a cheerful giver." We find this same criterion, intact, at the turn of our century, in the teaching of the "little way" of Theresa of Lisieux, and not, by chance, does Hans Urs von Balthasar see Pauline traces in her theological approach.

Even in this martyrdom, the point is not the record of suffering but the *intensity of love*. Every penance that increases true love is good; any penance that narrows and preoccupies the soul is harmful. "Certainly every penance is laudable and meritorious if one is convinced that the good God requires it of one. Even if one errs in doing it, [God] is touched by the intention. But I could never bind myself to anything if it became a constant preoccupation ...; as our mother Saint Teresa says: God is not concerned with a heap of trifles, as we too easily believe; and we should never let anything narrow our souls."[17]

We must keep this criterion in mind in our approach to certain passages of the New Testament. In the Acts of the Apostles, for example, a certain Barnabas is exalted because he sold a field he owned and gave the proceeds to the apostles. However, a married couple, Ananias and Sapphira, are deplored and punished because although they too owned a field and sold it, they offered the community only half of the proceeds maintaining that was all they had. And so the sacrifice they were forced to make generated a lie in regard to the community and the Spirit, and Peter severely condemns this. The absence of obligation, joy, and that cheerful heart Paul extolled among the Corinthians are not just exterior traits or a superficial mask of contentment: we can make a sacrifice that costs us so much effort that it makes us weep. However, ultimately it can be done with a certain spontaneity. It can be done willingly, in short, as if it were the ineliminable urge to express something we want to express, with passion, like the expression of something that is worth living, and therefore, manifesting. A scholar of Judaism and of early Christianity, Luigi Moraldi, confirms this point of view concerning the communion of the primitive community, just as Luke describes it for us in the Acts:

Firstly, it should be noted that the division we commonly make between the material and the spiritual plane is not biblical. There are no examples of it in the Bible, and it does not correspond well to Christian thinking: man is always considered in his concrete oneness, the result of matter and spirit indissolubly joined. Moreover, the summaries of the book of the Acts, our starting point, stress with evident approval how in the Church of Jerusalem, there were no needy and how as believers they were united with one heart and one soul, which means that the dynamic core of their personalities were in perfect unison. ... This communion does not impose the juridical renunciation of property, but is motivated by the union which reigns among believers. Neither the apostles nor Christian tradition imposed this communion, this sharing of things; however, it remains the natural expression of the reality of the faith. ... It is none other than this personal tension, this profound spontaneity which characterizes communion.[18]

This is the opposite of moralism, of the sacrifice conceived and made in the name of a formal sense of duty. This is the gift of self to God, the gift as the true fruit of a person's adherence to the great fact based on the recognized state of communion: sharing the same reason for living.

b) An Institutional Connotation

The word *communio*, or *koinonia*, used as an expression of sharing and lived in a state of dependence on Jesus Christ, also assumes an institutional connotation, for, as we have seen, this word does not only describe the ethical mark of the mutual relationship of Christians in their common belonging to the Mystery by which they are saved. Rather, it also illustrates a combination of factors which gradually structure the Christians as a social group, primarily that a new institutional phenomenon was taking form within society, characterized by elements particular to it. It was not merely an expression of fraternal sentiment.

In his letter to the Galatians, Paul recounts a journey he made to Jerusalem to verify his preaching with those who were considered points of reference for the emerging Christian community. "I laid before them the Gospel which I preach among the Gentiles," and after this "comparing of notes," since there were ongoing discussions as to whether or not converted pagans were obliged to be circumcised and to follow other stipulations of Judaic law, Paul makes a point of telling the Galatians that he had won explicit consensus: "I went there as the result of a revelation ... so James and Cephas and John, who were reputed to be pillars, gave to me and Barnabas the right hand of fellowship" (Gal. 2:2,9). This gesture, made official by a hand-shake, is significant of an institutional fact, an act of acknowledgment of joint participation in the same mission, the same reality. And this is one of the clearest and most explicit examples of documentary proof – even to our mentality – of the fact that the Church has always had within its ranks people whose objective role was to confirm or verify the truth.

In this sense then, the word *koinonia* or communion, described the outcome of a new way of life in terms of established social forms. It illustrated how the new relationships were so evident and constantly sought out that they became the first, fundamental features of an institutional system. In this sense, the word *koinonia* or communion was presented as a synonym of the word *ecclesia*. It was used to refer to the Church as Church and was indicative of the unity of the people of God as a social factor, a unity that assumed its own form, like an institution, like a new social structure. Besides defining a way of life, then, the primitive Church used these words intentionally because they would immediately suggest a fixed bond, both for the local communities and for the Universal Church: they would highlight social, organic unity.

The emergence of stable forms and structures facilitates a striving to share in freedom and constitutes the ground upon which it rests. These structures reduce the disorderly eruption into our experience of isolated impulses doomed to die away, impulses so often prone to become the easy prey of a disproportionate subjectivism, unless the touchstone of a context is always at hand.

In this sense, the Christian community gradually came to use other moving *synonyms* – beginning with a special value they had pinpointed and experienced – to describe the entire reality of the Church. One of these, the word *eirene*, which means peace, is used to define the bond uniting all Christians. Quoting Saint Paul, Fulgentius of Ruspa offers this recommendation: "This one heart and one soul were the work of him who is the one Spirit of the Father and the Son as he is likewise, with the Father and the Son, one God. That is why the Apostle asserts that this spiritual unity is to be preserved by the bond of peace."[19] The other synonym is the word *agape*, or love. To the early Christians, *agape* meant Church, and love meant that reality which, by its fraternal institutions, made the healing love of Jesus himself take root in the lives of men. It is interesting to note that the word *agape* in its strict sense also signifies a particular institution: a banquet held by affluent people who invited the neediest people of the community to their table. As Adalbert Hamman has remarked:

This word, forged by the Greek community ... meant fraternal community centred around the *Kyrios* in his glory. The *proprium* of the charity banquet is the concrete form of the meaning of community applied to a type of subdivision of all the Christians owned for the benefit of the poorer people. ... The concrete perception of all that charity implies was such that a discreet, unobtrusive form of assistance gained momentum in regard to the members of the community who were more disadvantaged and more tried by misfortune.[20]

c) A Ritual Expression

The Eucharistic Act was the third analytical factor which gave the ecclesial reality its characteristic as communion. The word *koinonia* fully embraced the Eucharistic Act because the first Christians felt it to be supremely expressive of the unity of the Church as Church.

It is important to note that there has never been a type of Christianity that did not originally express itself in the form of ritual. The rite was an integral part of the expression of the primitive Church and of its life in *koinonia*, the reality of new life, a social group constituted and distinguished also by a new form of ritual. The significance of this observation becomes clear if we think just how fundamental the rite is in human experience as we live it. "The rite," wrote Jacques Vidal, a religious science and theology scholar, "is a symbolic act whose aim is to give life to figures of a given order at the crossroads formed by nature, by society, by culture and by religion. ... Thus, in life the rite is a foundry for forging balances in the search for unity and fullness in a history brought back to its beginnings and made to go beyond itself."[21]

The Eucharist, then, which in Greek means the giving of thanks, was the mark of the community's whole life:

The most salient mark and the most incisive co-efficient of their union as a community was the *breaking of bread*, which they celebrated in private homes made available to the community by the wealthier among them. There is sufficient proof to validate the opinion that the Eucharistic rite took place at the end of a communal meal, or however, in connection with it. ... It would have been natural, too, for the first Christians to want to imitate the "Lord's Supper" ... also as regards the circumstance surrounding it – the context of an evening meal together.[22]

And so, in those early times, at the end of a communal meal, they did what Christ had asked them to do. They followed his example just before he was taken prisoner and killed in the gesture and sign that held all the ontological density of the real presence of Jesus. In Latin it was called "sacrament," while in Greek it meant "mystery."

To our modern mentality, the word "mystery" means the unknowable, the inaccessible, or the still unknown. In Christian language, too, the word "mystery" denotes the inaccessible and the elusive. However, in the Christian sense, the word assumes a different meaning – and while it does maintain its infinite content, it also in some way reveals itself in our finite state and makes itself a part of our experience. The mystery in the Christian sense is mystery that as we live it, makes itself known to our senses. Christ is the Mystery itself for the very reason that he is God who makes of himself a human experience, because, as Saint John preached in his first letter, he is the infinite Word that became man, a man we can listen to, see, and touch. Again Jacques Vidal observes in one of his treatises on the symbol-history relationship through the rite: "The sacrament takes the symbolic experience to the limit and it allows it self-fulfillment in this rite of rites which procures the presence of the humanity of Jesus for us, in the mystery of his Church in times visible and invisible."[23]

From the very beginning, the excellence of the Eucharistic celebration is immediately striking to the Christian consciousness, and explains certain episodes in the life of the primitive Church. Polycarp of Smyrna "was already bishop of that Asiatic see when he met Ignatius. As a bearer and transmitter of apostolic traditions he ranks high, for he had been, according to the testimony of his pupil Irenaeus, in direct contact with several of the apostles, whose eyewitness accounts of the life and teachings of the Lord he knew well."[24] About halfway through the second century after Christ, Polycarp went to Anicetus, the bishop of Rome, to discuss a problem concerning the dating of Easter. The controversy was not settled on that occasion, but it is interesting to note that, even when the debate was at its height, Anicetus invited Polycarp to celebrate the Eucharistic liturgy among the Roman community, as a mark of unity despite divergencies.

However, this is not the sole instance underlining the importance of the Eucharist, of the fact that the first Christians lived the celebration of the Eucharist as the supreme, distinctive mark of their one faith. The "communion letters," a procedure quite common to the early communities, provide another example:

When a Christian set out on a journey, he received from his own bishop a letter of recommendation, a type of passport, and on the strength of this, he would be welcomed as a friend and accommodated free of charge in any Christian community he would visit. This institution, whose traces we can find as far back as Apostolic times, was not just to the advantage of the laity, such as Christian traders, but to the bishops themselves. For at not much cost they could send messengers and letters throughout the Empire. ... These passports were called letters of peace, or communion letters since they certified that the traveller belonged to the *communio*, and could, therefore, receive the Eucharist.[25]

Incidentally, it is interesting to note the original meaning of the term "excommunication" in the history of the Church. It means "outside the communion," the mark of those who were not recognized by the bishop, and were therefore not admitted to the Eucharist.

d) A Hierarchical Factor

The community of Christians, then, never presented itself as a sponta-neous event left to the subjectivity of each individual. Yet neither did it appear as an amorphous aggregation. Rather, it is the deposit of special functions. All individuals are called to echo Jesus Christ's function in man's regard. However, some reflect it in an exceptional way, as teach-ers, while others possess the power to communicate divine reality.

In the reality of nature itself, it may be observed that as the biological structure of an organism gradually becomes perfect, its functions multi-ply, and the oneness of the organism assigns itself specific expressive functions. This is also true of the Christian community. The Lord made the best possible use of our natural components and therefore desired diverse functions in the community experience, an experience to be rooted in him, an experience within which he would always be present. According to Daniel-Rops,

the institutional foundations laid by Him are clearly visible in the primitive community. We got the impression that the Apostles, His first witnesses, the men whom Jesus had Himself chosen and established, enjoyed, naturally enough, enormous moral authority. ... Peter clearly occupied a leading place among the Twelve. We shall often see him acting as he acted on the occasion of his election to this position: he is the one with whom the initiative always lies. ... This pre-eminence of Peter, which was to have considerable importance, on account of its consequences for the entire history of Christianity, was yet another fact which rested on the express declaration of the Master. He had wanted to give His organization a hierarchic principle, and He had deliberately chosen Simon, this prudent, generous-hearted, steadfast man, as "the rock ... upon which I will build my church."[26]

This is not the time to return to the famed debate surrounding the authenticity of the passage from Matthew (Matt. 16:15ff.) referred to above. However, it is enough to note that even on the Protestant side its authenticity is no longer questioned. On this point, the Protestant theologian, Adolph Bolliger, commented: "the verses fit together as aptly as the members of a body. They have the quite inimitable flavour of a great historical moment. Moreover, they are expressed in words such as come only to the great ones of this world, and even to these only in the greatest moments of their life. No interpolator can write in this fashion."[27] And it is worth adding to this debate this acknowledgment by the celebrated Protestant theologian Oscar Cullman:

If, however, Jesus actually assumed a time interval between the two events, between his atoning death, decisive for salvation, and his Parousia, then he must have intended that in this intermediate period – whether it is of longer or shorter duration is here not essential – his disciples were to play a role. From this insight light falls upon the saying concerning the Church in Matt. 16:18; there is no longer any substantial reason to deny its genuineness.[28]

It is clear then that the Church, at its foundations, at the basis of Jesus' precise teaching, is founded on the apostles, grounded in the special primacy of Peter. But, as the early texts tell us, the apostles needed helpers almost immediately, and in light of this, it becomes certain that here lies the origin of the authoritative figure over each individual community. Let us examine this more closely.

The word "bishops" appears in Peter's first letter. To understand the meaning of this word, its relationship with "shepherd" is interesting, and in his commentary on Peter's letter, Rudolf Schnackenburg makes this comment:

The example of the love and concern for the flock that the Head of the shepherds has, love and care which are no longer visible but which are still at work in a living, real way, surely arouses a burning zeal in the leaders of the community chosen by God, a total gift of self given meaning by abnegation and the desire to guide by setting an example rather than by dispositions and recommendations. All of this is expressed by the word *episcopein*, indicating the concerned watch of the shepherd over the flock in his care with an eye trained to spot dangers from outside. It is almost certain that something of the richness of such a living image of pastor as this has come to make up the word "bishop," a word that gradually made its way into the language.[29]

We have already seen how bishops possessed a network for contacting each other through the "letters of peace" or "communion letters" or "letters of recommendation," which were the concern of the bishop as the head of the community. And, if they were necessary for a person to be recognized as a believer, and therefore admitted to the Eucharist in the far-off city where he was bound, then it is clear that the bishop's authority was important in his community, and that, in any case, it was his responsibility to acknowledge a man as an adherent to the faith or not. We have also seen how one among all the bishops – that of Rome – occupied a special position. To him, controversies were submitted. It was also desirable to be at one with him, in ultimate unity, so as to transcend the questions under debate. The bishop of Rome was the hinge of a whole network of relationships among bishops and, therefore, among communities. This is why Ignatius of Antioch, Polycarp's contemporary and a prisoner awaiting martyrdom, would declare in a letter to influential Christians working to have him released that he considered it a great honour to die for the Lord, who died for us. In addressing the Christian community of Rome, Ignatius calls it "the community which presides over love" (love or *agape*, was a synonym of the universal Church): the head of this community, then, was a point of reference for everyone.

Ludwig Hertling reminds us that this is true even in the middle of the third century: "Even the pagans knew that the real Christian was the one in communion with Rome. In 268, the bishop of Antioch, Paul of Samosate was deposed by a synod for his erroneous teaching and scandalous conduct. Paul ... did not submit and refused to hand over the church and the episcopal house to his successor. But when the Emperor Aurelian reached Antioch ... the Christians looked to him for a judicial ruling. Aurelian ruled that the episcopal house had to be handed over to the man "with whom the heads of the religion in Italy and the bishop of Rome keep written contact." The Church historian Eusebius, who reports this information, describes the ruling as "perfectly just."[30]

e) A Fervor of Communication, A Missionary Ideal

The word *koinonia* describes a reality of life, an institution, a *societas*, not closed in itself, but powerfully animated by a fervor of communication. Indeed, the first Christians felt that, as Christians, they were called to communicate the news of Christ to all those who did not yet know him. At no time in the history of the primitive Church did the community not feel it was determined and judged by the missionary dimension. And it could have been no other way, as Henri de Lubac suggests in this invitation to us to reflect: "'Go: teach all the nations': for twenty centuries this command has launched the Church on all the roads of this vast world. ... The Church only became self-aware when it was aroused to the missionary task its Founder had indicated and it was mainly through this task that it was revealed to its own eyes."[31]

Indeed, the primitive community felt the urgency to communicate to be so essential to its very existence that it immediately began to dedicate its life, with true intent, to transmitting the exceptional news to whomever it encountered, spreading news of a God so involved with men to the extent that he became man, never to abandon those who recognized him. This urge to communicate led to the existence of Christian communities scattered throughout the empire after just a few years. Without the hypothesis of an intense missionary zeal lived as the dimension essential to the Church's very existence it is impossible to explain how as early as the second century Christianity had been disseminated in the countries ringing the Mediterranean and had penetrated from these to the more distant regions of the Roman Empire. Besides the original apostles there were also professional missionaries, apostles in the extended sense. But they also are not at all to be regarded as the sole carriers of Christianity. The Christians in their totality became active in the world which surrounded them and spread the gospel of Jesus Christ. So the gospel of salvation traveled with merchants, soldiers, and preachers along the roads of the Roman Empire.[32]

Moreover, Jesus Christ also reached out to men in history. How did he do this? He did this through those who recognize him and those whom he himself has chosen. But, his ultimate aim is to reach out to all, and the nucleus of those who were the first to recognize him is to accomplish this – the only adequate, all-embracing motive of our faith is that we must become the means for communicating to others all that we have been told. The moral dimension of the Christian man is measured, in short, by the testimony he offers to others; it is measured, in short, by the love for Christ before men, and for men in Christ's name (cf. Matt 10:32–33). This impetus to communicate is not bridled by any ideological or social motivation. "The Church," says de Lubac, "is the body of love on earth. It is the living bond of those who are burned by this divine flame. ... But we have no love if we do not feel the desire to spread it universally. It cannot be something good that we want to keep for ourselves alone to enjoy or whose extensions can be confined within closer limits. No fire that is closed off could delude itself that it is keeping its heat to itself."[33] This is why the duty to communicate to others was and remains a decisive one. It determines the authenticity of the Christian life (cf. 2 Cor. 5:14–21). Even in the most normal of men's experiences, which is affection, love, by its very nature is communicative, while aridity, the lack of love, incapacity to focus on anything but ourselves, cuts our ties with others to the point that we no longer even savour the taste of an expressive relationship.

Many widespread objections in our age have surfaced against the missionary approach, as if its very existence constituted violence against those to whom the message is brought. But such an attitude obscures the root aspect of the problem, because it does not understand that missionary zeal is a communicative fervor belonging to the experience of love. Although forms of force and violence diminish the authenticity of this experience, and sadly, are always a possibility, they cannot be said to sustain that serene, respectful but impassioned proposal of one who has experienced a great encounter or made a great discovery. This inevitably constitutes an attack on the conscience of the interlocutor. Let me explain by means of an example. Imagine I am a mathematics teacher and that as I walk up and down the rows of desks during an important test in class, I realize that my pupils, whom I have taught with dedication and growing affection, are all becoming "bogged down" in a glaring error. Imagine that they are all looking at me with the typically anxious, questioning eyes reserved for teachers in these situations. If I were to offer them a few words of warning or give them a clue as to the solution to the problem, would this be considered violence? On the contrary, it should be considered a help. In fact, the communication of a certainty is an aid in any circumstance for one who is seeking, even though that individual may not yet think of himself as an adherent to the proposal being communicated. Certainty is a possibility, and the communication of it can serve as a working hypothesis. Jesus is none other than God who came to help, to make it easier for us to find what, on our own, we either would grope for in a confused way, without ever finding it, or more likely, would no longer even seek.

f) Morality as the Dynamism of a Journey

Saint Paul declares in his letter to the Philippians: "Not that I have already obtained this or am already perfect; but I press on to make it my own, because Christ Jesus has made me his own. Brethren, I do not consider that I have made it my own; but one thing I do, forgetting what lies behind and straining forward to what lies ahead, I press on towards the goal" (Phil 3:12–14). This declaration of imperfection is thought-provoking, given the frequent apparent use that the primitive community made in its texts of the word "saint." Paul himself, for example, opens his letter to the Romans with the ensuing greeting to the "saints": "To all God's beloved in Rome, who are called to be saints ... grace to you ..." (Rom. 1:7). Moreover, he ends his letter to the Philippians in the same way: "Greet every saint in Christ Jesus." (Phil. 4:21a) ... and he begins his epistle to the Ephesians in a similar manner: "Paul, an apostle of Christ Jesus by the will of God, to the saints who are also faithful in Christ Jesus" (Eph. 1:1). In fact, the communities of primitive Christians called themselves communities of "saints." It must be said that this never fails to disconcert us, especially in the light of the image we have of these first Christians as racing towards an unattained perfection. We inevitably sense the use of this word as a contrast because, in our mentality, "saint" means perfect. However, we must remember that this was not how the first communities viewed the word: its meaning, to them, was biblical, and in this sense, "saint" meant someone who was part of God's Covenant with man, who followed the pathway of life according to God's will. And while Israel, then, was the holy people, how much more holy must someone be deemed who was directly involved with the presence of Jesus Christ, the fulfillment of that Covenant? Such an individual, therefore, must journey, as a matter of principle and urgency, towards self-identification with God made man. He must hasten in his imitation of the true humanity of which Jesus, with all his powers, was the materialization. Only then does Christian morality assume its true face at last: a dynamism of tension generated by belonging to Christ, the unfolding of a journey within the personal mystery of Christ, in whom, with the help of his Spirit, we are chosen and in whom we realize our own humanity.

In this sense, then, the image of the community of saints does not contradict the self-image of a primitive Christian community openly acknowledging that it was made of sinners, for the New Testament does not paint us a picture of the Church at the beginning as comprised of people who felt "righteous." On the contrary, it was the place in which God's mercy embraced and corrected ordinary people, weak as they were and all too ready to fall into error.

Examples of the fallibility of the early community appear throughout the writings of Saint Paul. In his first letter to the Corinthians, Paul takes the community to task: "It is actually reported that there is immorality among you, and of a kind that is not found even among pagans" (1 Cor. 5:1). And although he is obliged to condemn violent rows, divisions, scandals, and abuse, in spite of it all, he has no fear in saying, as he ends his letter: "Thanks be to God, who gives us the victory through our Lord Jesus Christ. Therefore, my beloved brethren, be steadfast, immovable, always abounding in the work of the Lord, knowing that in the Lord your labour is not vain" (1 Cor. 15:57–58). Similar sentiments appear in his second letter to Timothy, where Paul is embittered by the failure of Christians to help him when he was held prisoner: "You are aware that all who are in Asia turned away from me, and among them Phygelus and Hermogenes (2 Tim. 1:15). And again: "At my first defence no-one took my part; all deserted me. May it not be charged against them" (2 Tim. 4:16). And yet, despite the understandable sadness of the imprisoned apostle, he does not neglect to thank those who were generous in his regard, and he fervently urges his disciples to know no limits: "I charge you, in the presence of God and of Christ Jesus who is to judge the living and the dead, and by his appearing and his kingdom; preach the word, be urgent in season and out of season, convince, rebuke, and exhort, be unfailing in patience and in teaching" (2 Tim. 4:1–2).

It is obvious then, that if we leaf through the early texts – Paul's letters, the Acts of the Apostles, and the Gospels themselves – we discover that they abound in appeals to sinners, in alarm for the shortfalls increasingly manifest among the communities, and in the offer of a forgiveness and acceptance that are not of man but come from the God who lives among men and did not want to abandon men to themselves.

The primitive Church, then, certainly did not think of itself as the place of perfect people. Polemics arose over opinions within the community that truly risked schisms. Mutual hatreds surfaced, people proposed themselves as charismatics, thus disseminating confusion in the group. Pagan vices persisted and people drew away from the apostles' message to follow their own or others' interpretations – all this truly happened in those communities of "saints." But within such a banal human reality, a reality as wretched as the symptoms of it we have listed, there was the certainty of a new humanity, the humanity of Christ capable of transforming any kind of miserable humanity, providing it runs the "race" the apostle described, providing it sets out on a journey, according to its own possibilities, but supported by grace. The certainty is that Jesus Christ can cut through all our powerlessness with his strength and can transform it into an energy that works for the good. This is the certainty we inherit, together with the potential for evil, from those who have gone before us.

The testimony of the first Christians is a warning to us that we cannot affirm an ideal value unless we desire it, and we cannot desire it unless we apply it. In the long run, whoever recognizes himself as a sinner, with all the pain involved – the mark of intensity of one's desire – must surely be on the road to true self-realization as a real human being, one who belongs to Christ. As the apostle John wrote: "Everyone who thus hopes in him purifies himself, as he is pure" (1 John 3:3).

Conclusion

In this first part dedicated to the Church, we have tried, on one hand, to understand the difficulties that make the journey to it and in it difficult for human beings. On the other, we have sought to shed true light on the true face of the Church as it appears to us, according to the structural factors the Christian phenomenon bore as it emerged in history.

In the second part of our journey, we will outline how, with the passing of time, the Church became aware of the implications of these fundamental factors, and how, as its life evolved, it developed a more articulated definition of itself, based on these same factors; for the Church is like a living personality gradually becoming more conscious of its state of being as it travels through time.

At this point, I would like to conclude this step on the road with two points. The first regards the weight of words. As we travelled along, we found ourselves assessing words used in the experience of the first centuries of Christianity, words which we, 2,000 years later, still employ. However these words, because of ignorance, force of habit, or distraction, have been emptied, and in so doing, we have clouded, even destroyed them. One such word is "Church" itself, along with communion, mystery, saint, truth. However, our concern here is not with philology, but with attentiveness to the reality these words imply. And this leads us to the second point.

Some words have been a means to approach the fundamental factors which rooted the phenomenon of the Church in the terrain of history. These foundations were immediately and explicitly revealed in Christian history, and they express a reality which is a judgment on us even today. For the Church of today is fundamentally the same Church it was then. It is only a few centuries older.

In view of this, therefore, it is important to understand that a return to these foundations, a drawing nearer to the tradition of the Church, helps us first of all to judge a way to conceive of ourselves and the world. For if it is true that "there has been the same readiness in all the Christian centuries to drink at the springs," it is also true that "fidelity to a tradition, moreover, is never servile repetition,"[1] this, in reference to the primitive Christians or to the Church Fathers need not be mechanical and repetitive. It can only be fruitful, however, in the event of a different personal dimension: if we look on ourselves, on others, and on all things with different eyes.

A great figure of the last century, John Henry Newman offers us an emblematic suggestion on this point. Precisely because he explored the fundamental characteristics emerging from the origins of the primitive church, this Anglican priest and scholar of Christianity's beginnings, eventually converted to Catholicism. It was a long and terrible crisis which beset him, but his inquiry was on the mark for one of the most pressing issues involved Anglicanism's accusation that the Catholic Church had altered the origins of the Christian experience. In his own narration of these interior developments, he proposed two observations, which deserve to be remembered as we conclude our reflection. One regards a criterion which we have already had occasion to mention, a criterion essential to our search for self-transformation on our path to obtaining a new dimension of mind and life. This is the criterion of the unity of our being, played out entirely in the arena of the search for and recognition of the truth: "For myself, it was not logic that carried me on: as well might one say that quicksilver in the barometer changes the weather. It is the concrete being that reasons; pass a number of years, and I find my mind in a new place; how? The whole man moves."[2]

Newman's second noteworthy point concerns none other than the organic development of the Church as a living reality, and this remains the one great interpretative point of view, basic to any aspect of the Church in any age. Moreover, Newman scrupulously takes the comparison between the primitive Church and the Catholic Church of his day further and reaches this consideration:

I saw that the principle of development not only accounted for certain facts, but was in itself a remarkable philosophical phenomenon, giving a character to the whole course of Christian thought. It was discernible from the first years of the Catholic teaching up to the present day, and gave to that teaching a unity and individuality. It served as a sort of test, which the Anglican could not exhibit, that modern Rome was in truth ancient Antioch, Alexandria and Constantinople, just as a mathematical curve has its own law and expression.[3]

In conclusion, we have been trying to delineate precisely this unity and this character so that today they will still inspire self-questioning, pushing us on to a personal comparison from which our lives will surely emerge richer and fuller, that is to say truer and more human.

BOOK TWO

The Effective Sign of the Divine in History

Introduction

We are about to embark on the final stretch of our itinerary, and consciously go deeper into what the Church says it is, in order to become more conscious of the awareness the Church has of itself.

What, then, does the Church claim to be? How can we decide what it is? We cannot form a judgment about someone unless we first take note of what that person poses as a problem. It is, therefore, very important that we understand what the Church claims to be, that we actually comprehend the substance of the Church's proposal of itself to the world. Let us ask ourselves then: how has the consciousness of the Christian people, of the Church throughout history, been formed? In what terms has the Christian people understood itself? By reflecting on itself and on the nature of the phenomenon it represents, how has the Church reached a self-definition?

So far, we have considered[1] the essential factors of the phenomenon, as revealed by texts which describe the emergence of Christianity in history. We have discovered that what came forth was the reality of a socially identifiable group and, from the interior point of view, an awareness persuading Christ's first followers that what was happening in them came from a strength, not their own, but a strength that was a gift, the gift of the Spirit, the energy of God made man who was at work in history and who affirmed his presence by mobilizing their lives. And, lastly, we witnessed the fact that this mobilization engaged and implied a conception, a sentiment, and a praxis of life that was "different." It was indicated by the word communion or *koinonia*.

It must be understood that although from the very beginning the Church presented itself as a social fact, a reality given form by men, at the same time, this earliest community always affirmed its conviction that "ontologically," that is, in terms of its value, in the depths of its being, it surpassed the human reality of its components. In fact, it presented itself as the community of salvation, the place where man might be saved. Both Peter and Paul can be cited for their comments on salvation. Peter, after being arrested for teaching to the people, answered the questions of the elders and the priests in this way, referring to Jesus: "Only in him is there salvation; for of all the names in the world given to men, this is the only one by which we can be saved" (Acts 4:12). And Paul, preaching in a synagogue one Sabbath day, launched this fervent appeal: "My brothers, sons of Abraham's race, and all you godfearers, this message of salvation is meant for you" (Acts 13:26).

I would like to dispel immediately any notion that this word, "salvation," refers to something vague and abstract. Rather, it implies what we, in our analysis of the religious sense, called man's fulfillment, his total meaning, the answer to his ultimate questions. Fulfillment, answer, and meaning – the primitive communities believed that these could be found within their own number, that they were the place where the presence of the divine fulfilled its design for and in the world, where the spirit of Christ, given to whomever believes in him, began his reign over the world as Lord, the fulfillment of the meaning of history. Therefore, that expression – community of salvation – summarizes the awareness of the early Christian: by affirming the Church as the community where man is saved, they were affirming its value as totally transcendent of all the factors composing it, and they were also acclaiming it as the place where man is reached by his destiny and where this same destiny makes man part of himself.

In this, the primitive Christian communities were in syntony with what the Old Testament had prophesied as a whole: that in his plan for salvation, God uses an instrument – an identifiable group of people, a history within history, which brings salvation for all history. Thus the idea of God's choice, of election by God, remains a fundamental concept of the Christian life too. This is why the expression, "people of God," but particularly and more profoundly, the "Mystical Body of Christ" – mystical because it is constituted by the ontological bond with the mystery of God – describe the content of the Christian consciousness, both then and now. This consciousness is dominated by Christ's prolonged presence throughout history, the Lord's mysterious permanence in time and space. This is why the people who gathered together in the first communities, while struggling daily with their own painful limitations, were nevertheless aware, in an unmistakable, irreducible way, that they were a new fact in history, a locus where the Spirit of Christ worked through their wretched humanity to mobilize the whole world according to his design. This is why they presented themselves as a community of salvation: they were the true people of God, Christ's successors, the extension and continuance of the Saviour's person in human history and, therefore, their very existence was an instrument for all men. They are God's people, however, and they prolong the Lord's presence in the world, insofar as they are his "mystical body," insofar as they are part of Christ's personality, "his body," to use Saint Paul's expression (Eph. 4:16). And it is for this reason that the crucial problem of the Church as the continuity of Christ cannot be grasped unless it is seen as analogous to the problem of Christ himself. The Church is the method Christ uses for self-communication in time and space just as Christ is the method God felt he should use to communicate himself to men and so establish their means of salvation.

I remember how many years ago I was asked to give a lesson to a group of priests who taught religion in high schools. The theme was the method of Christian living, and I started the lesson by commenting somewhat brusquely: "Christ is not the truth," – a remark which sparked an immediate and noisy rebellion in the whole assembly. I then proceeded to clarify this startling comment: because truth is the Word and Christ represents the method by which truth communicated itself to men, he *is*, therefore, the truth incarnate as he himself asserted: "I am the truth and the life." But his premise to these words was: "I am the way" (John 14:6). Christ, then, is the truth insofar as he is the way, the method, a man accessible to all, God who walks with men. He could have chosen another method to communicate himself to men, such as through an individual's personal choice, as rationalism affirms, or through an interior experience dictated by the spirit, as Protestants stress. But he chose this other way. He took the mind and imagination of humanity by surprise by becoming a man and claiming himself as the way, as the method. Christ is the method God chose for man's salvation.

The Church is Christ's continuance in history, time, and space, the means by which Christ continues to be present in history in a particular way. It is also the method by which the Spirit of Christ mobilizes the world towards truth, justice, and happiness. In summary, the Church stands before the world as a social reality filled with the divine. In other words, it presents itself both as a human and a divine reality.

This is the crux of the problem: a human phenomenon claiming to be the bearer of the divine, whereby, through the Church's presence in human history, the problem Christ raised is reproposed in all its scandal. The Church challenges history, just as Christ challenged his own time. Better still, through the Church, Christ continues to challenge time.

We shall now proceed to analyze the two factors constituting this scandal: the human and the divine in the Church, always bearing in mind throughout our brief analysis, that the criterion enabling us to penetrate the heart of the matter is the fact that these terms must be considered as one within the same reality. They are distinct and yet united, not merged together, but copresent. And, lastly, we shall move on to demonstrate how the problem of the Church presents itself to each one of us, as our problem to verify its ever-present claim to be human and divine at the same time. We are referring here to *this* Church, not merely in its generic reality, but as it is today, with all the good we immediately see in what it tells us, and with all the perplexities it creates within us, with all the reactions it provokes, and all the objections it stirs. How then can we "verify" this present Church, with the claim it makes? How can we discover it in its truth, satisfying, at once, both our reason and our conscience? What path should we take in order to see its credibility?

Verifying this will be the final step on our way.

PART ONE
The Church's Self-Definition

6 The Human Factor

Let us now briefly analyze the two factors we have introduced – the human and the divine. The divine communicates itself through the human, initially reflecting on the characteristics of the Christian method, the vehicle of God's communication, the chosen instrument: in short, the human factor.

The Church's most specific claim is not just that it is the vehicle of the divine, but that this vehicle works through human reality. Indeed, this is Christ's own claim, It was an insurmountable objection to the religious leaders and the educated people of his time, and it caused great scandal: "Is he not the carpenter, the son of Joseph?" (cf. Luke 4:22). "Surely he is one of us," they said, "one whose background we can trace, whose identity we can check, as we can anyone else's." Moreover, the height of the scandal was the fact that not only did his identity present nothing mysterious at first – he was a carpenter, the son of Joseph – but that his human personality displayed a disconcerting openness towards all sectors of the population. He did not hold back from the most unworthy of them, the lowest of the low, those most open to criticism. On the contrary, he clearly leaned towards them: "Why does he eat with tax collectors and sinners?" (Mark 2:16b). And such a man dared to say: "I am the way, the truth and the life. No one can come to the Father except through me" (John 14:6), daring to involve God with his own person to the extent of identifying himself with him.

And this is the scandal which the Church, in its essence and its existence in history, reproposes today and forever.

I THROUGH HUMAN REALITY

We have seen that what characterizes the Christian mystery is the revelation of the fact that God communicates himself to humanity through man, through human life. To illustrate and support this, I would like to quote a few passages from the New Testament.

The following passage, from Paul's letter to the faithful in Thessalonica, in which he expresses his satisfaction at this community's response to his message, is significant: "Another reason why we continually thank God for you is that as soon as you heard the word that we brought you as God's message, you welcomed it for what it really is, not the word of any human being, but God's word, a power that is working among you believers" (1 Thess 2:13). Here, Paul is giving a very clear description of the phenomenon: the divine word which communicates itself through the voice of a man, the word of God brought by a man and accepted for what it really is, the word of the living God, active and creative in the lives of men. As noteworthy is another of Paul's letters, where he is careful to underline that this word is so human a vehicle that it can even appear totally devoid of attraction, lacking the slightest wit. "Now when I came to you, brothers," the apostle admits, "I did not come with any brilliance of oratory or wise argument to announce to you the mystery of God ... I came among you in weakness, in fear and great trembling and what I spoke and proclaimed was not meant to convince by philosophical argument; but to demonstrate the convincing power of the Spirit, so that your faith should depend not on human wisdom but on the power of God" (1 Cor 2:1, 3–5). And the letter he wrote to the Christians of Ephesus, attributed to his first period of imprisonment in Rome, reiterated a similar notion: "I, who am less than the least of all God's holy people, have been entrusted with this special grace, of proclaiming to the gentiles the unfathomable treasure of Christ and of throwing light on the inner workings of the mystery kept hidden through all the ages in God, the Creator of everything" (Eph. 3:8–9).

Paul, then, was perfectly conscious of the innate disproportion in the phenomenon of the Church. By bringing its message through the vehicle of human reality, it is, therefore, exposed to all the individual instances of human wretchedness, including his own – in short, the human word might well be dull, as he knew his to be. Jean Daniélou made an acute observation in his commentary on this passage:

Minimo – ... "less than the least" – for St Paul was a bad speaker: and ... he made no great impression in personal encounters. The Corinthians said of him that he wrote "powerful" letters from a distance, but when he came himself, there was nothing to him. So he had no special aptitude for his work – rather the reverse. *Minimo* – less than the least; he might well wonder why God had chosen him: but all this was of no consequence; the question did not arise, for he had in fact been chosen, and must now get on with the work, ... Indeed he was all the easier in his mind for knowledge that he himself had nothing to do with the arrangement, that he was not to rely on his own resources, that, humanly speaking, everything was against him. How was he, a Jew, to deal with all these Romans and Hellenes? What equipment had he, to dispute with the stoic and epicurean philosophers of the day, at Athens? He had neither health nor strength, he suffered from an obscure complaint (probably of nervous origin) – how could he stand up to the rigours of constant travel by sea and land, often in terrible conditions?[1]

Paul's awareness of disproportion becomes more acute in the ensuing moving passage in which he outlines some aspects of the lives of the evangelists at the time of the first communities:

For it seems to me that God has put us apostles on show right at the end, like men condemned to death: we have been exhibited as a spectacle to the whole universe, both angelic and human. here we are, fools for Christ's sake, while you are the clever ones in Christ; we are weak, while you are strong; you are honoured, while we are disgraced. To this day, we go short of food and drink and clothes, we are beaten up and we have no homes; we earn our living by labouring with our own hands; when we are cursed we answer with a blessing; when we are hounded, we endure it passively; when we are insulted, we give a courteous answer. We are treated even now as the dregs of the world, the very lowest scum (1 Cor. 4:9–13).

And yet these same apostles, Paul continues, "let light shine out of darkness, that has shone into our hearts to enlighten them with the knowledge of God's glory, the glory on the face of Christ," for "we hold this treasure in pots of earthenware, so that the immensity of the power is God's and not our own. We are subjected to every kind of hardship, but never distressed; we see no way out but we never despair; we are pursued but never cut off; knocked down, but still have some life in us" (2 Cor. 4:6–9).

Paul was clearly aware of his own and others' limited humanity, of an incapacity totally disproportionate to that whose instrument, nevertheless, it is. However, as Paul comments in the above passage, this highly fragile humanity is destined to reveal the sublimity of a power, the invincibility of a presence which must be recognized, without the shadow of a doubt, as something that comes, not from us but which uses us, and which has begun, irresistibly, to change the world.

This was not, however, the only dimension to the lives of the evangelists, as the second part of the above passage shows: they were experiencing an existential tension connected with living a paradox, the simultaneous existence of a weakness and a strength, a paradox whose two contrasting elements are therefore ineliminable. The poet Charles Péguy uses a wonderful expression to depict this paradox when a character in one of his plays comments: "All the saints have always borne the glory of God in the folds of all their cloaks."[2] Treasure in earthenware pots, glory nestled in the folds of a mantle are images which must suggest to us the impossibility of renouncing the Christian tension, of which Paul's image of the athlete running the race is a powerful metaphor: "Do you not realise that, though all the runners in the stadium take part in the race, only one of them gets the prize? Run like that – to win. Every athlete concentrates completely on training" (1 Cor. 9:24–25).

It is obvious, then, that the first individuals who spread Christianity were perfectly aware that the divine shone forth in the world from what they said and did, that their words were insufficient, their gestures weak, their personalities inadequate, their human condition wretched. However, this did not mean that they were acquiescent and resigned. No, they proudly ran the race, fought the daily struggle, constantly reaching out for the gift of salvation. Moreover, it was not merely the people through whom God communicated himself who were human in a perfectly ordinary way. The circumstances were also unexceptional. We are reminded that in the day-to-day life of the first Christian communities, man's encounter with God – the supreme aspect of the problem of life – and his participation in his being took place, above all, in situations we might call vulgar, in the most normal of suppers, a simple, shared meal. This was the context in which the deepest, most mysterious involvement with the Lord transpired, the communication of divine life with all its gifts came through eating bread and drinking wine. Certainly, man may well feel such a method to be the most banal of approaches; he may show a type of subtle resistance to God's mysterious method of wanting to pass through human reality (while man, in contrast, tends to codify all his thinking and doing as divine!). However, this is the chosen method: God communicates himself in the human realm, even the banal and even the word that pardons sin (and who can pardon sin except God?) is a human word, channelled through a pathetic human voice. " If you forgive anyone's sins, they are forgiven; if you retain anyone's sins, they are retained" (John 20:23).

It is not so easy to realize in existential terms that this is precisely the problem of the Church: God *wants* to pass through the humanity of all those he has taken hold of in Baptism. Charles Péguy expresses God's unimaginable method in the following way:

Miracle of miracles, my child, mystery of mysteries.
Because Jesus Christ has become our carnal brother
Because he has pronounced, carnally and in time, eternal words,
In monte, upon the mountain,
It is to us, the weak, that he was given,
He depends on us, weak and carnal,
To bring to life and to nourish and to keep alive in time
These words pronounced alive in time.
Mystery of mysteries, this privilege that was given to us,
This incredible, exorbitant privilege,
To keep alive the words of life,
To nourish with our blood, with our flesh, with our heart
The words which, without us, would collapse fleshless.

O misery, o happiness, that it would depend on us,
Shivers of happiness,
We who are nothing, we who spend a few years of nothing on earth,
A few wretched, pathetic years,
(We immortal souls),
O danger, the risk of death, it is we who are responsible,
We who are incapable of anything, who are nothing, who are uncertain of
    tomorrow,
And even of today, who are born and who will die like creatures of a day,
Who pass through like mercenaries,
And yet it is we who are responsible,
We who in the morning are uncertain of the evening,
And even of the afternoon,
And who at night are uncertain of the morning,
Of the following morning,
It's folly, it's still we who are responsible, it depends on us and us alone
To assure the Words a second eternity
An eternal eternity.
A remarkable perpetuity.
It belongs to us, it depends on us to assure the words
An eternal perpetuity, a carnal perpetuity,
A perpetuity nourished with meat, with fat and with blood.

We who are nothing, who will not last,
Who practically speaking won't last at all

(On earth)

It's folly, it's still we who are responsible to preserve and to nourish the
eternal

On earth

The spoken words, the word of God.[3]

Let us summarize: the Church is characterized by the divine which
has chosen human reality to communicate himself. This implies that
we accept human factors as part and parcel of the definition of Church.
Given our human limitations, it seems absurd that God would choose
us in this way. But if we recognize that *this* is the Church's definition of
itself, then no objection to Christianity that makes a point or pretext of
the disproportion, inadequacy or error of the human reality which
forms the Church, can ever logically be raised. In the same way, in
reverse, a true Christian will not be able to use his limits as an excuse,
even though, by definition, he will have limits. As we have seen in Saint
Paul, a Christian, while being intent on asking for the Lord's goodness,
will, at the same time, be sincere and sorrowful in judging his own
incapacity, which, nevertheless, is used by God.

I would now like to formulate a few corollaries in connection with all
we have said so far, corollaries which will help us tackle more closely
the implications of the fact that the Church is a human reality, an
instrument of the divine. I would also like to insist on proposing
something that will help us to adopt the most adequate position from
which to judge the Christian problem. What I mean is this: if the
Church is a human reality, then we might well find in it unworthy men,
incapable parents, rebellious children, liars, cheats. And the list could
go on and on, starting from the long series of grave shortcomings to be
found even in the first Christian texts. But anyone seeking to verify the
announced presence of the divine in the midst of this human wretchedness cannot dwell on this wretchedness and conclude that the divine
cannot possibly be present. For this reason, another criterion will have
to be adopted, for there is no wretchedness that could ever annul the
paradoxical nature of the instrument chosen by God.

2 IMPLICATIONS

These implications, which this section shall detail and clarify, are
interesting in my view because they assume a practical nature. They
contest a mentality, a way of judging and feeling that generally sur-
rounds us, is in our midst and, therefore, is, to some degree, or at least
potentially within us too.

a) The Inevitability of Various Temperaments and Mentalities

If the divine chooses the human as a means of self-communication, the man who accepts this method, the Christian, becomes and remains just that – at once an instrument of the divine, but also a man who maintains his own particular temperament. This might seem tremendously banal, but I feel I should point this out in order to indicate the error contained not only in the rejection of this point, but also in the objection often raised to it. We can refer to the Old Testament to clarify this. Two of the forty-six books form a curious contrast – Ecclesiastes/Qoheleth and Ecclesiasticus/Ben Sira (Sirach in some translations) – a contrast once much more evident because it was customary to read them in sequence. The writings of the first author seem to be veiled in a veneer of sadness. They almost read like Leopardi's *Operette morali.* The biblical author, of course, concludes by inviting man to trust in God. However, when it comes to depicting the human condition, he is induced to make some bitter considerations.

This laughter, I reflected, is a madness, this pleasure no use at all (Eccles. 2:2).

When the author reflects on man's actions on earth, he feels he must say, "What futility it all was. What chasing after the wind!" (cf. Eccles. 2:11). This particular view of life essentially stresses the emptiness of things, the nothingness of appearances: "Sheer futility, teacher says, everything is futile" (Eccles. 12: 8).

But at the turn of a page, we find the other book of wisdom, and its tone is quite the opposite. It is serene, positive about creation, and in its entire vein, it is benevolent towards its interlocutors. It is also totally intent on praising God with joy because, throughout Israel's history, God scattered the seed of many men in whom he "displayed his greatness" (cf. Eccles. 44:2). The author concludes his long text in this way:

May your souls rejoice in the mercy of the Lord,
may you never be ashamed of praising him.
Do your work before the appointed time
and at the appointed time he will give you your reward (Eccles. 51:29–30).

The contrast we mentioned prompts us to reflect on the fact that God, having chosen humans as a vehicle for communicating himself and bringing salvation to man, utilizes both of these two opposite temperaments, expressing one value through the first, and another through the second. The melancholic temperament warns of the transience of things, while the sunny, enthusiastic temperament emphasizes the logically positive fact of existence. However, in spite of this contrast, it is the value being channelled that counts and, since God uses man as his "instrument," this value will never be found in its pure state. Quite simply, the communication of God is incarnated in the human temperament. It constitutes a "condition" which God accepts, transforming it into an "instrument" of his plan of salvation.

In the same way, the Christian, transmitting his message to those around him today, makes use of whatever resources he has, and if his temperament is of good stock, the results of his efforts will be dynamic and alive. But if his resources are frayed or fibreless, then his action will be all smoke and no fire, generating only uneasiness.

But no matter what the temperament of the individual, the power of God passes through the conditioning of the person he chooses. And this is what we are called to understand. A few examples should serve to illustrate this point.

I remember that in the early days of my priesthood, I was always beset by a strange sensation every time I had to preach in Church. The church, in my eyes, seemed to be divided into blotches of light and shade, as if the congregation were grouped into points of light and darkness. In fact, there were people whose faces, as they listened, would gradually open up, while others, in contrast, would assume a withdrawn, irritated attitude as I spoke. Much later, as the years went by, I understood what it all meant. It was my own temperament, my own tone of voice, the way I expounded and approached issues that produced this effect of shedding light on some and perturbing others. Because of this, I made a note to remind myself and others of the inherent risk in judging a sermon, a message, the expression of a value, according to such factors as personality, attitude, expressive capacity, or incapacity. For to do this is to risk forgetting that the point at stake is one's own love for the truth. In effect, an individual must possess a profound desire for truth in order to overcome the scandal of the instrument communicating it.

The second example concerns the first time I ever went into a school classroom as a teacher of religion. I was taking over from someone with special qualities: he was an exceptional person, with distinguished, fine features and a quiet manner. When I went into the class and started the lesson in my way, with these features of mine, with my own characteristics, it was as if the whole class drew back at first, as if they were irritated or almost insulted. Evidently, in that situation too, certain characteristics of mine hindered the communication of the truth that I, too, was so anxious to transmit.

We often hear it said: "If only all Christians were like him," or: "If only all priests were like that." Such comments prove the error I mentioned and are symptomatic of an attitude which impoverishes the person who adopts it. For it is an illusion to think that we would automatically react differently to a truth if we had met it through another type of person. This conclusion is illusory because it means endowing a simple and often understandable reaction of like or dislike in regard to a given person with the dignity of a judgment. A gold prospector would never have been daunted by the mud of the river bed where he hoped to find nuggets. Rather, he would have been motivated by the probability of finding gold, not by the conditions he might have to face in order to come across it. It is terrible then to think how easily, in contrast, man can be detached from the problem of his destiny, to the extent of renouncing the gold because of the mud that comes with it. But as we were saying, the problem is one of judgment: a man, daunted by the mud of their rivers, has not taken into account the fact that it is the gold of life which is at stake.

We could make similar observations about the mentality of an individual or a society – the whole series of attitudes habitually adopted in response to the problems of life. A man's mentality is the fruit of his temperament, his formation, and the particular circumstances that have left their mark on his existence. Mentality is a capacity of our consciousness. And in the history of the Church there are many enlightening examples of the variety of temperaments and the diverse possibilities posed by differing mentalities. For example, in the history of the papacy, we could contrast two particular figures in terms of their personalities, formation, and, above all, the specific features of their mission: Sylvester II and Gregory VII. Sylvester II, pope in the year 1000, was considered to be "the most universal intelligence of his age."[4] "He had studied mathematics, astronomy, Latin literature, music, and above all the religious sciences of philosophy and theology."[5] In short, he was "the greatest scholar of the day ... Educated in his monastery of Aurillac, then at Vich in mathematics and science, and finally at Reims, and appointed *scholasticus* of the Reims cathedral school, [he] had made such a name for himself through an amazing mastery of all branches of the trivium and the quadrivium."[6] He was the master and friend of the young Emperor Otto III, with whom he shared the dream of a Christian empire, although "this cooperation occurred, it is true, in the form rather of a subordination than of an equality of the pope."[7] Sylvester had been elected to the pontifical throne with a great deal of support from the emperor and, during his brief reign, the young Otto seldom failed to interfere in many ecclesiastical questions. But we must remember, as

Daniel-Rops pointed out, that "Christians in the year 1000 were men of temperamental extremes ... but still capable of deeds inspired by a touching faith ... the German emperor Otto III, who remained throughout his life a disciple of Gerbert [Sylvester II] as he had been in his youth, and when the interests of their respective thrones were at variance he submitted to the pope."[8]

Although their imperial dream was short-lived, Otto and Sylvester left their mark on the history of the Church. The cultural sensibility of Gerbert, the former monk, had been placed at the service of a Church he was anxious to consolidate in the furthest regions and whose universality he felt he had a duty to express. Hungary and Poland were thus definitively won for the Christian West, and Gregory VII himself would later remind the Hungarian Church of the role his predecessor had played in this important event.

If Sylvester's papacy bore the mark of concord with the empire, in the sense that both entities nurtured the same plan, the pontificate of Gregory VII, while still stressing the unitary ideal of Christianity, is best remembered for emancipating the papacy from its submission to the empire and for separating the spiritual authority of bishops from their commitments as members of the feudal hierarchy. Animated by the need to renew the Church, Gregory pursued holiness and purity with zealous vigour. "He was not likeable or pleasant by nature and was often as bitter as the 'North wind.' Perhaps the rigour with which he fought so excessively (at least to our minds) to extend the prerogatives of his office was rooted in this side of his character."[9] Thus, conflicts with Henry IV assumed proportions that perhaps the pontiff himself would not have desired. But, independently of all the dilemmas that Gregory VII's actions in history pose for scholars "one thing, however, is not to be doubted: the Pope felt himself to be one seized upon by God and acted accordingly. If, even in the most extreme distress, he made no dishonourable compromise with Henry IV, it was not obstinacy that guided him but his faith, able to move mountains, in his mission."[10]

And it was precisely his faith in the Church, a church which he believed had to be free and holy, which was recognized as heroic by his successor, Paul V, who canonised him at the beginning of the twelfth century.

The unity of the Church, its propelling strength in regard to all men, its innate need to be as effective as possible in bringing a unique message to mankind, all of these facets are helped by different temperaments and even, as we have seen, plans which are in complete contrast, cultural imprints which highlight widely diverging perspectives of action. However, none of this can be either an objection to or reason for adhering to the Church's message: we cannot dwell either on the magnetism of these great figures or on their limitations. We adhere to or reject something because of content, because of its truth in resolving a problem as it presents itself. If God has chosen to use men and women as instruments of his self-communication, then they are to be judged as such. To return to our metaphor: it is the responsibility of each one of us to desire the gold of the message. If one truly desires gold, then he is not scandalized at finding it in mud. He must dirty his hands and work hard to extract it. But if one does not want to get his hands dirty, then he is not all that interested in the gold after all; he is more concerned about keeping his hands clean.

Another example from Church history, one much closer to our times, demonstrates the incisiveness and limitations, of temperament and mentality as instruments of God's providential design. This can be found in the papacy of Pius IX. Throughout his long pontificate, which witnessed great social changes in the latter half of the nineteenth century, he demonstrated not only the goodness of his nature and temperament, but also the limited horizons of his mentality, understandably overshadowed by anxiety, fear and emotion. And yet Pius IX:

was genuinely unpretentious and good person, equipped with a sensitivity which permitted him to make charming gestures and have happy ideas, without excluding, if he considered it advisable, a sometimes rude frankness. ... He failed to adapt the church to new conditions. These were on the one hand the profound evolution which was in the process of completely altering the structures of bourgeois society, and on the other the totally unchanged perspectives by which certain theological positions needed to be viewed in light of the progress made in the natural sciences and historical research. ... After he became Pope, he kept abreast of modern inventions.[11]

It is noteworthy, however, that the Church of that time certainly did not lack great figures and great saints: in England, John Henry Newman converted from Anglicanism; in France, the Curé d'Ars died thirteen years after Pius IX's election; in Germany, Bishop William von Ketteler was pointing the way to new tasks for the Church through his sensitivity to workers' conditions, while in Italy, John Bosco was drawing public attention to the plight of young people in modern cities. At this juncture, God wanted a good man at the head of the church, a man of great impulse but not long-sighted enough to come to grips with the new age. And yet he, too, Pius IX, with all his qualities and faults, served the Church as others would no doubt have done, his qualities and his limitations acting as instruments and stimuli for making the Christians of his time more aware of their responsibility.

b) Through Freedom

The importance of the implications we are detailing here becomes even more penetrating and profound as we approach this second statement: man is Christian with all his personal freedom. This means that the Christian ideal will be actuated only to the degree that a Christian, with all his freedom, chooses. In this way, then, an individual could be the bearer of the ideal and, at the same time, contradict it in the way he lives. The Christian message depends on the seriousness of man's moral intent and on his moral capacity.

This, therefore, is the dramatic implication of the method God has always used: everything depends on freedom. In no other sphere, either of thought or of achievement in history, does freedom play such an important role as in the vision Christianity proposes of man, of society, and of history. However, if, as we have seen, the divine message the Church proposes to us must pass through human reality – through a limitation, something finite – it is for this very reason that we know for certain that human freedom will never be able to realize this ideal to its fullest extent: the human vehicle in the Church will always seem inadequate in comparison with all that it presumes to bring to the world. But the point we are making is precisely this: God has bound himself to this, the individual's highly personal application of freedom, to the specific way in which every single man responds to the capacity for the infinite which is in him, and to the requests of God. This is why any of us may well encounter generous Christians and not so generous ones, just as in the early Christian community, for example, people shared all their possessions, while others were willing to share only some. All were Christians in their freedom, and if we recall the episode of the elderly couple, Ananias and Sapphira, who were punished after maintaining that they had given all they owned to the community, we will remember, too, that they were not punished for having really given only half of their possessions instead of all of them, but for attempting to tell a lie.

The divine passes definitively through the channel of personal freedom in its communication of self. It is interesting to observe the Christian way of life from the point of view of freedom. If, in fact, a man says something that is right and does not put it into practice himself, we who notice it have our backs to the wall in the face of *our* ultimate responsibility.

i) ANALYSIS OF AN OBJECTION

We must recognize, first of all, that this paradox whereby the divine communicates itself through human beings, whereby the infinite chooses a finite, free instrument as its tool, raises certain questions for everyone. However, the real problem involves directing our efforts to answering the right question, to asking ourselves if this paradox, once it has been recognized as a paradox, responds to reality or not. The second part of our reflection will try to outline the coordinates of the answer to this question. But the immediate question which, in terms of logic, would send us off on a tangent is the following: how would I judge the Church, using man's behaviour as my criterion? And the answer to this is quite simple: any judgment of the Church based on human conduct, whoever they may be, is formulated from a basis of erroneous premises.

Let me explain. If the Church says of itself: I am a reality made of men and women, the vehicle of something exceptional, of something supernatural, of the divine, the Divine that saves the world; if the Church, then, gives this definition of herself – and it has done so since the very beginning – its value cannot be truly judged by listing the crimes and behavioural limitations of men who are part of this Church. On the contrary, if the definition of Church incorporates human reality as the channel chosen by the divine for its self-manifestation, then these crimes are also a potential part of that definition. This does not mean that we must resign ourselves to accepting them. What I mean, in this context, is that wickedness and wretchedness are not worthy subject matter for formulating a judgment concerning the truth of the Church.

So how do we approach this problem? On the one hand, from the point of view of moral attitude, in the face of the shortcomings of members of the Church, a person's duty is not, either out of personal weakness (as if to say: "Yes, Christianity would be a good thing, but I'm not up to it"), or out of a sense of shock at the behaviour of others, to withdraw. Rather, it is one's duty to intervene, to make a personal effort, first, with the most ardent commitment, to improve one's own shortcomings, and then to mitigate the weaknesses of others with all the wisdom and goodness of which one is capable. On the other hand, from an intellectual standpoint, the most adequate position to adopt is to ask ourselves exactly what the Church aspires to be, and then verify if this claim is grounded in reality. This is why the following famous phrase of Nietzsche's – where he told his hypothetical Christian interlocutors that he would be willing to believe in their Saviour more "if they looked more like people who were saved" – is very understandable from a psychological point of view. This phrase must also surely be a reminder to Christians of their duty to bear witness. However, from a logical, objective, and critical perspective, it does not delineate any well-grounded judgment and, morally speaking, betrays an attitude indifferent to tackling the crux of the problem the Church presents, a problem far too serious, as it is, to cling to such positions of dubious foundation.

ii) THE UNVEILING OF THE WAY TO FIND TRUTH

We have seen how any judgment of the Church, beginning with human conduct, starts off on the wrong foot. We have also seen how such judgments are doomed to miss the paradox – of the divine channelled by human reality – the paradox on which the Church bases its definition of self. The following words, from one of Henri de Lubac's famed works, are words which flowed from his pen like a song, and will introduce us to this paradoxical reality:

What a paradox in its reality this Church is with all its contrasting aspects! How many irreducible images of it history offers us! In nearly 20 centuries, how many changes in its demeanor, how many strange developments, how many turning points, how many metamorphoses. And even today – quite apart from the separations which certain rifts have forged – and in spite of the new conditions prevailing in a world tending towards uniformity, how great the distance, how great the abyss, sometimes, between the Christian communities of various countries in their attitudes, in their way of living and thinking the faith! ... The Church. ... What features would I give it if I were to draw its portrait? Can all these so disparate of elements – each of which belong to it – form one face? Yes, I believe, the Church is *complexio oppositorum*; but, at first sight, surely I ought to recognise that the jarring *opposita* hides the unity of the *complexio* from my view? ... They tell me it is holy, and I see it packed with sinners. They tell me that its mission is to tear man away from earthly preoccupations, to remind him that he is called to eternity, and I see it unceasingly occupied with the things of this earth. ... They assure me that it is universal, as open as divine wisdom and love are open, and often I note that its members, fatalistically almost, withdraw timidly into closed groups ...

It is proclaimed as unchanging, the only stability on a higher dimension than history's turbine, and then suddenly, before our very eyes, it disturbs numbers of faithful with its brusque renewals ...

Yes, paradox is the Church. Mine is not some vain rhetorical game. Paradox is the Church, made for a paradoxical humanity to which it sometimes adapts too much. It espouses the characteristics, in all their complexity and as inconsequential as they are – it marries all the endless contradictions that live in man. ... From its first generations, when it had only just gone beyond the confines of the old Jerusalem, the Church's face was already reflecting the features – all the wretched features – of the community of man.

But let us sharpen our focus. Let us try to see beyond the over-superficial, rough-hewn facade. ... And then we will discover the characteristic paradox of the Church, and it is this same paradox which will introduce us to its mystery. The Church is human and divine.[12]

In view of this, and in the attempt to sharpen our focus, let us then ask ourselves that, if we exclude human conduct as a basic factor, what would be the most suitable attitude to adopt for expressing an opinion about the Church? And we must emphasize that human behaviour really must be excluded from our consideration, not only because, as we have seen, of its inadequacy in front of the object in question, given that the Church's definition of self incorporates potential and inevitable human wretchedness, but also because it is not consistently applicable as a factor at all. The American bishop, Fulton J. Sheen, once made this acute observation: those who flee the Church because of the hypocrisy and imperfection of the religious individuals in it, forget that if the Church were as perfect as they would like it to be, then there would be no place for them at all.

It is certainly true that the power of the Church, the power to recreate man, is not given its fullest expression because we ourselves prevent it. It is equally true, however, that this paradoxical nature of the Church, of which de Lubac spoke, calls upon us as individuals, to live lives of moral clarity, lives in which the real object of our seeking is unveiled. When Jesus said: "Blessed is he who will not be shocked by me" (Luke 7:2) he meant, do not be shocked by what I might say and do, however paradoxical that might appear. In the same way, we can say: blessed is the man who does not reject a value because of an imperfection in its bearer.

We can seen, then, that even when Jesus was still alive, the problem presented itself, just as it presents itself to us today. The disciples noted this dynamic in some who stood listening to Jesus, and the Gospel reports it in the following way: "Then the disciples came to him and said, ?Do you know that the Pharisees were shocked when they heard what you said?'" (Matt 15:12). What Jesus had said was that impurity lives in man's heart, it has nothing to do with the food he eats. "Leave them alone," he answered in a premptory way, "They are blind leaders of the blind" (Matt 15:14).

But what is it that this particular category of Jesus' interlocutors do not see? They do not see what they do not seek; in fact, what they seek is not the truth, as it presents itself, to which they closed their eyes, making themselves blind. Even today, if we are intent on finding fault with those who proclaim Christianity, or if we are waiting to be shocked, this is only an excuse for never adhering, for never having the need to change. For, in any case, there will always be faults, and to opt to fix one's gaze on them only means to make the fatal choice not to scan our horizons searching for what is worthwhile. Jesus again stigmatizes this excuse, when he replied to a new objection raised by the Pharisees that his disciples did not observe the tradition of washing their hands before meals: "How ingeniously you get round the commandment of God in order to preserve your own tradition" (Mark 7:9) – and this is the unhappy attitude of which we can still become prisoners today.

However, the Church was saved throughout the centuries by all those who, in their pursuit of the truth and reality, in their love of value and the ideal, were not shocked by the limitations, by the grip of circumstance, by the apparent incomprehensibility of human affairs, and who set out resolutely in the search for the object of their love, to find the treasure hidden in the mud. In this way, they showed the world and history that their eyes and their hearts were trained on the treasure and not the mud.

Saint Francis of Assisi, for example, was not shocked at the divisions and violence shaking the foundations of the Church in his time, at the fratricidal wars which set Christian against Christian. Rather, touched by God after a frivolously spent youth, he hurled himself headlong into a struggle which was not "against" anyone. It was "for" Someone. A famed historian of the Franciscan movement, Kajetan Esser, described his gaze, fixed on the goal in this way: "He was oriented not on the life of the apostles or even on the life of the first Christian community in Jerusalem, but directly on all that the Man-God, Jesus Christ, had experienced and fulfilled on earth. The life of Christ is the ideal model with which Francis aspires to identify as far as possible. God himself called him to this life and, with simplicity and candour, he responds to this divine call and he does not let himself be waylaid by anyone or for any reason in the world."[13]

Neither was Catherine of Siena, over a century after Francis' death, shocked at the wretched situation into which the Church had sunk, despite the vital sap brought by the mendicant orders. The Papal court at Avignon was increasingly the minion of the French crown, its clergy often unpopular and pleasure-seeking, and the climate was one of strife and conflict between cities and families. In this context, this dynamic Sienese woman strove to fulfill the mission she believed was her calling: the mission to renew the Church, a mission for which her other contemporaries also strove, through prayer and mortification, in the flow of mysticism that was traversing Europe at the time. Heedless of obstacles, Catherine launched her impassioned appeals for monarchs, popes, and criminals alike to convert. Direct and frank, she faced all that for her was value, the "treasure" to seek and to save. "Take heart in Christ gentle Jesus, for I trust that his help, the fullness of divine grace, will come soon to your support ... Don't let your holy desire falter on account of any dissent or rebellion you might see or hear about on the part of the cities. ... Be a courageous man for me, not a coward. Respond to God, who is calling you to come and take possession of the place of the glorious shepherd, Saint Peter, whose representative you still are."[14]

The great error is to allow one's own error, or that of others, to be an obstacle; the fully human reaction, the "virile" one, to use the saint's words, would be "to want to act immediately." Personal commitment, although it does not terminate at it, does not exclude a critical attitude. Rather, it is a problem of elementary morality. Let me explain this with a small example. Let us imagine a woman who is married and has a small child. Let us suppose that she is already a little disappointed, as can happen, with her companion for life, who comes home at night and immediately starts to read the newspaper, or watch television, or perhaps even go out again to the bar, without as much as a glance in the direction of his wife or child. One day the child falls ill. The house is some distance from the town, and the young woman cannot leave her little boy alone to fetch a doctor, who cannot be reached by telephone. At long last her husband arrives and she asks him to lend a hand. He, however, thinks his wife is over-concerned. Because he has been working all day, he sits down to read the paper, assuring her that everything will be fine. Now what will be the reaction of this child's mother? Will she say, perhaps: "Well, if it's not important to him, then I won't bother either"? Or, is she more likely to take charge herself, refusing to allow her husband's laziness to stand in her way? If a person from whom one may quite rightly expect a certain commitment fails to fulfill it, and if another person loves the object of this commitment, the second person will be the one to multiply his efforts without hiding behind the other's lack of action.

It also would be useful to recall once again the words of Simeon to Mary, when she presented her son in the temple. Simeon prophesied that the reason for her son's presence in the world was "so that the secret thoughts of many may be laid bare" (Luke 2:35) – a phrase synthesizing the dynamics the Christian message sets in motion in man. In its paradoxical reality and potency, the Christian fact makes man's true desire emerge. If someone aspires to what is right, he does not stop short at the perhaps ignoble way in which it presents itself. Rather, he lets himself be led by the attraction this right thing holds; all the more so because such a painful awareness of the disproportion between what we passionately believe and our own limitations, our meanness and fragility, can rarely be found outside the sphere of life in a Christian community.

It is generally easy to adopt an erroneous attitude to our own limitations, plausibly to justify ourselves by saying something like this: "That would be great, but I can't", and to fall prey to a form of desperation. But within a sphere of Christian living, the clear consciousness of the ultimate value burns and judges first of all those who try to live it – in fact, the Mass begins every day with: "I confess." This is the most intensely true position conceivable from the human point of view: a clear love for one's ideal in the awareness of one's disproportion. Using an etymologically interesting word, the Christian tradition calls this attitude "humility." Its root is *humus*, which means the earth or what we come from and of which we live. The humble attitude is nothing other than a recognition and a love for what is real, for the earth that we are. But it is an earth – and this is also part of the reality – in which Something Other is implicated, from which Something Other grows.

Let us conclude these particular observations on the way man's profound desire is unveiled, the way the Christian fact has acted in history, by citing this impassioned plea of de Lubac's:

Nothing that is human is ever fault-free. Never, in any synthesis, are all things totally coherent – just as there are never perfect circles or squares in the nature of things. But why should we suppose *a priori* that the thoughts and works of man are like a bag of tomatoes in which even one single rotten fruit is enough to make the whole bag bad? Why bet that the faulty element of a thought is always the dominant one, the strong one, the element which will carry all the others along with it in the future? Why do we never believe in the strength of the truth and of good, in the possibility of straightening things out, indeed of the profound transformation, of the "conversion" of the lesser elements by the action of the better ones?[15]

And we will find the answer to this question by posing another: "What are we really looking for? A value such as to change us, to make us more true, or self-affirmation, blaming our inertia on the series of others' faults?" No evil will be able to deviate our search for the truth and the good if it is really oriented to finding them. But it would be very difficult for anything true and good to overcome the obstacle of our soul if it is not decidedly steered in that direction. It is a curious fact that the phrase of Jesus' we cited above in which he said that all those who were not shocked by him were blessed, is not reported by Luke, the evangelist, as the conclusion to one of those episodes in which the Lord, with his teaching, astounded and overturned his contemporaries, the scholars and the religious. Rather, it is reported after the simple list of miracles and good deeds which Jesus asks be relayed to John the Baptist in prison. They were facts to which anyone could have testified: "Go back and tell John what you have seen and heard: the blind see again, the lame walk, those suffering from virulent skin diseases are cleansed, and the deaf hear, the dead are raised to life, the good news is proclaimed to the poor" (Luke 7:22).

c) By Means of the Era and the Historico-Cultural Environment

Man is conditioned by the historico-cultural era in which the affair of his earthly life unfolds, and by the environment of which he is a part. Because he lives his Christianity in this fabric of variegated needs, stimuli, great things, and worries, the values the Church presents will, from era to era, bear the features of the limitations and the characteristics of the particular vision of life of the moment. The most concise of Paul's epistle, known as the Letter to Philemon, is particularly significant in this respect. It is "a short note addressed to a Christian, Philemon, the master of a fugitive slave, Onesimus. The apostle took Onesimus under his wing and is now sending him back to Philemon with a recommendation that he be treated as a beloved brother; the note was written during Paul's imprisonment and was probably sent to Colossae."[16] This short "letter of reference" focusses on an issue of interest to our own reflection here: the attitude of the first Christians to slavery. Paul sends Onesimus back to Philemon, whose slave Onesimus was. Paul probably knew this wealthy gentleman and had probably converted him. In the letter, he does not tell him that since it can be deduced from Jesus' teaching that all men are equal, Onesimus must no longer be his slave. Why not? Because as children of their time, as Philemon and Onesimus were, "slavery is an accepted fact which in this instance, does not constitute a problem. It falls within the framework of the established social order, although it is obviously not the best of orders."[17] So even though Paul seems to be subject to the social conditioning of the time, he nevertheless, expresses a belief in the value of the person, asking the master to welcome back the fugitive slave and telling him that all this happened "so that you could have him back for ever, no longer as a slave, but something much better than a slave, a dear brother. ... So if you grant me any fellowship with yourself, welcome him as you would me" (Phil. 15b–17).

The true innovation ... lies in the new relationship which slave and master have with God, and which transforms the common slavery, perchance, of the human condition into rational devotion to a God who frees all those who serve him for love. This concept was liable to clash with the arrogance of a proud society (which had also been irritated by the declarations of the pagan Roman, Seneca) but it was not in conflict with Roman law. ... For unlike classical Greek philosophy, Roman law acknowledged that a slave could be potentially equal to his master, and granted slaves citizenship as soon as they became freemen.[18]

It must be understood that Christianity is not in the world to hollow out the dynamic of historical evolution. Rather, its purpose is to communicate certain values, such as the value of the person, and if these values are preserved, then every evolution has the means to become more useful as an expression of man. Without values, every evolution is contrary to and goes back to degrading the dignity of human life. The value brought by Christianity is something that concerns man as man in any circumstance. A Christian, while not resigning himself to negative turns of events, is, when conscious of this value, capable of affirming human things, even in the worst circumstances. Circumstance, therefore, seen in the light of values, is mobilized in time to become work able to transform. In this way, the completeness of the Christian's mission will present itself in such a manner that it exalts – either by highlighting or by not denying – the cultural characteristics of the historical age in which he lives. And he will do so precisely through his own vigilant consciousness of the values which, in their perfect form, are faith's points of reference, despite the fact that every age will be tempted to yield unilaterally, factiously, or partially to the values of the dominant culture.

Thus, the structure of the Church as a human instrument always notably bears the mental and cultural mark of the age in which it operates. However, as opposed to other structures, the accentuation of a factor – right or wrong, justifiable or incomprehensible as it may prove to be – will never be able to elude the presence of the truth in its entirety. Allow me to clarify this point with a few examples which illustrate how the history of the Church has always given birth to widely diverging Christian experiences, in which Christianity was manifested according to the developments of the times.

The first example pertains to the Society of Jesus. In an age of triumphant individualism, the society's Christian experience placed a strong accent on individuality by highlighting the anthropological, historical, and cultural factors characterizing the times. It, therefore, insisted on rationality in the life of faith and will or desire as the necessary factor for belonging. Not that these values had been overlooked by preceding movements. On the contrary, in each of them we find different emphases. The Benedictine movement, for example, which stressed the phenomenon of faith as an all-embracing event specifically, celebrated the social and liturgical dimension.

The monastery offers the monk everything. It is his world and he has no regret for the world outside. The monastery is not a prison. It is comfortable and beautiful and it is a rather better producer of things than would be found outside its walls. The abbot is the father of the monastic family and he governs not according to a penal code or by coercive strength but with paternal author-ity. Liturgical service, the monk's principal occupation, is rich and edifying and does not oppress him with long hours of prayers. The monk loves his monas-tery, which is his homeland. Here the Benedictine *pax* reigns.[19]

However, in the different cultural climate which greeted the birth of the Jesuit experience – in an age which was the prelude to modern rational-ism – it was no wonder that Ignatius imposed different characteristics, that the perennial thrust towards Church renewal should also have assumed a form that accentuated the vigour of individualism and the strength of rationality, as the following quotation underlines:

Ignatius combined cold reason with mystical devotion to Christ, the military rigor of his idea of obedience with great liberty in the shaping of the interior life, imperturbable foresight in regard to the worldwide tasks of the Society with a tender sympathy for the individual person, the courtesy of a man of the world with the practical good sense of the Basque peasant. Constantly maintaining an aristocratic reserve, he was never on familiar terms with even his closest asso-ciates. He made a point of considering his decisions long and carefully, of listening to others' advice, of seeking divine guidance in prayer, and then, when the decision had been reached, of enforcing it without respect for people and even with severity. In his *Exercitia Spiritualia* he shows himself to be one of the great teachers of the spiritual life, thoroughly familiar with human nature, and a master in the handling of men.[20]

But what aspect of this interesting example is the typically Christian one? While the type of individualism born of the Renaissance tended to "reduce" man to mere "individual," a Christian experience, such as that of the Society of Jesus, "cannot" forget the whole series of factors that makes a human being, placing the individual in the context of an or-ganic reality, and transcending the purely individualistic concept of the person. By its very nature, any Christian experience tends towards this "fulfillment" independently of the specific emphasis of the age which serves as its springboard, since "its members are chosen with care, receive an intensive education, and are subjected to numerous tests. ... This and the 'Exercises,' show that Ignatius affirmed the ideal of an original and powerful personality ... that he excluded all subjectivism: he formed his disciples rigorously, according to the fundamentals common to the rule of the order and to the entire Church."[21] And if Saint Ignatius's exercises do pursue an ideal of perfection developed in a given age and embossed with the brand of his exceptional individual-ism, the "reflection of his personal struggle to reach God ... was peculiar to this ideal of perfection and [what] made it appropriate to its age was its intimate relationship to the visible Church."[22] "We can then agree that the religious attitude of mind of St. Ignatius and his order is radically ecclesial and papal. ... Here is the fundamental Catholic attitude of mind in all its objectivity: which is to say, an energetic reaction to humanistic and Protestant subjectivism, the categorical affirmation of the theocentric position."[23] In the end, therefore, the intent of this particular Christian experience is the utilization of all human resources "for the glory of God," resources and energies to be discovered and fine-tuned. As von Balthasar comments:

The "attunement" of man to the mysteries of salvation plays the greatest roles in the *Spiritual Exercises*: man's disposition is to "correspond" and be harmonised, and this correspondence must be prayed for ... however as far as possible, it must be created and acquired by man himself ... so that, in his spiritual-sensual totality, man may come to experience and realise the contemplated mystery by "applying his five senses" ... This total attunement to revelation is subservient to the goal of coming to understand God's being and will in order then to correspond to him. For this reason, we can no more speak here of a religion of feeling than we can of a rationalistic religion: the aim is that higher middle way which we can call "existential Christianity."[24]

We have seen, therefore, how a particular aspect of the Christian experience was born in the climate of an age. However, being authentically Christian, the experience extracted the right aspects of the age and proposed them in the context of the Church's own concept of man, which had been carried on throughout history.

However, it must be pointed out that the Church certainly does not presume to empty the human affair of all that historical evolution injects into it. The Church's task is not to take the place of man's work. No, faith tailors and determines the personality of the individual, of the subject about to act, enabling the individual to use the means which his personal talents and historical conditioning will prompt him to use, and if he knowingly lives the universal context of the Church, then he will do this with an equilibrium, watchfulness, and patience that he otherwise would not have had. The Christian of any historical age will always have some means at his disposal that his predecessors did not have, and he will be deprived of others, a limitation lying at the very core of the approach of the Christian message. God-made-man has communicated himself from "inside" human reality, from within the confines of precise historico-cultural contexts. This is a fact not easy to accept, but it is the way of the Christian message. In his earthly life, it was impossible for Jesus to take advantage of technologies which only later epochs would bestow on man. However, because he made the fullest possible use of his own tradition, his own historical moment in time, this does not negatively effect the universal claim of the Christian message. Rather, it exalts it and in a concrete way, too.

Years ago as a teacher of religion in a Milanese high school, I was trying one day to explain precisely this relationship within the Christian message of the mutual need between its claim and its historical conditioning. A student, brandishing a small book, interrupted me. It was an anthology of the Syllabus, that undisputed late nineteenth century symbol, for rationalists, of the Church's "obscurantism. " That little book was designed to represent the supreme list, almost, of clerical aberrations. I asked the student to hand me the book and I began to comment on some of its phrases. One said, quite literally: "Any man may choose the religion which he believes in all conscience to be true." Now, the Syllabus condemned such a statement. I then began to explain to my listeners that the Church's principle of morality is to follow one's own conscience: an act is moral when it is the expression of personal oneness, and personal oneness is affirmed when an individual is consistent with his conscience. I naturally pointed out that, considering that Catholics are particularly "conformist," this affirmation is studied in moral theology textbooks worldwide, in all seminaries; moreover, considering that Catholics are also "conservatives," this framework had been in place for four centuries. So, I asked my students: should a Catholic sanction this affirmation? Should he adhere to that condemnation?

When the class had finally split into opposite camps, I gave them my answer. First, I pointed out that even a minimum of historical sensibility demands that any declaration should only be recalled for scrutiny within the context in which it was made, and that all circumstances which had motivated it should be considered. And this includes the Syllabus. The Syllabus was written in 1864 as a compendium of the "errors of our times," and it proposed to address Catholics, pointing out to them the various instances when the thinking of the day diverged from Catholic dogma. Concerning the particular phrase just quoted, the Syllabus had no intention of responding to some kind of ethico-subjective concern. On the contrary, the Syllabus' concern was historical and objective, anxious to show Catholics that this phrase, in that particular context of man's history, was designed to negate Christianity's historical factor, the truth of Revelation, for if it is true that God became man in order to point man in the right direction, and there is no doubt that this is the pathway he indicated, then no man has the right to adhere to whatever religion his own conscience may have dreamed up. This is the historico-objective meaning behind the Syllabus' phrase and, in light of its own particular context of concerns, the phrase is more than correct.

But, you may ask, what of someone who does not know that God became man? If someone does not understand? What if someone explained to it to this individual in such a way as to render it incomprehensible? In that case, it is legitimate for him to act according to
conscience, thus respecting the ethico-subjective meaning. But this was
not the intent of the Syllabus' condemnation. It was historico-objective
one. In any case, the Second Vatican Council stated forcefully that
religious freedom was proper to human dignity. In this, it applied an
ethico-subjective criterion which a Catholic of any historical age would
be able to sanction under any circumstances, by the very fact of his
tradition.

We will conclude this reflection on the implications of the idea that
the Church is made of men by reiterating that each of the forms of
conditioning we have mentioned – temperament, mentality, environ-
mental and historico-cultural factors – constitute an element of the
incarnation of the divine, through which the Church claims to define its
nature and the content of its message. The divine really does become
incarnate. It really does use human reality as its instrument. It does not
annul its contingent factors but uses even them as instruments of
salvation, as the means, that is, of reproposing the true relationship
between man and his destiny. In a particularly beautiful passage,
Jacques Leclercq comments on Jesus' earthly life in the following way:

Come to bring men salvation, he subjects himself to the laws of nature: he
preaches, and his voice travels as far as the human voice; he knows all nature's
secrets, he would have been able to pre-empt the discoveries of this age of ours
carrying man's voice through space, and he did not want to; the men of his day
did not speak to each other across continents, and he did not want his voice to
travel further than the voices of others. ...

He speaks in the language of his time, he expresses himself according to the
customs of his country; his manner reflects the manner of thinking and of
feeling of his country and of his time. ... There are miracles, yes. ... The
miracles are the manifestation of his transcendence and, in the ordinary course
of his life, they do not stop him from accepting the human order and submit-
ting all he does to it.[25]

7 A Mission of the Church: Towards Earthly Man

Let us now draw conclusions about everything we have said so far concerning the place human reality occupies in the global reality of the Christian phenomenon. We have pointed out human reality, chosen by God as the existential instrument of his self-communication, as the expressly desired conditioning factor of this communication in time and space. We have also detailed the implications of the Church's awareness, from the moment it began, that it is made of men, that it is a phenomenon within history, in society, in the world. Let us now ask ourselves: given the Church's presence in history, society, and the world, how then is its role defined in regard to this history, this society, and this world? What function does it claim to have in the course of historical events? We need to think carefully about these questions.

To begin with, the Church's function on the world scene is already implicit in its awareness that it is the protraction of Christ: this means that it has the same function as Jesus in history, which is to educate all men and women to the religious sense, precisely in order to be able to "save" them. In this context, the religious sense or religiosity means, as we have already pointed out, man's exact position towards his own destiny in terms of conscience and his attempt to live it in practical terms.

Now, within the horizon of this formula lies the question of the liberation that Jesus, the Saviour, came to bring. Salvation is generated by the truth of man's position in regard to himself and his ultimate destiny. The definitive word on the structure of each individual person

– of our "I" – and on the history of man cannot come from any impassioned introspection, any scientific analysis, or any of the ideologies which every epoch creates, as the projection of its efforts and limits. This is because all ideologies in history will be hindered by the conditions in which they are born; they will be irreversibly slanted according to the very point of view from which they draw life. The final word on the structure of each human being, and, therefore, on his immanent destiny and history, was made to emerge in history by God: the Word communicated himself to man by becoming flesh.

I THE DEFINITIVE WORD ON MAN AND HISTORY

This definitive word can be traced back to two expressions: the term "person" or "soul," to use the Gospel expression, and the phrase "kingdom of God." The first expression stresses that the "I" cannot be reduced to any scheme or category. The person is a source of values and is not subject to any kind of dependence other than the original one constituted by God. The second term, "kingdom of God," coincides with the affirmation of a *meaning* towards which all things tend, towards which all of life's fragments reach out, fragments which dazzle and blind us to the degree that when, in a favourable situation, we are able to seize one of them, we think we have reached the apex of our destiny, and presumptuously we try to affirm the meaning of everything in this small part that we can measure with only the span of a hand. This *meaning* also incorporates the meaning of all those segments, and because we cannot understand its orientation, one generation cannot even see in the subsequent generation the logical outcome of all it has produced. It is a meaning through which all things flow into a design whose name and face we already know, and whose memory we have by no means worn out (just as one in love cannot wear out his loved one's face): it is the name and face of Jesus who, as Saint Paul taught, will draw all things unto himself, and in whom all things have their substance.

This definitive word saves man and steers him to a correct position in regard to both himself and the world. It removes him from the dangers of a labyrinth of cruel and wild trickery, and it sets him on the path to his true freedom, to his humility and, therefore, his religiosity.

The Church, as the prolongation of Christ, claims to give man this definitive word: the *person*, immortal man, untouchable, irreducible, who can be exploited by no one; man, in function of the *kingdom of God*, the secret order of things which time may sometimes help to obscure, but which will, nevertheless, lead towards its ultimate clarity.

2   A CONTINUOUS REMINDER

What, then, is the substance of this religious education of mankind the Church proclaims as its aim, the very reason why it recognizes itself as the protraction of Christ?

This is the pressing pedagogical concern: to make man aware of what God is. It is expressed in continuous reminders urging man to live the awareness of his total dependence on the Mystery which speaks to us. For the law of life is this: dependence on the Father who shapes our life in every instant, who is the continuous source of our existence. These reminders, therefore, are impassioned pleas: they call me back to the reason why I am irreducibly "I;" why I am an ontological participation in "Being." Man's independence is drawn from living his dependence on God. Nor does the paradoxical nature of this situation detract from its truth: it is my dependence on God which makes me be myself; it is my dependence on Another that frees me from all others. This is the same educational concern we saw in Jesus,[1] in the way he proposed himself to the disciples so that they would recognize him: it is a concrete, lovingly cautious, educational approach, but it is a demanding one too, never neglecting to address the constant need to make the best possible use of the situation within which the freedom of the person lies. It is the pedagogical approach of revelation.

The Church has never forgotten this, its educational vocation. Ever since the first centuries of its history, its faithful have incarnated this conviction in the image – in many hymns and songs of praise – of a mother. In fact, the Church is still called Holy Mother Church today. Let us take a look at some of these hymns, collected by Hugo Rahner[2] and taken from the first millenium of Christian history. In this Church, this watchful mother, lauded by martyrs and Fathers of the Church, Christ continues his pedagogical mission to lead man back to himself, that is, to the Father who loves him and does not want to lose him.

Let us first look at these words of Ambrose of Milan:

Here is the woman, mother of all living souls.
Here is the spiritual home.
Here is the city which endures in eternity because it is
loosed from death.

The image of a mother is not far removed from the familiar image of the walls of a home and the protective walls of cities within which danger is not so near. These are images of attentive care for human life, the care of God himself made man. Gottschalk of Limburg, an early mediaeval author, says as much in the following, a sequence of praise to Christ composed for the octave of Epiphany:

> Providing,
> Moulding,
> You give us form
> In multicoloured beauty
> Like an artist.
> ...
> You make human life strong when it is only an earthen vase.

So the Church is the heir of the loving concern of God himself and therefore earns the name "Mother." Thus came the song of Quodvult-deus of Carthage:

> In the Spirit she generates sons for God, in the Spirit she nurses the
>   children
> with the milk of her teaching and she instructs the young in holy wisdom.

> To men she gives vigorous strength in the battle against Satan.
> For people who have reached maturity she is wise.
> She makes the elderly who are weary of their years venerable again.

> She sets erring sons on the right road once more.
> She weeps bitter tears for the dead.
> As a shepherd, she is unceasing in her protection of her whole flock of
>   faithful.

Moreover, this is how the monk Anastasius of Sinai described this continuity with Christ:

You alone are "blood of the blood" of his steadfastly solid divinity. You are flesh born of the flesh of his human nature, harbour of his divine nature. ... You alone have become the "help" of man: of God himself who is your help and your protection. In fact, he is your concern, you teach, you proclaim, you baptise, you convert, you procure everything for him since he is the light of men in the darkness and shadow of death.

Constantly you generate, you rear your children on the bread, you give them the cup to drink. You always flourish anew, you bear fruit, you sprout new branches, fresh and green. Every day you feed the flocks of your children with the fruit of your garden and your vines.

And in one of the most beautiful hymns he ever dedicated to the Church, Saint Augustine exclaims: "Truly, O Catholic Church, you alone are the mother of Christians. You teach us how to worship God in a limpid and pure way, and you tell us that a holy life consists in returning to your dwelling place. In fact, you show us that there exists no creature to which we should bow in a submissive attitude of adoration." Augustine composed this hymn while still in the first flush of his conversion: it is the sigh of relief of a man who has found the way home again, of a man who now knows himself to be in the hands of a mother brimming with tender care, capable of facing daily life. But, above all, the Church is a mother through the prayers, prompted by the spirit of Jesus, which she raises to God, because we ourselves are incapable even of asking.

And finally, is the following hymn of Cyrillona, a Syrian poet who lived at the end of the fourth century:

The Church stands before the tribunal of God,
to invoke him in prayer like a mother full of compassion ...
"Hold back justice, O Lord of the world,
your strength must cease! Men are too weak.
Goodness inspired you at the beginning to establish the earth,
love guided your hand when you gave man form,
now that he is there, made by you, be indulgent towards him.
For, a father tolerates even the affront of his son,
and a mother is calm when her children speak in harsh tones,
in the same way, my God, be tolerant of the sins of men!
...
For you see, O my Lord, even in our day
the earth is home to numerous of your faithful who strive only for the truth.
Monasteries have been built and behind their walls
live men of strong, pure heart.
Look and see, in the cracks of the rocks live hermits
and in the desert live great men of prayer who work
for reconciliation in this way.
...
And listen, your psalms resound from sumptuous rooms,
and your praise is raised from the fields of the farmers.
Loving service is offered to you from the sea,
the ships echo prayer,
the cities proclaim your holy word, and the judges
emit a just verdict for fear of your sentences.
Behold, your holy light floods even into mirky hearts ..."

...

It is for this reason, O Lord, that the holy Church prays before you,
prostrate in the dust, she beseeches with all her children:
that your birth in the flesh, which came for love of the Church,
may still generate mercy for your creatures today!

The Church's function in history, then, is that of the mother calling
back her children to the reality of things: man's dependence on God, a
merciful God. And just as a mother gives concrete help to her little
ones, the call of the Church – as we will see later – is not a theoretical
one. It is, as one of Bruce Marshall's characters claims, something that
is a beacon of salvation to a drowning man, vital support to a lame man:
"The mercy of God is a long and a strong rope and it's never too late to
catch hold of it."[3]

For this reason, the Church's unceasing calling for the authentic
religious education of humanity is a dimension which, in the honest acknowledgment of humanity's dependence on Another, also finds hope
in the mercy of the creator. It sees salvation held out like a rope, and
does not conceive of the human person alone, but, by definition within
the company of Another who is Father to him. This is why, when the
disciples asked Jesus how they should pray, he found that the best way,
within the horizon of human experience, was to illustrate the individual
as a child in his parents' arms; he told them to pray to God, calling him
Father, "Our" Father. Thus man is defined in terms of a company, he is
implicated in the very origin of things and remains with other men. If
this bond is obliterated, man will lose himself in the social web. The
Church's ceaseless urging is necessary to defend us from that isolation
which makes us such easy prey for exploitation. Only true religiosity is
the boundary blocking any type of invasion and exploitation, including
the ecclesiastical variety.

Let us conclude with this succinct observation of Romano Guardini's:

The Church is always confronting man with the Reality which creates in him
the right attitude of mind: namely, the Absolute.

She confronts him with the Unconditioned. In that encounter he realises
that he himself is dependent at every point, but there awakens in him the
yearning for a life free from the countless dependencies of life on earth, an
existence inwardly full. She confronts him with the Eternal, he realises that he
is transitory, but destined to life without end. She confronts him with Infinity,
and he realises that he is limited to the very depths of his being, but that the
Infinite alone can satisfy him.[4]

3 THE BEST POSITION FOR FACING HUMAN PROBLEMS

The Church, then, urges us to adopt the "right attitude" towards ourselves and life. It calls us back (as does a mother who is experienced in life) to realism and to a type of behavior in which we are reminded how things really are. Only the Church pronounces the definitive word on our personal make-up, our destiny, the common destiny of humanity (this word that God himself sent into history).

But all of us feel the brunt of problems which are the fabric of our days and our every hour – problems large and small, and if there is any impetus which marks all our lives, it is the impetus to resolve these problems. And although philosophies and ideologies, social and political realities all propose solutions, the Church indicates the best position to adopt for facing human problems. If we live the consciousness of our original dependence, which is the first supreme truth, then all problems will fall within a framework which will make solving them easier. This does not mean that they will be suddenly resolved. However, they will be in a favourable condition to be so.

Resolving humanity's various problems might be compared to the construction of a building: the religious sense, to which the Church recalls us, is like a test done to find the most solid piece of ground on which to erect a building. If the test yields clear indications, then building can begin and the construction will endure the test of time. But if it is improperly done, or work starts despite uncertainty about the suitability of the terrain, the building, after a few years, will betray this fundamental error. This is the same comparison Jesus himself made (cf Luke 6:46–49). And this too can be expressed in another way. If we find we have to lift a heavy weight, certain positions can be adopted to facilitate the task (using a lever for instance); other positions are less suitable and still others would make it impossible for the weight to be lifted at all. Similarly, if man puts himself in the right position, he can face a problem and try to resolve it. If he is not in the proper position, the very approach to the problem becomes more complicated. In fact, Jesus told his disciples: "In truth I tell you, there is no one who has left house, brothers and sisters, mother, father, children or land for my sake and for the sake of the gospel, who will not receive a hundred times as much, houses, brothers, sisters, mothers, children and land – and persecutions too – now in this present time and, in the world to come, eternal life" (Mark 10:29–30). Jesus said this in reference to an episode of a young man, who, from the beginning, Jesus had looked upon with love. In response to Jesus' proposal to leave everything and follow him, the young man sadly declined, because he was very attached to his wealth. In other words, the right attitude could also mean being detached from our own point of view or from that fragment of life we might want to hold on to, as if it were everything. Yet, if this detachment transpires, it generates a new and true wealth, a new and true possession of things and affections. Therefore, the salvation wrought by that right attitude begins, in abundance – "a hundredfold" – in the present time, according to the particular commitment and life story of each one of us.

This is what the Church's appeal means as far as the multitude of human problems is concerned: it is a reminder of the fact of a Relationship which constitutes, right from our origins, the fundamental capacity of our person and of the entire history of humanity. The respect, adherence, seriousness, and love, which are the features of this relationship, also constitute the stability and foundation of all man's attempts to build, to find solutions to his problems.

Having so many different problems that change within our very hands is part of everyone's experience, and even as we struggle to resolve them, they do not fade away. Rather, they increase. Nor do they reveal their real origin in a simple way. No, they become still more complicated. And this is because we are not oriented towards our own origin. If we were, we would view those same problems in a way that would highlight their workable side, or in a manner that would allow us to accept them, or else, in a way that, looking at ourselves, we would find the strength to ask for help. And because this method of looking, in fact, would be focussed on Something larger than the individual problem, it would confer on everything the prospect of a constructive path to pursue.

4 THE PROBLEMS OF MAN

In summary, we can trace the whole gamut of human problems to four large, fundamental categories. The first problem falls within the horizon of the category of culture, and here lie all problems related to man's search for *truth* and the meaning of reality. This is the category which reveals man's conception of self in the face of his own destiny, according to which he mobilizes and utilizes the elements of his own existence. The second problem is that of *love* and here falls all of the problems man experiences in relation to his constant search for personal completeness. The third problem is related to man's need to express his personality, all his hopes of leaving his mark on the reality of time and space that is his to live, and this can generate problems under the category of *work*. And lastly, is the political problem of human co-existence with its whole comprehensive and difficult spectrum. Each of these categories groups different facets of the obstacles and problems that man must face on his journey. And although conditioned by them, an individual thinks he can resolve, forget, or even repress the fundamental needs they represent.

If the Church were to proclaim that its aim was to take over the human effort of self-advancement, self-expression, and human searching, it would be acting like the kind of parents – to return to the mother image used before – who are deluded into thinking that they can resolve their children's problems by taking their place. This would be an illusion for the Church, too, because it would mean falling short of its educational task, a task I have defined in regard to individual educators and which is, in fact, also valid for the Church: "to the mystery of Being, to the Measure that made us, that far surpasses us in every direction and that we cannot measure – it is to This that an educator's love must entrust the ever-widening space of unpredictable pathways which are opened up by the freedom of the new man in his dialogue with the universe."[5] Moreover, this illusion would also diminish the essential history of the Christian phenomenon, and it would impoverish man's journey. Commenting on the Church's role in this unique enhancement of history, Henri de Lubac observes:

For Christianity ... the course of history is indeed a reality. It is not mere barren dispersal but possesses, so to say, a certain ontological density and a fecundity. ... Facts are no longer phenomena, but events, acts. Forthwith something new is wrought. ... Creation is not merely maintained, but is continuous. The world has a purpose and consequently a meaning, that is to say, both direction and significance. The entire human race, the child of God, sustained through all the disconcerting variety of its activities ... by those two hands of God, the Word and the Holy Spirit, that despite its mistakes have never entirely loosened their hold, in this one great movement sets forth to the Father.[6]

5 THE CHURCH'S TASK IS NOT TO RESOLVE HUMAN PROBLEMS

The Church's direct task, then, is not to provide man with solutions to the problems he encounters on his way. Rather, as we have seen, its proclaimed function in history is to educate us to the religious sense. This implies the appeal for man to adopt the right attitude to reality and the questions it poses, an attitude which constitutes the best condition that man can have for finding more adequate answers to those questions. We have also emphasized that the spectrum of human problems could never be removed from the realm of man's freedom and creativity. It is not the Church's task to provide him with a prepackaged solution, and, if it were to do that, it would fall short of its own foremost educational attitude. It would devalue "time," which man, who has been engaged by God's initiative "in history," is called to consider deeply "sacred."

The Gospel contains an enlightening episode on this point. "A man in the crowd said to him, 'Master, tell my brother to give me a share of our inheritance.' He said to him, 'My friend, who appointed me your judge, or the arbitrator of your claims?' Then he said to them, 'Watch, and be on your guard against avarice of any kind, for life does not consist in possessions, even when someone has more than he needs' " (Luke 12:13–15). Although Luke is the only one to report this incident, it cannot have been unusual for people to look to Jesus to resolve quarrels and controversies, as they often did with people acknowledged to be masters. How instinctive it is in man to think he has found the source of solutions to his problems! However, Jesus immediately clears the air of this misunderstanding; he who showed himself to be the authoritative judge of man's sins who challenged public opinion and dared to forgive those sins makes a decisive declaration in this case: it is not up to him to arbitrate on the matter. Undoubtedly he must have disconcerted his interlocutor. However, Jesus does not neglect to fulfill what he is there to do. Do not become attached to anything on which your life does not depend, he reminds them, and with this remark he reveals what the right attitude for the two quarrelling brothers would be: do not let yourself be taken over by the desire for wealth – remember that your life depends on God, as he explains in the parable he relates immediately afterwards, teaching that it is wiser to become rich in the "sight of God" than to store up treasures for "yourself" (cf. Luke 12:21). And perhaps that love of money, which made one brother keep part of the inheritance not his by right, was the same love of money that made the other brother claim what should have been his. Jesus came to teach us the authentically religious attitude (and, therefore, true in its origin) to be adopted in the face of all problems. When confronted by the brother ignobly disinherited by the other, Jesus feels he must call them both back to their freedom, defining the type of attitude we must have towards the world's riches in the following way: "Life does not consist in possessions."

Christ, like the Church – which is the continuation of him – did not come to resolve problems of justice. No, he came to place the condition in man's heart without which the justice of this world could have the same root as injustice.

6 FACILITATING ASPECTS OF A TRULY LIVED FREEDOM

It is not that Christ and the Church have no function at all as far as men's problems are concerned. As we have already said, both urge man on towards certain principles and conditions, and, if man does not lose sight of them, he will find that he can face everything in truth and therefore, more *productively*. This solicitation, for example, reminds an individual of the value of the other person – of charity – or of the context in which money will be given its rightful, reasonable place. And if that reminder is heeded, it is not so easy for a person to fall prey to hate or greed-inspired crimes. Of course, this is not a magic formula for the mechanical avoidance of such crimes, Yet it is the basis for which the solution may more easily be more human rather than fictitious and one-sided. It is like yeast. It is indispensable and without it life's bread would be indigestible. However, it is just the beginning for constructing; it is not yet everything.

Solutions to our problems must strive to maintain a kind of humanity. They must include all aspects, a balanced solution, stability in the resulting solution, and afterwards, fertility. And if this humanity is overlooked in some of its aspects, something of this construction could collapse, threatening to bury man himself under its rubble.

Finally, I must repeat that the essential symptom of the humanity of a solution is freedom – freedom in its most powerful, full sense, a freedom to which Christ and the Church recall us, the freedom of the man who keeps vigil, with a watchful eye and a soul wide open, to his origin and his destiny. It is the type of freedom in which our intelligence cannot be blocked by any obstacle, wherein our will is not curbed by any term of equivocal love, and where our sensibility accompanies both of these things with the vigour of inexhaustible patience. In this sense, then, it can indeed be said that the Church leads man to the solution of his problems in that – under the same conditions – man, to the degree that his attitude, at least implicitly, is the authentically religious one which Jesus came to show us, attains his goal in a more lasting, complete, and realistic way.

7 THE WORK OF EVERY MAN

In the course of earthly events, man must seek the solution to each problem, making an effort to resolve those four categories of problems mentioned above. The task of each individual person and, indeed, of all those in their socio-historical context is to look for solutions in the concreteness of their own history, within the given circumstances of their own social and political history. This task is entrusted to our freedom, within the freedom of God's plan, which is enacted in history. Describing man's attitude towards this work in time, Henri de Lubac makes the following comment: "Time is vanity only for one who, using it unnaturally, desires to establish himself in it – and to think of nothing but a "future" is to establish oneself in time. Of necessity we must find a foothold in time if we are to rise into eternity; we must use time. The Word of God submitted himself to this essential law: he came to deliver us from time, but by means of time. ... Following Christ's example, ... every Christian must acquiesce in that state of engagement in time which gives him part and lot in all history."[7]

Freedom and history. Because God did not insert us in the flow of time for no reason, man lives within the possibility of solving problems. However, the complete potential for solving problems does not lie within a mechanism conceived by man. Nor does it come from the outside – from things. Rather, this possibility is entrusted to man's freedom to link himself – and the things or circumstances creating the problem – with the foundation of life. God does not oblige man to be himself if man does not so wish. But he does ask him, he does urge him, he does remind him constantly to be himself. Thus, the Church spurs us to live the conditions of the religious attitude, conditions which carry out this linking and facilitate man's work in history. In fact, if we sincerely confront the state to which the Church calls us, we soon start to experience an energy and pride in settling down to work, and we carry out our tasks with a special kind of intensity. If, on the contrary, a Christian believes he can resolve his problems and live the religious condition to which the Church calls us without a commitment to apply it to himself, the Christian fact is suddenly cast outside the sphere of time. This is due to the fact that anything avoiding problems is external to the realm of time, and because destiny is played out within time and space, everything in time and space poses as a problem.

The Church is a living thing; it places itself in front of an entire generation expressing the whole spectrum of its vital resources, resources revealed to the precise degree that Christians live the foundation of their religiosity and feel the duty to be committed within the context of time and space (which give form to their problem as men). The pertinence of the Gospel today, as Marie-Dominique Chenu said in one of his pamphlets, passes through the problems of men; the more a Christian is committed to resolving human problems, the more he becomes the sign of the Gospel's consistency with the hopes of men.

From the Church, then, we have this absolute and intransigent affirmation of religiosity, the cornerstone of our lives and our society. Not only is it not abstract (because it is the foundation of a construction which is the task of each one of us), but, the equilibrium, security, solidity, and fecundity of this affirmation make it easier for us and even push us into the folds of history, into the concreteness of problems in search of solutions. In a history in which God has become flesh as the proof of his love for men, to be committed to the problems time presents us is the first form of charity.

8 RELIGIOSITY WILL NEVER BE WHOLLY LIVED IN HISTORY

Like an attentive mother, however, the Church has an extremely realistic conception of man and history, and although it insists on respect for the condition of a religious attitude, it knows that the path history will follow in its evolution – the path which could be simplified by that attitude – will be complicated by man's lack of freedom. Throughout history, man will often refuse to live this religious attitude and, even when he does accept it, he will not always manage to keep to it. Religiosity, therefore, will not be lived adequately in this world. In fact, we repeat this, at every Mass, every day, all over the world, by beginning with the confession of our sins, by acknowledging a state of freedom which has not kept to the right attitude. As long as the world endures, the Church will invite communities of believers to begin their gathering together with the "*confiteor*," the sign of human freedom's inadequacy in front of destiny, of its immanent disproportion, a disproportion which will accompany the history of man until the end. This is the mysterious, albeit experienceable doctrine of "original sin."

The figure of the anti-Christ, or false Christ in the New Testament is placed at the end of time to point out that in the Christian vision of history the struggle between good and evil will be fought right to the end of time. The anti-Christ is the symbol of an ambiguity which will always exist and, indeed, will grow, and the more the evolution of humanity progresses, the more this progress will display ambivalence: the capacity for good and the capacity for evil, the value and nonvalue. It is an ambivalence which will always manifest itself in order to put our freedom (adherence to the truth) into play. Thus Christ, imagining Jerusalem's eleventh hour (which embraces the meaning of the decisive hour of all our lives and of all history), warns his own: "If anyone says to you, then, 'Look, here is the Christ,' or 'Over here,' do not believe it; for false Christs and false prophets will arise and provide great signs and portents, enough to deceive even the elect ... because the coming of the Son of Man will be like lightning striking in the east and flashing far into the west" (Matt 24:23,24,27). In this ambiguous context, in the presence of both good and evil that will follow us to the end, we are

warned that there is something in which we must not believe, something false, something which claims for itself the attributes of another.
Moreover, we are also told that something else will propose itself for us
to trust: lightning across the sky, the light of Christ. However, we are
warned, this will not be imposed in a mechanical, automatic way. We
will never be "forced" to acknowledge it. False prophets will always be
able to deceive, and the Christ who will come could be considered less
dazzling because the miracles worked by the false Christs seem to be
more so. To be certain in our recognition, nothing can take the place of
our humble and continual return to the right attitude to which the
Church has called us throughout the ages. And although religiosity
makes us wise to the enigmatic figure of evil awaiting them at the end
of the road or at the end of every stretch of his journey, it does not
eliminate this figure. This is because of what Church tradition calls
original sin, this limit added to our freedom (apart from the limit
inherent in its created nature) this limit derived from the original
choice made by the first man, which renders man unable to sustain the
rectitude of the religious attitude for long. In fact, man is so incapable
of sustaining it that the Church, in its keen foresight, insists that
Christians continually beg God for it.

It is mainly because of this shortcoming of ours that human problems will always have unresolved aspects. They will always be burdened
with the weight of complications because, when facing reality, we do
not always adequately respect the right attitude, inspired by Christ.

9 THE CHRISTIAN'S MORAL TENSION

We may then ask: what can be done, given that a good solution to problems requires a religious attitude of which the Church reminds us, and
given that our freedom will never fully live this religious attitude? The
answer is: the Church proposes a concept of human life, one of tension,
a watchfulness, like that of a sentinel who, from the castle walls, takes
notice of even the slightest rustle. Or, it might be the tension of a
pilgrim journeying towards his destination. And to the degree that we
love our humanity and live the depth of Christian awareness, every one
of us must make a constant effort – and this is why we use the word
"ascesis" – to tackle human problems from the standpoint of authentic
religiosity. Romano Guardini describes the Christian's moral tension,
as urged by the Church, in the ensuing manner: "The Church continually arouses in him that tension which constitutes the very foundation of his nature: the tension between being and the desire to be,
between actuality and a task to be accomplished. And she resolves it for
him by the mystery of his likeness to God and of God's love, which
bestows of its fulness that which totally surpasses the nature."[8]

Thus the Christian – *homo viator*, the wayfaring man, to use that beautiful expression of mediaeval Christianity – is conscious of the fact that life is a journey, a travelling towards a goal, where at the end of all problems lies the total solution – not our work, but God's. We are powerless in the face of our unquenchable thirsting for our destiny and our goal, and only the power of God can make us whole. But the search for ever greater completeness, the search for the best, – as far as possible – characterizes a Christian's greatness at every moment; and this, at every moment, is the characteristic of the Church's invitation to us, and with it is the measure of our being Christian. It is a boundless commitment, without end.

Let us recall Jesus' parable comparing two moral attitudes: that of a Pharisee and that of a publican. Remember that the Pharisees considered themselves the faithful custodians of the divine laws, while the publicans, who collected taxes for the Roman Empire, were generally publically exposed as sinners. It is Luke who reports this well-known story: "Two men went up to the Temple to pray, one a Pharisee, the other a tax collector. The Pharisee stood there and said this prayer to himself, 'I thank you, God, that I am not grasping, unjust, adulterous like everyone else, and particularly that I am not like this tax collector here. ...' The tax collector stood some distance away, not daring even to raise his eyes to heaven; but he beat his breast and said, 'God, be merciful to me, a sinner' " (Luke 18:10–11;13). We know that Jesus condemns the moral attitude of the Pharisee. And why? Because the Pharisee is proud of himself. He evades and repudiates the tension of his life. However, if we look carefully at the publican, he expresses himself in a most basic formula – a sorrowful uneasiness with himself, a tension which incorporates the moral concept the Church indicates for man. Nothing more starkly contrasts to this than a person who is complacently self-satisfied or hopes for a possible contingent happiness.

This constant searching by the Christian for self-truth and, therefore, for the truth of the world, bears an experienceable mark. Jesus indicated it with the word "peace," and one of the most moving commentaries on this aspect of Christian anthropology is the prayer which the priest says at Mass after the assembly has recited the Lord's prayer together: "Deliver us, Lord, from every evil and grant us peace in our day. In your mercy, keep us free from sin and protect us from all anxiety as we wait in joyful hope the coming of our Saviour, Jesus Christ." All of the elements of a moral tension are contained in those lines: acknowledged dependence on God who created me, in whose hands I fearlessly remain; an affirmation that because the substance of life is Another, so my hope for my destiny is Another; and the need to live life as expectancy and therefore, searching – as a journey in which an emptiness is ever to be filled.

Thus the tension to affirm reality, as did Christ's gaze, is the foundation of peace. This peace cannot last if it does not rest on the ultimate substance of reality, on the Mystery, which makes all things, on God, the Father.

Without this final context, peace will be fragile and brittle. It will crumble into anxiety. The effort of faithfulness in following the truth is very different. It is a struggle, which is not the opposite to peace. And although it might be painful or weigh heavily upon us, it is not anxiety. Anxiety is a lie which continuously reemerges and nests in us to impede our adherence to all that in our conscience has emerged as truth. Peace is a war, but it is with ourselves.

This is why one cannot bear witness to the Christian message by appeasing oneself with some easy affirmation of faith; the authentic religiosity which Jesus brought to human history and which his Church continues to propose to us marks history profoundly. Through the Church, the human subject faces problems with an attitude befitting his humanity and his destiny. And within the realms of this attitude, he is called to apply his freedom, he is called to work. This happens in the awareness that his journeying is tentative, open to correction, and that his freedom is fragile, in need of forgiveness. And because of all of this, he is always beginning again.

8 The Divine in the Church

The human factor, whose implications we have been outlining, is valued as a method in the Church, a means by which something greater is channelled in our direction. In fact, because human reality is God's means of self-communication, what reaches us via the human factor is more than human. It is divine. The Church has always lived this certainty in a close bond with its awareness that it is a living reality, the prolongation of Jesus Christ. As commented by Karl Adam:

If we ask the Catholic Church herself to tell us, according to her own notion of herself, ... what is the substance of her self-consciousness, she answers us through the mouth of the greatest of her teachers, "The Church is the realization on earth of the Kingdom of God." "The Church of today, of the present, is the Kingdom of Christ and the Kingdom of Heaven": such is the emphatic assertion of St. Augustine (*De civitate Dei* xx, 9,1). The "Kingdom of Heaven" and "Kingdom of God" taken up from the prophecy of Daniel (Dn 7:9–28) and proclaimed by Christ, that Kingdom which grows great like the mustard seed, and like leaven permeates the world, and which like a field of corn shelters both wheat and cockle until the harvest, this "Kingdom of Heaven" is, so the Church believes, implanted in her own being and there manifested. The Church believes that she is the manifestation of that newness, that supernature and that divinity which come in with the Kingdom of God, the manifestation of holiness. She is the new supernatural reality brought by Christ into the world and arrayed in the garment of the transitory; she is the divine attesting itself under earthly veils.[1]

Primarily, our considerations concerning the human factor as essential to a definition of the Church should take into account the judgment that the Church cannot be reduced to that same factor. The Church consists of men and women, with their temperaments, attitudes, and greater or lesser degrees of freedom in a given historical and cultural context, and, as such, cannot be judged in a way that reduces it either to those people, their characteristics, or to their particular historical context.

In view of this, then, let us try to analyze, however summarily, this divine content which the Church claims to communicate. It would be useful, however, to make one observation first. In calling itself the conveyor of a divine reality via a human vehicle, the church is claiming to be the bearer of an absolute value which uses an innately fallible and imperfect instrument. In this way, a Christian, with all his limitations, could well live the experience of being a bearer – for someone far better than he is – of a value superior to both himself and the others. Should this person then, conscious as he is of his own unworthiness, renounce the task? In this case, too, Jesus Christ highlights human nature. By asking those who follow him to live this dramatic experience, he is simply exalting all that is imperiously required of our nature if we pay close attention to it. Would parents, who sincerely love their children, renounce the task of transmitting a value to them on the pretext that they themselves do not possess it completely? No, they would be more concerned that their child acquire as much good as possible than in measuring their own degree of perfection. And there is no doubt that, in the simple recognition of their own faults, they too would be encouraged to do better. When urged by nature towards authentic love, man is much better at expressing his attachment to the truth concerning himself than with his own self-consideration. Jesus expressed the importance of this direct pursuit of all that is valuable when he said: "unless you change and become like little children you will never enter the kingdom of heaven" (Matt. 18:3). Totally trusting, the child instinctively pursues the goal which nature suggests to him – to learn and grow.

I THE SELF-COMMUNICATION OF TRUTH: COMMUNITY, TRADITION, MAGISTERIUM

Man cannot reach for knowledge of something if he does not understand its meaning, if he has no grasp of its relationship to all other things and the condition for acquiring knowledge of any reality is clarity and a certainty of the meaning of life itself. This is truth: a definition of all the ultimate meanings of our existence, of this life of ours which is so simple and yet so complex. The first level at which the divine in the Church communicates itself is that of the transmission of the truth. God, through the Church, helps man to attain objective clarity and security in his perception of all the ultimate meanings of his existence.

In a previous step of our itinerary,[2] we had occasion to discuss man's ceaseless search for the meaning of life. Let us remember here, too, that man as man, in some way, comes close to the truth. He senses it, but only with difficulty and in little bits. On this point, we cited Thomas Aquinas, who observed that the truth reason seeks, with no assistance, would be accessible to just a few. It would be interspersed with numerous errors and attained only after a long time. In fact, the experience common to most men is that they run the risk of becoming confused just when they are faced with the most pressing of issues, precisely because they stand before the ultimate values, individuals feel their judgment obscured, their assessments clouded. And the more essential these issues are for them – the more vital they are for the knowledge of self – the more acute this feeling will be. So people need help, as they usually do in living the important experiences of their lives, experiences in which they would be in grave difficulty if they were alone. In fact, the Church proposes to help at these very times, presenting itself as capable of making clear and routine all that the human mind, at its maximum potency, can attain only after much striving, only after a long time, and with many errors. Gertrud von Le Fort was addressing the Church directly when she said in one of her hymns to it:

Who would dare speak as you speak? Who would not
be crushed by the anger of the Almighty?
But you lift your face up to heaven
And your head is not invisible in the heights.
You go right up to the edge of Hell
And your feet are unharmed!
You proclaim eternity and your soul is unafraid.
You impose sincerity and your lips are not silent.
...
For you thrive in your boldness
Like a palm tree in the desert
And your children are like a field full of ears of corn![3]

Man begs for help such as this. The height of man's reason can only reach the threshold of the meaning of existence and, perhaps implicitly or unconsciously, it asks for divine help in its searching. Or, it might ask more explicitly that the divine reveal itself. But independently of all that the history of humanity, of man's religious efforts and thought tells us, even personal experience, provided it has not been allowed to grow cold, is enough to perceive one's burning desire for a meaning which could link all the elements of existence and speak the truth about every step of the way. So, again Le Fort has the Church say:

> ... in the deepness of your yearning
> the springs of this earth no longer flow.
> And where your ultimate longing surges
> All clepsydras stop.[4]

It must be emphasized here that the communication of the divine as communication of truth is not a response to a philosophically abstract problem. Rather, it concerns the way we conceive of and perceive our lives, our personal relationship with reality. Let us examine, for example, what they used to have us learn by heart in the Catechism. One of the questions was: "What are the principal mysteries of our holy faith?" And the answer was: "There are two principal mysteries of our holy faith. First, the unity and Trinity of God; second: the incarnation, passion, death, and resurrection of Our Lord Jesus Christ." Now, what claim is the Church making when it declares itself the bearer of the divine in its communication of truth? Its claim is that these two phrases identify the ultimate truth about humanity, that these expressions hold the ultimate meaning of "my" existence and "yours." This means, for example, that the "One and Triune God" is not an abstract formulation but something pertinent to the root of every man's existence, explaining and clarifying his ultimate meaning. In this way, then, one cannot understand man except in the light of this one three-personed God, except in the light of the fact that Being cannot be defined as a oneness in the mechanical sense, understood on the basis, perhaps, of our natural experience. Rather, we must intend being to imply a state of communion within its own mysterious substance. And there is no doubt that it is mysterious and therefore we cannot understand it. But, as Jesus said to Nicodemus, an influential member of the Sanhedrin who, desiring to learn more of Christ's message, had gone to see him one night: "The wind blows where it pleases; you can hear the sound of its voice, but you cannot tell where it comes from or where it is going" (John 3:8a). The mystery remains but "you can hear the sound of its voice," this is to say that it is possible not to be able to explain it. But it is also possible to discover it in its capacity to give us a better understanding of the reality of our own experience.

Another example here will perhaps illustrate my point. The message that Being, on whom all things depend, in whom all things end, and of whom all things are made, is both the absolute one and communion at the same time, an explanation like no other of the formula of co-existence – first of all, of the relationship formula between the "I" and the "you," between a man and a woman, between parents and their children. No analysis by the power of reason alone can ever explain this paradoxical nature of the "one" and the "many," which is man's experience. Man never says the word "I" so intensely, never perceives the unity of his own identity with the same passion as when he says "you" or when, with the same love with which he says "you," he says "we." As Charles Moeller observes in the conclusion to one of his books on modern literature and Christianity:

In love, our freedom gives itself totally to the one we love. Only then is man conscious that he is complete. With this "dual creation" it was God's wish that man be complete only in a context of dialogue in which two people abandon themselves to each other. In the union of love – "joined in the flesh" – the person is himself or herself at last, in freedom. It is so because God is Trinity: the relationships which are the substance, the very life of God demonstrate that freedom and self-giving are synonymous. There is a divine family, a heavenly fatherhood of which all earthly fatherhoods are an image and of which they are all part.[5]

This is why no theoretical effort can offer a better explanation for the peaks and the most characteristic aspects of the human experience, made in God's image. Moreover, what we have said about love also holds true for another of man's supreme yearnings – knowledge – which is all the more powerfully united, the more the subject and object remain distinct. No philosophy can pinpoint the ultimate mechanism of this paradoxical oneness, however rightly impassioned in the pursuit of that one ultimate explanation that philosophy might be. For philosophy, in identifying the thread of synthesis, is always tempted to eliminate one or other of the terms at play.

The communication of truth by which God reaches us in the Church, the mystery of Being revealed to man, explains the profound convergence of the "I" and the "you," of the "I" and the "we," of the unity of the individual and the presence of others. Without this explication, the identity of the "I" and the presence of "other" would both be mere pieces of an absurd existence. This is why the mystery of the Trinity has a "voice" which lets itself be heard as a clarifying factor within our experience. It belongs, in a profound way, to the ultimate meaning of life, or better still, the ultimate meaning of life belongs to the mystery of the Trinity.

Thus, the second mystery of the Christian faith that we used to recite in Catechism formulas – the incarnation, death and resurrection of

Jesus – is the most enlightening of the hypotheses which give unity to human history. Unifying categories have always been sought in attempts to interpret the affair of history, because everything in us tends towards this unity. But the various elements of an experience, of an age, of an event remain painfully separated from us and often, to assuage this sense of uneasiness, we force together facts impossible to unify. Then, all of a sudden, the annunciation of an event – a child, a human being – presents itself as the meaning of all history. He affirms his profound involvement with everything man might do, that all things belong to him. The Christian message of the Word made flesh, who died and rose again, fulfills what often surfaces in man's conscience as presentiment or prophecy. The Risen Christ acclaims that all things in history are redeemable, that nothing is lost in the vortex of events. In concluding his synthesis of human history, René Grousset shares his own questions with us:

As for human history, what historian, judging from on high, would dare to look upon it without horror? ... But if, at the end of so much agony, there is in fact nothing but the tomb? Ah, then indeed the last man, on the last night of mankind, were he without hope of resurrection, might well utter in his turn the most tragic cry that has every rung across the ages: *Eli, Eli, lamma sabachthani?* Christians know the response which, throughout all eternity, the Eternal One has made to that cry. They know that the martyrdom of God-made-man was intended only to bring Him back to the right hand of the Father and, with Him, all mankind by Him redeemed. Apart from the Christian solution, ... there is henceforth no other – no solution, that is, acceptable to both the reason and the heart.[6]

This solution is acceptable because all humanity is recapitulated in Christ, all-mindful, but without arbitrary detractions, without censorship. The great thinker, Sören Kierkegaard, wrote in his diary that the relationship of "polemical negativity" which paganism wedged between present and future life was well represented by the images of souls who, before arriving at the Elysian Fields, fulfilled their obligation to drink the waters of the River Lethe. By doing so, their earthly struggles were cancelled, leaving only oblivion. This means, then, that it is impossible for man on his own to arrive at even a notion of peace without forgetting (or reneging) something. On the other hand, the truth the Church teaches about the value of a humanity redeemed by Christ is the exact opposite: everything has value for eternity, nothing falls into oblivion. We are called to account for all things, for announcing the Risen Christ, once more at the right hand of the Father, means bearing witness to man placed within the sphere of a companionship so strong that there is no need to forget evil or contradiction: he redeems, transforms all things, with man's freely given consent. However, according to the Church's authentic tradition, this transformation is not postponed to the life beyond. Rather, it is an experience a person already begins to live in the present. In this way, life acquires an interior proportion with the eternal already transpiring in the present time. This makes the appeal to the Christian idea of "merit," or of human reality in proportion to the eternal revealed in Christ.

We must remember at this point, however, that an hypothesis may be considered true and functional if it is able to explain all the factors at play. The communication of truth which the divine in the Church transmits to men proves its validity precisely because it overlooks nothing in its highlighting of the good or in its judging or transforming of evil. Let us ask ourselves, then: how does this communication of divine truth, the message of confidence and certainty about the ultimate meanings of life, come about in the Church? Although the dynamic is one and the same, we can describe this in the following two ways: through the ordinary and the extraordinary magisterium.

a) The Ordinary Magisterium

In channelling to man the supreme truths that Christianity communicates, the Church uses a method best described as the phenomenon of osmotic pressure. This is when one of two liquids, mixable but separated by a type of membrane, is transferred, along with some particular properties, to the other side of the membrane. In this way, the phenomenon of diffusion comes into play. This is very similar to the manner in which the Church's concept of truth is communicated: it is by remaining within, by living within the ecclesial community that, almost by continuous osmosis, these truths penetrate the membrane of our consciousness, day by day, in an incalculable way, enabling us to attain that certainty and clarity of truth which we need in order to face life.

This is to say: fidelity to the ecclesial community is the first way in which the true message that Christ came to bring to the world comes to pass. Traditionally, this method is expressed by the phrase: *ordinary magisterium.*

The Christian arrives at the divine truths the Church proposes in an ordinary way, through the very life of the community. However, the one condition for this is that this community must be truly ecclesial, that is, *united to the bishop* who, in his turn, is supposed to be united with the bishop of Rome, the Pope. This is the normal source of ultimate, sure knowledge; not by theological study or biblical exegesis – which will be tools in the hands of guiding authorities – but through the shared way of life of the Church, bound to the ordinary magisterium of the Pope and the bishops in communion with him.

There are various basic means of recognizing the conscience of the community as it lives its life. They might be encyclicals or Papal addresses, the texts and letters a bishop writes to his diocese in his unity with the Pontiff's pastoral teaching. Or they might be the texts of a community which bear the signs of the ecclesial life, with the implicit approval of the bishop.

Now, if the ordinary magisterium is the guarantee of the development of the community as a living thing, the greatest means of all for the communication of truth in the life of the Church is that life's continuity. This is called *tradition*, the conscience of the community living now, rich in the memory of its whole history. Commenting on the *Dei Verbum* constitution of the Second Vatican Council, Henri de Lubac wrote the following: "The idea of tradition expounded upon here is derived from the idea of Revelation: the Church transmits in its doctrine, 'in its life and in its worship' all that it has received; it is not just a matter then of 'oral tradition,' but of a concrete, living tradition, which bears fruit time after time so that, while it conserves the truth revealed, it applies it to the here and now according to the needs of every age." And he went on to observe: "Tradition is always more to the fore in our minds than Scripture in respect of chronological order and because, at the root of everything, lies 'this Tradition that comes from the Apostles,' and it was within an already constituted community that the sacred books were composed or received."[7]

The Christian community, insofar as it is Church, is like a person who, as he grows, becomes aware of the truth that God placed within and around him. Its memory is a fundamental element of its personality, as it is for every man; in the absence of memory, in contrast, a grave symptom of mental hardening, sclerosis, sets in. This is why a Christian's unity with tradition is one of the great marks proving his religious authenticity. He should be impassioned by this ecclesial life and by the teaching that has traversed the centuries for 2,000 years. And he should be proud to be the heir of such a tradition.

Tradition is of decisive importance because it comes to us through the life of the community, the continuity of Christ in history, whatever it teaches now, cannot be in contrast with all that it taught a thousand years ago. As the annunciation of truth, as the ultimate meaning – not necessarily ritual formulations or practices – it cannot come to represent the decline of its first message. John Henry Newman had this to say:

When we consider the succession of ages during which the Catholic system has endured, the severity of the trials it has undergone, the sudden and wonderful changes without and within which have befallen it, the incessant mental activity and the intellectual gifts of its maintenance, the enthusiasm which it has kindled, the fury of the controversies which have been carried on among its professors, the impetuosity of the assaults made upon it, the ever increasing responsibilities to which it has been committed by the continuous development of its dogmas, it is quite inconceivable that it should not have been broken up and lost, were it a corruption of Christianity. ... That its long series of developments should be corruptions would be an instance of sustained errors so novel, so unaccountable, so preternatural, as to be little short of a miracle and to rival those manifestations of divine power which constitute the evidence of Christianity. We sometimes view with surprise and awe the degree of pain and disarrangement which the human frame can undergo without succumbing; yet at length there comes an end. Fevers have their crisis, fatal or favourable; but this corruption of a thousand years, if corruption it be, has ever been growing nearer death, yet never reaching it, and has been strengthened, not debilitated, by its excesses.[8]

Alfred North Whitehead once said that a philosophy or ideology could only be coherent with its origins for a generation at most. Well, the Church, with its millenary history, dares to affirm that it has never contradicted itself and never will. Such a claim is a miracle by itself.

b) The Extraordinary Magisterium

A second way exists for the truths of the faith to be communicated in the Church, and this is when its teaching assumes an extraordinary position – when the Pope, that is, intends to state something with all the authority at his command. This can happen in a solemn, historical way, by, for example, convening an Ecumenical Council, the assembly of all the bishops under the guidance of the Bishop of Rome, or, the Pontiff might intervene personally in an initiative called an *ex cathedra definition*. Understood in this way, then, the extraordinary magisterium is a teaching which is exceptional both in terms of its formulation and its contingent cause. To put it briefly, this magisterium has as its subject the Pope's authority, both when he makes a personal *ex cathedra* definition and in the event of a council – neither of which can be valid without the Pontiff's approval. And because this extraordinary means is used to define values which are proposed as historically definitive and irreversible, it therefore represents the height of Christian conscience in regard to society.

On this point, I would like to make a few observations:

i) AUTHORITY AS A FUNCTION OF THE COMMUNITY'S LIFE

The supreme authority of the magisterium is an explication of the conscience of the entire community as guided by Christ. It is not some magical, despotic substitution for it. It is functional to it. The truth defined by means of either ordinary or extraordinary exceptional intervention concerns something that is already part of the Church's life. The authority highlights it, defending and clarifying what has always been lived (at least implicitly); by its nature, this truth is not something invented, preclusive of the life and conscience of the community. As Father René Latourelle specifies: "The Church must faithfully preserve (as a deposit) and infallibly proclaim that revealed doctrine. And in the second text: she must holily preserve (as a deposit) and faithfully explain (as a doctrine) the revelation handed down to her. ... But for the doctrine of Christ to be taught without addition or corruption, the Church necessarily needs not only to preserve it, but also to denounce the errors which threaten it."[9]

The expression the Church uses for these explications is "dogma," whose Greek root lies in the verb *dokéo*, to believe, to retain. The noun signifies opinion, decree, maxim, and throughout the centuries, it has come to refer to specifically the points of doctrine which the authority of the Church defines with precision. The Church expresses itself in this way when it is certain that it is explicating the maturity of the common conscience in Christ.

In the life of the Church, as regards the communication of the truth, authority is like a channel, like a river bed, with a twofold function. The first is an ideal function whereby the Church indicates the direction of the river towards its mouth. In the second, the Church delimits, like a river bank; it must judge when a statement or teaching goes against or beyond the flow, flooding the banks whose purpose is to keep the water coursing in the direction of the ideal. So when a dogma is proclaimed in the Church, it is never the fruit of some hasty conviction or ill-considered reaction. Rather, it is similar to what happens to us when, after an encounter or a particularly significant event, a clear awareness of impressions, convictions, or intuitions that we have been harbouring for a long time dawns on us, enabling us to give expression to them. For the life of Christ in the history of the Church is a life that grows. The whole richness of the truth is Christ: the life of the Church is increasingly conscious of all that Christ brought to it and, therefore, of all that it itself holds. The dogmatic formulation coincides with this leap of quality in terms of the conscience of the Church and, therefore, of the people in it.

Nevertheless, when it proclaims a dogma, the Church takes great care to sound out the conscience of the community. When, for example, in 1950 Pius XII proclaimed the dogma of the Assumption, he did so only after repeated consultations with the bishops and communities worldwide, until he was certain that a doctrinal definition would merely give voice to something that the Christian people since ancient times had never ceased believing. And it appears, in fact, that the Feast of the Assumption was already celebrated in the fourth century. It has been handed down to each generation ever since Our Lady was raised to heavenly glory in body and soul at the end of her earthly life, and because she did not have to wait for the final resurrection of the body, her mortal remains were spared corruption. This is exactly what Pius XII proclaimed when he defined the dogma of the Assumption.

Of course, it was particularly significant to affirm this in a society where the value of life was being increasingly made to consist in success in the here and now. It was also a challenge to announce that the Christian event proclaims the value of the body's existence in eternity and that the value of life – even of a totally unnoteworthy life – lies, as the figure of Mary suggests, in living the moment as an aspect and in function of the love for everything. This is to say that the value of the moment does not lie in its immediate success but in the love for all things with which it is lived. In this way, then, nothing, not even a hair of our heads, will be lost. This is the affirmation of man's true dimension, which pressures his materialistic narrow-mindedness and, spurred on by his spirit, opens him up to the infinite.

The dogma of the Immaculate Conception, proclaimed in 1854 at the inception of the materialistic wave mirrors a similar provocation. Duns Scotus, the late thirteenth-century Franciscan philosopher and theologian, was already, in his time, teaching that the Virgin was preserved from original sin in some way, which is to say, that she was redeemed in advance by him who would be her son. It is surprising, then, that almost six centuries later, the Church reproduced precisely the same explanation in defining the dogma of the Immaculate Conception? The Church proposes that we look to Mary as one who lived her humanity in a complete way, without the mark of our original ambiguity. We are invited to look, that is, to a woman whose life can be summed up in her own phrase – *fiat voluntas tua* – in accepting her mission. Thus, in the face of the proud sons of the Enlightenment, the fragility of man who becomes great only in adhering to God was reasserted, as was the doctrine of original sin, already defined by the Council of Trent. And undoubtedly the thinking of the day, like our own, viewed "this image of weakness and in-built incoherence to be repugnant," this "warning of the irresolvable incapacity of man acting alone to allow the steps he takes in life to be determined by true destiny." But then, "this revelation is a glorious affirmation of the seriousness of human responsibility (the condition of fragility is asserted as the outcome wrought by the first man); it is also a proclamation of the organic, deeply rooted relationship that exists man to man, and so there is no better affirmation of the unity of men, the dimension that defines the make-up of each one of us."[10]

Clearly, then, the vast majority of people have no idea of the Church's procedure leading to the proclamation of a dogma, never mind comprehending the meaning of the expression. But, as we have seen, it defines a value when that value has become a sure and living part of the conscience of the Christian community. In this perspective, a truth taught by the ordinary magisterium may have the same characteristics. However, strictly speaking, the word "dogma" is applied to an exceptional proclamation. It indicates that at this ultimate level, the Church is driven by the urgent need for clarity in the eyes of the world, and the issue is no longer open to interpretative doubt. In a family, for example, it is futile to clarify an obvious issue in any formal way. However, it does become necessary when divergent, confusing interpretations arise concerning important aspects of family life.

ii) IN THE CHURCH NOT EVERYTHING IS DOGMA

It is evident from our brief summary so far that it would be wrong to interpret the life of the Church, guided by the authority, as being marked all over by dogmas. Not everything is dogma because, firstly, if it were the solemn clarification we described above might not be necessary and, secondly, not everything can possibly surface in the conscience of the Christian people as to become a certain and clear awareness. If this were not the case, history would no longer have any meaning.

The authority of the Church, then, does not frequently have recourse to the proclamation of a dogma in order to fulfil its mission of communicating the truth. Only three dogmas have been proclaimed, for example, in the last 150 years: the Immaculate Conception, in 1854; Papal Infallibility, in 1870; and the Assumption of the Blessed Virgin, in 1950. However, in the interests of being consistent with the educational role which, as we have seen, is proper to the Church, perhaps we should stress this point: the proclamation of a dogma has a primarily pedagogical function. But why, at a certain point, does the Church proclaim a dogma, no longer leaving the issue as a matter of the conscience of the people of God? The reason is that this step becomes necessary within the great pedagogical task of educating man to Christ, the mission the Church must fulfil.

This dogmatic explication of a truth may become particularly useful for the Christian community, for example, when a certain dominant culture negates that truth by grave and violent means. Take, for instance, one of the most recent dogmas: Papal Infallibility. Firstly, we should remember that the Pope, as the ultimate point of reference for the Church, is a proven fact, the documented experience of the Christian community from just a few years after Christ's death. As Joseph Lortz commented: "From the historical point of view, the definition of the Pope's 'Supreme Episcopate' and of his infallibility represented the conclusion of a great development. It started in the first century with the primacy of Peter and his function as bishop of Rome and it endured through two millennia, traversing an endless series of diverse circumstances ... And it never deviated from its principle."[11] But, of what does this infallibility consist? Primarily, it is a characteristic born of the fact that God communicates himself through the Church. It is not, therefore, some capacity of man, but rather a prerogative of the power of God, which manifests itself by guaranteeing his Spirit to his whole Church, under the guidance of Peter's successor. Therefore, considering that the dogma of Papal Infallibility is the ultimate specification of the help Jesus promised his Church, and that its root lies in the Church's very history, perhaps it need not have been promulgated at all. And in fact, most of the objections to it during the conciliar debate revolved not around its subject matter, but on whether or not it was an opportune time. As August Franzen has commented:

The debate was conducted freely and frankly and with the advantageous result that all arguments and counter-arguments could be expressed without hindrance and nothing was concealed or suppressed which was required for a clarification. As a matter of fact, the vehemence of the opposition, which was so brilliantly represented [at the council] caused their objections to be examined particularly carefully. Because this careful attention was given to the opposition views, absurd content was soon excluded and the remaining nucleus was so much more irrefutable and reliable. ... The final voting ... demonstrated that among the opponents the greater majority had voted against the definition for reasons of inopportunity.[12]

When the debate was over, the constitution *Pastor Aeternus*, containing the doctrine of the primacy and infallibility of the Pope, was put to the vote. This occurred in a society where a rationalistic concept of life had become the dominant one in people's minds, and within this milieu, the Church opted to make a provocative, solemn affirmation: that man is not the only measure of reality, that the bond between man and truth does not just span the short bridge of his reason. No, it flows between the banks of an authority which, assisted by God, is called to guide man to salvation. So in this case, the dogma, even though it was debated at length, was provoked by a shocking and total contrast with the surrounding world, a contrast necessitating clarification.

Let us conclude our résumé of this specific instance with the words of Jacques Leclercq:

Papal infallibility is just a tool of the Church's infallibility. The doctrine of the Church's infallibility was universally accepted in early Christian times. It was a corollary of Christ's promises, a consequence of the Spirit's assistance ...The Church's infallibility is expressed by Tradition ... and when this develops without problems there is no need for anything more. But when the Church is torn by controversies and Tradition is no longer clearly manifest, it becomes necessary for us to know which organ is the ultimate verification of this infallibility. Papal infallibility, then, is just a specification of the Church's infallibility ...: it is the infallibility of the Church which is manifest through the Pope.[13]

It seems evident to me from these brief explanations that the use of the adjective "dogmatic" to accuse the Church betrays a failure to grasp its real meaning, which is consistent with the proper concept of the Church.

In order to understand the Christian fact we must constantly refer to life. It is not true at all that the word "dogma" has the dictatorial meaning many commentators attribute to it. Rather, it merely indicates the definitive formulation of a consciousness of the truth of which the Church is custodian. And this is analogous to the most common of life's experiences. When we were five or ten years old, we had a certain attitude to life that corresponded to circumstances particular to our own experience, reflecting our personalities, even at that age. Yet, as we grew older, some of our ideas were subjected to expressive changes, although they remained within the unitary expression of our personality. The same is true of the history of the Church. The fundamental content of the Christian event, theologically called the *depositum fidei*, is to the history of the Church what the content of humanity is to the child. As time goes by and in the encounter with circumstances and events provoking it, the Church, like the child, becomes increasingly conscious of self. This is what happens when the conscience of the ecclesial community, certain in its adherence to authority, proclaims – "Now, we can be definitively sure about that" – when referring to a given aspect of the essential content of faith.

The Church, in fact, is a life, and it is so easy to miss this point. It is the life of One, the mystery of the Person in Christ that develops through time within the living organic nature of His People. The Church, then, is a life which becomes increasingly conscious of self as time goes by.

iii) THE PATH OF THE CHURCH'S SELF-AWARENESS

All that happens in each of our lives, as our self-awareness matures with the passage of time, also occurs in the life of the Church. Therefore it is important to remember that this maturing process follows a certain course. An enlightening example took place in this century in the case of the Dominican father, Marie-Joseph Lagrange. He was an eminent biblist, the founder at the end of the nineteenth century of the *École pratique d'Études bibliques* in Jerusalem, and the creator of a biblical study review of international standing. Lagrange did all these things at a very particular period in history.

At the end of the nineteenth century, the Church was totally unprepared for the shock arising from various developments in the methods of historical and literary criticism as applied to the texts of Scripture by rationalist and Protestant exegetes. It was a time of great intellectual upheaval and of new advances in scientific research, inducing many souls to wonder if the demands of science could be reconciled with the truths of faith. Within the Church itself, a conviction had started to form in some quarters that real research was incompatible with any authority and that authority could not be allowed to impose elements of the faith as *a priori* truth. And it was this drawing away from the fundamental facts of Catholicism that Pius X condemned as a heresy, calling it "modernism."

Now Lagrange, a pioneer of biblical studies, knew beyond a doubt that in his work he would have to utilize the various advances in the fields of philology, oriental archaeology, and textual criticism and that, in doing so, his theological steadfastness would not be shaken. Indeed, he believed he could bring new impetus and prestige to Catholic exegesis without detracting from the principles of his faith. However, given the climate of suspicion wrought by the strain of rooting out heresy, some of the fruits of his work were the targets of violent attacks from some Catholic circles. They reported him to ecclesiastical authorities, who, although not condemning him doctrinally, eventually subjected him to disciplinary measures, including forcing him to leave the biblical school. But Lagrange continued his research, never refusing to submit to the judgment of ecclesiastical authority in attempts to prove the correct nature of his overall approach. He worked hard and, by the time he died, his bibliography counted over 1,000 texts. In the end, Pius

XII's 1943 encyclical *Divino afflante Spiritu* on the advances in biblical studies can be considered as doing justice to the perseverance of Lagrange's work: he is quoted with approval, while, a good part of his recommendations were reproposed to Catholic exegetes.

Now, the means the Church uses to safeguard the expression of the faith may ultimately take the form of an affirmation such as: "At the current state of knowledge, we do not see how (or we see with concern that it is not ...) this attitude can be in harmony with the values of the faith." However, knowledge can well evolve and a deeper study of certain questions can reveal such concern to be unjustified.

Karl Adam commented on this tension between freedom and authority and its bond with a certain course in history in the following way:

Its new truth does not originate in humanity as its primal source ... but is essentially given from above. Therefore it can be communicated to men only by the way of authority ... Church authority is a necessary correlative of supernatural revelation. ... On the other hand the Church prohibits all blind faith, and merely external conformity. The affirmation accorded to the Church's teaching must be a convinced and inward affirmation, and so an affirmation of the free moral personality. ... And since this personal insight cannot be attained by a scholar without a severely scientific method, the Church cannot possibly be an enemy to a sober criticism, least of all to the so-called historico-critical method. Even the much attacked antimodernistic encyclical of Pius X ... does not forbid this method, but rather presupposes it. What they forbid is simply that men should make the affirmation of supernatural faith dependent *exclusively* on the results of this method. ...Our faith does not rest upon dead documents, but upon the living witness of that stream of tradition. ... By means of this life of hers, by means of the clear daylight of her revealed knowledge, the Church is ever throwing new light on the ever new problems. ... And when she believes that the central thoughts of the Christian revelation are menaced, then by means of her Congregations – not in the name of science, but in the name of faith – she utters *tuto doceri non potest*, the prohibition to teach them, ... It is possible that the teaching authority of the Church, as in the case of Galileo, may in the name of faith forbid a scientific opinion which is only in apparent contradiction with fixed dogmatic truth, which becomes later on an irrefutable certainty.[14]

It is probably useful to repeat this here: this failure to consider the Church as a living organism – therefore liable to grow in self-awareness and to correct and modify its awareness of the unchangeable deposit of the revealed faith – is the greatest source of misunderstanding in the way people judge and live the ecclesial community. In analyzing a person's life, we give due consideration to his background: to the conditions in which he grew up, his circumstances as an adult, and the contingency factors that might be incisive for his personality and cloud his consciousness. In the same way, we must remember that the Church lives and operates in the realms of time. It charts its itinerary of self-awareness, and in this, so that it may fulfill its mission and, therefore, avoid the trap of ever *defining* an error, it is assisted by the indefatigable Spirit of Christ. This assistance, however, does not spare the Church the fatigue and work of evolutive research for the precise reason that the Church's nature as a "body" that is certainly divine but also human is incarnated in time and space.

Let us conclude this reflection on the communication of the divine in the Church by quoting John Henry Newman: "Thus, a power of development is a proof of life, not only in its essay, but especially in its success; for a mere formula either does not expand, or is shattered in expanding. A living idea becomes many, yet remains one." [15]

2 THE SELF-COMMUNICATION OF A DIVINE REALITY

At this point, we must consider the second aspect of the divine which constitutes the Church, whose mission it is to channel it to the world. The first aspect concerned the ultimate meanings of existence and history – the truth – which the Church communicates to us with definitive clarity and certainty. We have also seen how it is very likely that we have to reconsider our usual way of thinking about dogmas, whose formulation and definition represent the highest and most profound pertinence to life and history imaginable.

Let us now move on to the heart of the Christian message: how living within the Church, living the presence of Christ, communicates a divine *reality*.

a) Supernatural or Sanctifying Grace

In the famous prologue to his Gospel, John announces that "in the beginning was the Word," and that he was "with God" and that he "was God;" he also communicates that the Word, without whom "not one thing that is came into being," was life and the light of men, life and light even of men who did not recognize him; and he affirms that anyone who does recognize that light and life will be given the "power to become children of God." After this, John sets before us the unprecedented fact: "And the Word was made flesh." In this way, he shows us that we do not find ourselves simply in front of the communication of truth, a revelation of the mystery of being, which is nonetheless, vital for our search for the meaning of life and history. No, we are before the communication of the divine itself, of man's sharing in God's life, the ontological density of which is only hinted at in the expression "children of God." We are dealing with a communication touching and transforming the whole being of man. Within the man to whom Christ draws near and who freely desires and accepts the relationship with him – and, therefore, within the Church – his nature as a man changes. This is an ontological "exaltation" of the "I," a leap in quality in the participation of Being. In the life of the Church, Being, God, the Word made flesh, Christ communicates to man the gift of a more profound participation in the origin of everything. In this way, man remains man but becomes something more. Man within the Church, is offered a "supernatural" participation in Being. This is the most fascinating element of the Christian announcement.

The Gospel calls this profound self-communication of the divine reality "being born again." We find this expression in chapter three of John, in the episode we have already cited of Jesus' conversation with Nicodemus, a prominent Jew: "Jesus informs his visitor ... that it is not primarily a matter of human effort and the accomplishment of law, but being 'born from above.' "[16]

Independently of the debate sparked by this expression, among old and new exegetes, the fact remains that what Nicodemus does not understand – "How can anyone who is already old be born again?" (John 3:4) – is exactly the point that Jesus immediately clarifies. As Rudolph Schnackenburg writes: "Prior to all human effort to attain to the kingdom of God, God himself must create the basis of a new being in man, which will also make a new way of life possible. ... The 'birth' or 'begetting' of which Jesus speaks is of a completely different nature. It comes about 'from water and Spirit.' ... Earthly man must be born 'from above,' which means in fact created anew out of the divine spirit of life."[17]

Christian tradition has an expression to describe the realization of this new way of being. It is "supernatural grace," or "sanctifying grace." The word "grace," which we have become all too accustomed to hearing, is the most beautiful word of all in our Christian vocabulary. It indicates the total gratuitousness of the phenomenon it defines, marking its divine value, because only the self-communication of the divine is "totally" gratuitous. The addition of the word "supernatural" establishes the link between this communication of self that Christ works in our lives (making us different people from the people we might have been) and the act of creation which gave us that life. Man is the same man, but he is different.

In this way, we are before a human novelty, whose dynamism remains mysterious. It is not for us to know "how," but if we return to

Jesus' conversation with Nicodemus we find that wonderful simile we mentioned earlier in reference to the Christian mystery – the comparison with the wind, which, in this context, applies precisely to the heart of the divine reality's communication. Again Schnackenburg comments:

> The central idea is that the wind is also a mystery as to its origin and goal, but it still remains a reality, perceptible by means of its sound ("voice"), recognizable through its effects. ... The positive affirmation is that the wind blows of its own power, according to its own law. This is also true of the man born of the Spirit. The origin and goal of the divine power bestowed on him, the nature and character of the process are divinely mysterious: but these powers are present, the divine Spirit is at work in him. And hence the Spirit is also recognizable through the effects which he produces in man.[18]

In this same perspective, another expression dominates the New Testament: *the new man, the new creation.* In his second letter to the Corinthians, Paul pronounces explicitly: "So for anyone who is in Christ, there is a new creation: the old order is gone and a new being is there to see" (2 Cor. 5:17). And he repeats this when he intervenes in the Galatians' discussions on the need for Christians to adhere to the Jewish custom of circumcision: "It is not being circumcised or uncircumcised that matters; but what matters is a new creation" (Gal. 6:15). In a similar way, he urges the Ephesians: "Your mind was to be renewed in spirit so that you could put on the New Man" (Eph. 4:23–4a); and reminds the Colossians of the new reality among and in them: "You have stripped off your own behaviour with your old self, and you have put on a new self" (Col. 3:9–10a).

Peter, also, in a letter to Christians scattered throughout Asia Minor, urges them to live holy lives, and establishes the possibility by referring to the same concept of "new generation" already mentioned in our commentary on John: "for your new birth was not from any perishable seed but from imperishable seed, the living and enduring Word of God" (1 Peter 1:23). And finally in James, it is as if this formula of the new man or the new creation has reached its full potential as a catalyst of humanity and of human history: "By his own choice he gave birth to us by the message of the truth so that we should be a sort of first-fruits of all his creation" (James 1:18).

These passages bring us to the second aspect qualifying the word "grace": sanctifying. The idea of the saint in our religious tradition indicates a person who adheres, who corresponds to God. This is why, in Jewish ritual, God is described as thrice holy: obviously, as the supreme paradigm of adherence to his most intimate reality. Now, for

Christians, this "grace" is sanctifying because it is God who, through his own person, began a new humanity, a definitive humanity according to his plan, a humanity which he will continue in history. The term, sanctifying grace, then, confirms that those who adhere to this gratuitous initiative of God shall enter into a more profound relationship with Being to the extent that they become, as Paul says, part of Christ, members of his body: "Now Christ's body is yourselves, each of you with a part to play in the whole" (1 Cor. 12:27).

Anyone who lives the mystery of the ecclesial community receives a change in his nature. We cannot understand how this happens, how it is that our person changes; yet if we take this phenomenon into consideration, if we live it, if we assume a commitment to it, then we will become different in a verifiable way.

This should be the curiousness of the Christian adventure: the birth and establishment in the world of this new creatureliness, the first fruits of a new humanity. And we are not called to announce this regeneration only with words. Rather, we are invited to live an experience. Thinking that Christianity could be reduced to mere verbal statements – and anyone, even someone who believes himself to be a Christian, might be so affected – means denying ourselves the fascination of a unique adventure – withdrawing from Christianity as life.

How the force of this announcement – that we have been recreated – has been weakened in our consciousness! How we have depleted the potential of this new self-awareness, of this different sense of ourselves, of our "I," which triggers all our energy for action like the light shed by a judgment! How the concept of "sanctifying grace" has been emptied through moralistic usage, and the two most perfect and most beautiful words in all theology no longer express their own power.

In any case, this new phenomenon which penetrated history and human society, the radical novelty of the Gospel revealed by the announcement of an ontological exaltation, responds to an unconscious need of all humanity. Paul says as much in his letter to the Romans: "For the whole creation is waiting with eagerness for the children of God to be revealed. ... We are well aware that the whole creation, until this time, has been groaning in labour pains" (Rom. 8:19,22). Without being fully conscious of what this implies – because of the impossibility of imagining God's initiative – man, in whatever age he lives, has been waiting for this new man. And, even more so, the Christian – or whoever wants to verify the content of the announcement which the Church has prolonged throughout history – cannot ignore that groan. He joins in it with all of his inadequate response, remaining a protagonist of the universal attraction of the Christian adventure.

In the Christian, the newness is called to awaken and, no matter how dimly, to manifest itself like the dawn of a new day. The comparison I like to make is, in fact, the dawn. Imagine a person who has always lived in darkness. If he were to see, for the first time, the first half-light of day, he would realize that what was unfolding before his eyes was something new. It was no longer darkness. And, even though he could never imagine the sight of the midday sun, he would certainly be attracted by this phenomenon, which for him would be so unexpected and indefinable – that the dawning would have dispelled the darkness, introducing him to something different from the obscurity to which he was accustomed. This person would gaze in fascination at that prelude of light, waiting for an even greater newness, even though he could not imagine its form.

This is Christianity in history, the Church in the society of the times, a Christian community in its environment, a Christian man in the circumstances of his day-to-day living; the dawning of a different humanity, of a different human community, a community that is, new, truer.

b) By Means of Effective Signs: The Sacraments

How is this supernatural grace, this ontological leap of quality communicated within us?

Just as the truth is transmitted by means of the magisterium in the life of the Church, so too this profound sharing in the mystery of Being has its beginnings in the objective life of the Church. This is to say, it is not born of sentiment or of the intelligent imaginings of the human mind. Rather, this new reality is communicated through a person's sharing in the life of the authentic ecclesial community, by means of gestures, called sacraments.

The word "sacrament" is a translation of the Latin *sacramentum* which, in its turn, was the Latin translation of the Greek word *mysterion* whose etymology is uncertain. Mircea Eliade reflects on this word in the ensuing way: "The Greek term, used chiefly in the plural, *ta mysteria*, probably derives from an Indo-European root *mu*, the original meaning of which, 'to shut the mouth,' refers to 'ritual silence.' Cf. Gk. *myō* and *myeō*, 'initiate into the Mystery,' and *myēsis*, 'initiation' (a term used only of initiations into Mysteries)."[19] Such expressions must surely have been familiar to the Christians of the early centuries. According to Gustave Bardy:

As the Christian age was about to dawn, all the countries of the Mediterranean basin had been invaded by eastern religions. There was no divinity that did not attract fervent worshippers in Rome or Athens. Isis and Osiris, Cybel, Attis, Adonis, Mythra are the best known but it would be a long list indeed if it were to include all their contemporary and successive counterparts to which restless souls turned in devotion. At the end of the fourth century pagan worship was more exasperated than ever. As a result, there was an infinite number of initiation rites to the foreign mysteries to which the Orient introduced Rome.[20]

This Greek antecedent of *sacramentum*, then, evoked the cults originating in Greece or the Orient, and whose rites were kept a rigorous secret. According to scholars of religion, the expression applies to a vast field of research. But pending our return to the argument later, it is enough for us here to keep in mind that for the cult worshipper, the access to the divine was only partial, that these cults offered the initiated the possibility of a degree of union with things divine. In this respect, therefore, the word *mysterion*, does not indicate the absolute unknowable, but rather all that can be known of the unknowable using special techniques, and, as a derivative of the theory and practice of mystical cults, this word was also applied to the search for illumination.

The New Testament also mentions this word, *mysterion*, but scholars have generally ascertained that its realm of meaning grew to assume an apocalyptic tone – the search for the key to God's ultimate intentions – as opposed to a mysterial sensibility (or participation in the presence of the divine). This word was translated into Latin, then, as *sacramentum*, and its root lies in technical and military terminology, suggesting a solemn pledge, a soldier's oath, a sacred bond – something similar to a vow. In Christian literature we first find it referring to a confession of faith, and then, by the third century, it was extended to other analogous acts.

We have seen briefly what the word "sacrament" – now so commonplace in Christian practice – entails in terms of historical reminders. At this point, it is enough to note that its link with the word *mysterion*, expands the meaning of the word "mystery" as we normally use it today to embrace a degree of possibility in the striving for knowledge. Also, on the basis of the origin of *sacramentum*, it evokes a sacred pact of fidelity, and the impression it leaves the Christian is that it is linked with the covenant God wished to make with man.

However, in both of the original connotations, we find the mark of an operativity, a type of effectiveness that the Church links to the sacrament. In the religious and philosophical language of human thought, that which is mystery is only to be found at the limits of our possible access, and only with the use of special techniques may we arrive at some of its fragments. However, for the Church, mystery also indicates what lies beyond our capacity for knowledge, insofar as the Mystery, by sovereign initiative, desired to make itself knowable within human experience, in a permanent, faithful way. Thus the sacrament is the first aspect of this self-communication of the divine within human experience. In this sense, the Church describes itself as sacrament, a place where the presence of the divine strength, of the person of Christ who conquers the world, is and will always be seen. The Church is the sacrament of that presence.

If, then, the Church – as the Mysterious Body in its unity – is the place where Christ continues indefatigably to exist in time, Christ's gestures are also bound to reverberate in Church history through the actions of the community. In the strict sense of the word, the sacraments prolong in history *Jesus' redeeming acts*, those fundamental signs Christ used to communicate salvation, which is himself. Karl Adam reflects on the sacraments in this way:

(Sacrament) finds its full sense and its entire consistency only in Christ and because of Christ. In the same way as Christ in His earthly life was not ashamed to connect bodily healings to visible signs (cf. Mk 7:33–35; Jn 9:6), thus, in a new and sublime sense, He raises even the sacraments to specific instruments of His redeeming power ... in order to sanctify souls by means of them, through their sensitive evidence. ... The Catholic concept of sacrament wishes therefore to protect what constitutes the intimate nucleus of Christianity, that for which St. Paul suffered and struggled, the full gratuitousness of grace and the thought that Christ is "all in all" ... The Christian sacrament ... ensures the vital, immediate exchange, without obstacles between the Head and his members.[21]

Moreover, Hans Urs von Balthasar underlines the concrete nature of the sacraments by referring to Origen in this way: "If the 'mystical body' is not pure metaphor, if this communion of the saints is truly incarnate, if also this body is distinct from every other body because it is the body of Christ, if these two conditions merge, then we should be able to touch this body just as people were able to touch Christ in the flesh."[22] We must note here that "mystical" does not have an abstract meaning. Rather it denotes something rich in mystery, not something intellectually vague. Indeed, all that the Church proposes, with its whole self, and with the gestures that perpetuate the gestures of the Saviour, is the true involvement of people with His Person.

We have seen how care for the tangible, for concrete teaching, was part of Jesus' pedagogy for his self-revelation. It is not surprising, therefore, that Jesus had his Church use elements of material living in its sacramental gestures. Jesus, too, had used mud, water, wine, fish, bread, and even the hem of his cloak to make himself manifest in miracles which healed man, yes, which assisted him in his specific needs, but which, above all, put him in contact with him. And he was the complete and perfect manifestation of God's love for man, the source of an energy that resolves life for the individual and for mankind's entire history. So, like Christ, who approached the sick and released a strength that gave not just health, but sanity, and just as that gift was, for Christ, the communication of his divine reality, in the same way, the company adhering to Christ, that lives in the place he created for his continuity – the Church, his Body or his visibility and self-evidence present with us – explicates the perpetuation of the Saviour's gestures by safeguarding all their elements: from the visibility of the signs to the effective action that is incisive for and, indeed, determines the individual's personal life.

The sacraments put us in contact with a reality more profound than the one we are able to see. They are the signs communicating a divine reality in which the presence of Christ lies. The sacrament, then, is a gesture of the Church. It is useful to reaffirm this, even if it is logical to assume that it is the gesture of Christ perpetuated in history, for a widespread current in Christian thinking today conceives of the sacraments as some kind of secret prescription, personal and individual, as if grace and salvation were a private reserve, quite apart from the individual's belonging to the whole community of the Body of Christ. Quite simply, this is not true, for if this were the case, it would contradict the very genesis of the sacramental structure of the Church as a locus of redemption. The acts of Christ's mystery are not the formula for one individual life of devotion. Rather, they constitute the action of Jesus himself who, in the Church, stoops to assist human weakness just as he used to stoop at the sight of the twisted body of a cripple, taking hold of that weakness just as it is, so that he can change it. Acts such as these are inconceivable outside the community of the Church. This is why we priests, when we celebrate Mass and stretch out our hands over the offerings, are stretching our hands over what must be changed into the body and blood of Christ. With that gesture, we are really incorporating all people and all their lives, for they comprise the mystical body of Christ. The supreme aspiration of the liturgical prayer is that we be one body: "We humbly pray that we may become one body."

Thus, while the Christian life cannot ever be conceived as an individualistic relationship with Christ, it is, nevertheless, a highly personal one, unfolding within the consciousness of fraternal relationships and within the bounds of personal responsibility towards the world. And here lies the difference between "individualistic" and "personal." Both refer to the attitude of an individual who either confronts things from the limited perspective of his isolated "I" or perceives himself as the subject of universal relationships because his essence is relationship with the Infinite and his task is to participate in the redeeming and triumphal sacrifice of Christ, who died and rose again.

There is a community of life, and it is immeasurably deep. The same current of grace flows through all alike, the same active power of God. The same real Christ is present in all, as the ideal and prime exemplar of perfection, our incentive to pursue it and the creative power which makes it possible. ... Thus the sacraments are forms and processes, in which the life of the supernatural community begins, progresses, recovers lost ground, and is continually propagated.[23]

And it is precisely this entire existence of a new creatureliness that we become aware of every time we look at the sacramental signs the Church proposes.

Within one fundamental act a man is made immanent to the mystery of Christ in the life of the Church. This act is baptism, the act by which Christ takes hold of man and takes him into himself. Water, a feature of the baptismal ceremony, was once used more abundantly – Christians used to be entirely immersed in it. But water is also an eternal and ambivalent symbol, the primordial sign of life and the words the celebrant speaks over it make the recreational force of the Spirit of God present. In addition, water is the symbol of risk and weariness, so man crosses the sea of life with a different kind of freedom. Through the sign of this immersion and regeneration, Christ takes hold of those whom he has chosen as his disciples in history. As Paul wrote to the Galatians: "Since every one who has been baptised has been clothed in Christ. There can be neither Jew nor Greek, there can be neither slave nor freeman, there can be neither male nor female – for you are all one in Christ Jesus. And simply by being Christ's, you are that progeny of Abraham, the heirs named in the promise" (Gal. 3:26–29). This is an identification with Christ which becomes decisive for man's physiognomy. It touches his most intimate fibres, transforming him. According to Jean Daniélou:

In the beginning the Spirit of God moved upon the face of the waters, and there was brought forth in them the physical life of the first creation. The same Spirit, according to the Gospel, overshadowed Mary, that she, in the power of the Most High, might bring forth the world of the second creation, the world of grace, wherein men become sons of God; the world whose orientation is towards Christ, the eternal sun-rising. Baptism is this same new creation of every living soul. That which comes out of the stream of living water, "water and the Spirit" regenerated, new-begotten, born again in Christ, belongs thereafter to the new creation.[24]

And the act that enables this newly created man to journey through life, this man remade by the power of God and now capable of new things, is the Eucharist, *viaticum*, food for the journey, the human being's real nourishment, the food of hope. Continuously in this act, Christ, in giving himself, perfects man in himself.

Let us look again at the Lord's encounter with Zachaeus, the rich publican who climbed up a sycamore tree for a better view of Jesus as he passed by: "Jesus looked up and spoke to him, 'Zachaeus, come down. Hurry because I am to stay at your house today. And he hurried down and welcomed him joyfully" (Luke 19: 5–6). This is the Eucharist: Christ gives us back a humanity capable of justice, of joy, of welcome – a true humanity; and he does this by coming to our house. We, too, would like to be snatched from the trees of our various plans and hear him say: "I am coming to you." Or, we might desire the familiarity of the youngest disciple who laid his head on Jesus' shoulder at the Last Supper. But there is nothing more profound than the type of familiarity that Christ makes me capable of by giving himself to me as food and drink. What the sign points to really happens within the material sign itself: he becomes one with me. In a sign, an unimaginably profound, ontological relationship is communicated to our lives.

This is why when we acknowledge our weaknesses, we too would like to hear the voice of Jesus say what he often used to say to people he cured or encountered: "Go, your sins are forgiven. I do not condemn you. Sin no more." And these words of Christ do resound through history in the sacrament of confession, which is literally those words, that gesture of forgiveness by Christ which continues throughout this history.

Christ, therefore, continues to be present and to fulfil those acts of salvation at the most significant, fundamental moments in the life of man, moments that represent a turning point – in man's happy fulfillment through baptism and the eucharist or in his struggles, through confirmation, such a solid and potent sign, reminiscent of the athlete or soldier (in fact, oil and perfumes were used to strengthen the muscles of men preparing for some kind of contest or competition). He also addressed aspects of the fragility of living, not just moral fragility through the sacrament of confession, but physical fragility too, by anointing, the sick with holy oil, the ill, whose social function as persons is always acknowledged until the very last instants of life. He wanted to be there to respond to the human need for the completion of the "I" and for the continuity of the race through marriage, in a family that procreates and educates. He wanted to respond to the human need to have present and active the ideal prophecy because of which it is worthwhile for man to give life and to teach life, and he created ordination, the sacrament conferring the priesthood. He truly is the Man-God who never forgets that he is a man. And he wanted to leave us his company in the fundamental aspects of living, almost entrusting them with the expressive development of our existence in him.

The sacrament, then, is the experience of a relationship with Christ contained in a concrete, physical act. This is why the catechism calls it the *effective sign of grace*: it is a sign because the physical is a concrete reminder of the aspect of life in which Christ communicates himself; and it is effective, because, through that physical element, he truly transmits his reality and divine power. The sacrament is the typical structure of every act of the new individual, the ultimate structure of a person's every action. Its dimension is the immediate relationship with Christ, the definitive man, and, in this sense, its dimension, then, is the truth of humanity. And even though we remain inept, incapable, sinners, we yet live his new dimension, his new identity fully belonging to the communion. The "I" is no longer an "I" torn out of a given context. It becomes a "we:" every action becomes charged with a responsibility we all share, and even the most secret act has the task of edifying totality.

Thus, the sacrament is the divine which makes an appeal to our senses through the sign, becoming a presence which reaches out far beyond the limits of the sign itself. It is a presence at work in us in an ineffable way. It confers upon us our new stature as new men. And it is a unifying power because the sacrament is only given in the context of the unity of all Christians.

The saving power of Christ in the world, his "name" in the biblical sense, his capacity to change the world and people, coincide with the Christian community, the Church, as the subject and sacrament of his power.

c) In Free Personal Participation

We have seen that the sacrament indicates man's ideal structure. It expresses the new man, so the continual drawing near to it allows these supernatural connotations slowly to penetrate man. This is the metamorphosis Paul suggests when he speaks of renewal of the mind or of putting on Christ. This happens by living the life of the Christian community because it penetrates our entire fibre through the sacraments, the gestures that Christ established.

This transformation does not, however, occur mechanically. Rather, it comes through our freedom. This is to say that it only happens if man makes that act a conscious experience, by accepting its significance, by making room for it, and by allowing himself to be invested by it. Man must participate in the sacrament as a free man, in full conscience. This is why the Church teaches us that we cannot approach a sacrament if our soul is shadowed by a profound rejection of God's presence, by a sin the Church calls mortal. For since a sacrament is also prayer, it must also be a plea to God, emerging from the tiniest aperture of desire for liberation, even if we are buried in our own personal wretchedness. And what the Church calls "grave impediment" is nothing more than what tradition has identified as the hindrance to that small opening, a hindrance we ask God to remove in the sacrament of confession.

The sacrament really is the divine act of the Risen Christ who knocks on the door of our personality. He presses on it, and unless man does not want to let him in, he will stop at the threshold. And it is this bond with man's freedom of conscience that precisely distinguishes the Christian mystery from the pagan mysteries mentioned when we addressed the word *mysterion*. But it is essential for man to be free if he is to acquire the salvation conveyed by the Christian mystery. In contrast, freedom is totally extraneous to expressions of the pagan mystery, a conclusion of Hugo Rahner in his celebrated study of Greek myths. And while he demonstrates the significance of some similarities between these myths and Christian worship in the early centuries, he also highlights the basic difference: "The Church, lucidly conscious, responds to the chaos of the Hellenistic cults by saying that man is called to communion, based on faith and grace, with God made man – Jesus Christ. Because of this Christian consciousness of the sacred freedom inherent in his new vocation, Paul rejected any kind of religious servitude."[25] Christian anthropology exalts freedom and personal responsibility, while non-Christian anthropology cannot help suppressing one human factor or another. Ultimately, it tends to obscure responsibility and freedom, eventually eliminating them.

In his commentary on Clement's writings regarding some Homeric passages, Daniélou observes that Clement: "enables us to grasp the sense conveyed by the transposition from the biblical to the Homeric imagery. ... A Homeric image has been substituted for those of the Bible; but the content remains that of Scripture. A striking contrast at the level of doctrine is combined with assimilation at the level of symbolism. And this, after all, is only what the biblical editors of *Genesis* did, when they made use of a Semitic imagery borrowed from the heathenism of their day."[26] All of the similarities between the mystical cults and early Christianity often sought by scholars are based on these analogous features. However, they omit the radical anthropological contrast distinguishing the Christian experience. As Gustave Bardy observed:

The mystery religions which, in the Christian era, make rapid conquests in all environments, do not demand interior piety. The initiation rites guarantee the gift of salvation to all those who agree to be subject to them. The revelation of secrets, of the code-word to triumph over destiny or of the doctrines for knowledge of the hereafter obtain the same result.

However, he does acknowledge:

Nevertheless, it is still true that ... signs of authentic piety in the strict sense of the word are to be found. Formalism is a problem which all religions come up against at a given moment ... The formalism of the pagan religions, both Greek and Roman, did not exclude any sentiment or emotion. ... But this is not the crux of the problem for us. The emotions we mentioned are essentially transient, accompanying the religious act. When this act has been performed, they fade to a memory of no consequence. They are not capable of generating the spiritual transformation which is the stuff of conversion, which is to say, they are incapable of renewing the soul from beginning to end.[27]

In fact, it is freedom that makes the act or the emotion linked to the act, a vehicle of transformation. Freedom allows full individual participation and commits man in a nonmechanical way. It involves him in the meaning of the act, *a meaning that will go beyond the threshold of the place of worship because it is the seed of the new consciousness that will be confronting life.* And within this process, the Church makes no promises that a formula or a procedure will have an automatic outcome, for every step on the Christian way implies the change of man's will. This, again, is what Hugo Rahner has to say concerning the originality of the Christian baptismal rite:

The mystery of baptism therefore involves a continuous process of decision – and one that lasts throughout our earthly lives – between light and darkness, between Christ and Belial, between life and death.

To put the matter another way and use a metaphor much favoured by antiquity, the man who has partaken of this mystery has already made harbour in the next world and is nevertheless still upon a perilous voyage; he carries upon his soul the seal that gives him clear passage upon his heavenward journey, yet during that journey his enemies, the evil spirits, still lie in wait for him ... it is precisely at this point in the fashioning of the words and gesture of the ritual of baptism that the expression of the profoundly Christian decision which that ritual embodies, was assisted by a plenitude of excellent but extraneous things, things that came from that common territory whence many of the symbols and usages of the mystery cults are also derived. ... The redemption of man in Christ is something other than a creative fiat coming from above, and in this respect if differs from the action of creation itself. It is an act of God that includes within itself the co-operation of man, though that co-operation is itself a matter of grace and does not imply any impairment of God's sovereign power. Man was not to be merely the object of redemption but a partner therein. The descent of God was to be met by a receptive and answering "Thou," the unconstrained "Yea" of the creature: in a word, by love. ... In this sense then the

Christian ... in baptism has already been raised from the dead and become a man freed from all corruption and from the dark compulsions that prevail in the regions that are below the moon, and all through the Christian literature of antiquity one can hear the echoes of the cry of joy: "No longer are we children under compulsion from the stars."[28]

I remember that in the high school where I taught years ago there was a teacher who was a lover of the phenomena of magic. His spiritual journeying had been very dramatic and, in the end, he converted from atheism to Catholicism. One day he recounted the part his studies of magic had played in his conversion. He had begun to explore the history of Christianity in terms of magical occurrences. However, as his studies proceeded, he was forced to admit that the Christian experience incorporated answers to the needs of human nature, without bearing the limitations normally inherent in such answers. In fact, he observed, there is no doubt that the cultural dynamics bound up with esoterism or the pagan mysteries highlight one particular human need that was not secondary, and this is the need for the truth, or the divine, to become a tangible, concrete, physical experience. Man feels the need for his ideal conception of life to take concrete form in a real life experience. More-over, it is true that affection too – to name one experience common to all of us – demands tangible proof. The mere notion, the intention to love is not enough. Thus the "sacrament" obeys this natural need for something we can "feel," although in no way does it reduce my gesture to the level of mere repetition: the freedom of God and the answer of man's freedom are affirmed as essential.

Man is a composite of perceivable experience and attitudes that come from within, and both these factors must be present if humanity is to be fulfilled to the utmost in the unfolding of a given event. And Christian-ity, in making its urgent appeal to freedom of conscience, and given its concern for tangible things, responds to both these factors. Indeed, God became man by corresponding in this same way to the all-embracing need of our nature. The pursuit of every human ideal is that it might become globally incarnated, protect freedom, and become experience-able. From Moses, who cries to God: "Let me see your face," to Leopardi and the hymn he raises to the woman who matches his ideal of beauty and whom he hopes to see incarnate one day in the streets of the world, it is the human need for an all-embracing experience that clearly emerges throughout history. Corresponding to this need and surprising man with its unprecedented sovereignty, the event of the Incarnation happened and continues to happen in history, in the form of the Church, and the sacraments constitute the ingeniousness of the Chris-tian method in this regard. According to Rahner:

That which the pious genius of Hellas vaguely guessed at was ... brought home by the Church into the light of that divine revelation of which she is the guardian. ... The Church alone has retained the element of mystery: by her sacraments she has consecrated sun, moon, water, bread, wine and oil and also the love of the flesh, nor will it ever be permitted to her to cease teaching mankind that behind the veils of the visible the eternal secrets lie concealed, and that it is only through the word of God which lives on in the Church, that we can recognize the true meaning of earthly things.[29]

And Albert Houssiau, an historian of liturgy who was also a scholar of sacramental theology, made the following comments:

For primitive Christianity, the condition for membership of the Christian community is conversion ... the radical change of the whole person. ... So initiation to Christianity consisted in a single act. It did not happen by way of a series of progressive initiations. ... Liturgical symbolism is undoubtedly reminiscent of pre-existing rites but a new meaning is conferred on them. ... The symbols of Christian initiation always refer to the events of Christ, to his death and his resurrection or to his "investiture" at the moment of his baptism. It is not the uninterrupted death-life cycle: the *efapax* of Christ and of the Christian mysteries is totally extraneous to the eternal theme of the mysteries of nature. ... Although mystery vocabulary was used, there was no initiation in the mysteries. Rather it was initiation, through the mysteries, in the reality that unveils the faith.[30]

Therefore, the free conscience of the individual who believes is required not to envelop itself in automatic gestures, in repetitive suffocating cycles but to discover a reality. Moreover, we would add, this conscience's calling is to enter, with all the resources of its humanity, into profound contact with this reality.

Outwardly, this might seem paradoxical, and some objection might very well be: how can this same Christian concept, which is so intransigent and peremptory in affirming the totality of the power of God, suddenly declare itself so indissolubly linked with an anthropological vision exalting freedom? If God is all, the one truth of which all other truths are a function, what "room" does that leave for man's freedom? And surely is it not that same Catholic concept of the sacraments, whose effectiveness the Council of Trent summarized in the phrase *ex opere operato* that proposes this very automatism, whose rituality is seen as a grace-producing machine, or, in short, just another form of magic? Hugo Rahner's reply is this:

In the sacrament with its basic form fashioned by Christ ... it is Christ himself, Christ crucified and glorified, who is at work. It is because its power derives in the last resort solely from the free personal will to save of the God-man that all task of the "magical efficacy" of the sacrament remains unworthy of serious consideration – at least circumscribed meaning it bears in religious psychology.[31]

Moreover, man is also a participant in the freedom of God, because he is invited by God incarnate to participate in his reality. If God is free and he can be nothing but free, and if God's will is to communicate his divine reality to man, then he will also communicate the dimension of freedom. And he has done so since the beginnings. Again, Rahner has commented:

For man is the incarnate dialogue with God, the dialogue of which the first words are – and here is the original authority for every kind of humanism –: "Let us create man after our own image and likeness." In that moment man was given the power to answer God, but only in him who is both *anthropos* and Logos, for man can only address God in the manner in which God himself has spoken to him.[32]

While it is true that the bond between the freedom of God and the freedom of man, between the dominant, intervening initiative of God and the part played by man, is a bond, it also holds that the elements of this bond are very clear indeed. As opposed to the state of the created person in the pantheistic image, the created person in the Christian vision participates in God's primary characteristic – which is that of being himself – for the simple reason that the person derives from God, and in this way, in his dependence, the created person affirms and distinguishes himself. To understand this better, we could draw an albeit fragile comparison with artistic creation. The more powerful a person's creativity is, the more that individual's creation has, so to speak, personality. It exists, lasts, and affirms itself as time passes. This, in fact, is the characteristic of a work of art, just as everything born of God's genius and infinite power acquires an unmistakable identity of its own, for the simple reason that it participates in God.

The effectiveness of the sacramental sign (which, by our tradition, depends on the rite as such, and not on the skill of any minister) is not designed to exclude the freedom of anyone who draws near to it. Indeed, it necessarily requires man's freedom. The intention is to underscore that these signs are effective because they are a gift of God, not due to an effort of the minister or faithful; to reiterate that grace is communicated in a real encounter with Christ, which is freely desired by man.

How do misunderstandings arise in this area? Man's need for salvation is such that the easiest way would be to find some kind of "saving" mechanism that would touch him, involve him, but not depend on him. It is a need for a certainty that is easy to come by. And so we see pagan man, who, even in his most moving experiences, since he imagines himself to be dependent on a mysterious force, strives to divine its secrets so that he might use them to ensure an automatically guaranteed salvation for himself. But notwithstanding all the deviations of form possible, this is not the Church's position. In the Church, a person is wholly engaged, body and soul. His actions are free and his will is committed to transforming his entire person and entering the definitive ideal. Christianity, of course, can be reduced to a mechanism. But in asserting the constant, articulated presence in the life of man of Another who created and recreated him, the Christian message requires that man freely adhere to this presence. And it ensures the type of certainty that does not depend on any special effort or any automatism. It depends, rather, on the Other's Love.

At this point, it might seem that the hypothesis of Christian salvation is somewhat precarious, left entirely to the will of Another who requires the commitment of man's whole personality. However, nothing could be further from the truth. Salvation for the Christian means freely accepting the companionship of a merciful God who wanted to intervene and remain in history. Naturally, this is not a mechanical formula, guaranteeing a result. Like any form of love, it implies the risk of one's freedom.

d) The Answer to an Objection

In discussing freedom as a condition of grace, I always expect some objection to be raised, and it often has been in the following manner: if there is so much insistence on freedom as the necessary factor for the mystery of Christ to act, why is baptism imparted to children when they are still too young to consent freely to the profound renewal of life that comes about through this sacrament? The answer to this problem highlights not only one of the most fascinating experiences in Christian anthropology, but also concerns the Christian vision of history.

Perhaps an example will illustrate my point. Let us imagine a missionary who encounters a small child in a distant country. Could this individual seize the child, without his parents' consent and sprinkle him with holy water in baptism? Certainly not. The Church would consider this an act of grave violence. In fact, if it is not morally possible to predict that a person will be educated in the faith, it would be wrong to impart baptism unless this person were on death's door. In other words, this means that the Church conceives of a person's freedom as something deeply inscribed within a context of community, in a body. If there were not even a minimum context of a community that could educate, freedom could not act. In this, Christianity has inherited the conception of man as a profoundly social creature, a tradition which has transpired from the whole biblical tradition. However, unlike the Jews, Christianity does not categorize the individual in terms of race or an ethnic community. Rather, Christianity steers clear of any abstract affirmation of the person according to a vision of independence which, in effect, does not correspond to reality. It views man as being pro- foundly bonded to other men, and the child, dependent as he is on his parents, as emblematic in this sense. And while it is true that the child is too young to give explicit form to his capacity for freedom, he cannot be extracted from the unity into which he was born and of which he is a part, for it is precisely this communital dimension into which he was born, which allows for the development, as an educative prospect, of his capacity for freedom. This capacity for freedom in the child is a poten- tial which must have the right conditions in order to realize itself and grow. Moreover, it is also a potential which would be stunted if the conditions for growth were to exclude the inevitable and decisive community dimension. Communionality is essential for a person's development, for his education.

In baptism, in particular, the child is seen by the Church as belong- ing to the Christian community, and since he is born into communion, it is thus a point of reference for him along life's pathway. He will come to know the grace of awareness, of sensitivity, of moral conscience that God works within him. And it is for this reason that – except in the case of the portentous occasion of death – the Church only imparts baptism to children if it can be said in all moral conscience that they have the possibility of receiving education in the Christian community. Other- wise, the freedom implied would have no future.

Christianity affirms two dimensions of the person: communionality and history. The personality is formed within communion and within history. Thus, the gift that God bestows on children who receive the sacrament – the gift of himself – will not be a seed that is wasted, but a premise for growth through time, a growth made possible by the com- munity. In this sense, it is clear that the primary responsibility of com- munity life lies within the family or within an alternative or additional responsibility which the Church recognizes and affirms in the figure of the godparent, the emblem of the community, who assumes the task of educating the child.

To conclude, then, both the freedom of the community itself, which recognizes a child as belonging, as a full member in all his dignity; coupled with the future development of the child's life, lived in full awareness, safeguard the freedom imparted to children in the sacrament of baptism. A faith which is convinced and, therefore, authentic and worthy of the dignity of man, implies that the whole of the personality is unified by the truth and the reality in which a person believes. In fact, the word "conviction" derives from *cum-vincere* which means "bonding." The existence of a person who believes must be bonded as one with the object of his faith, for man is only himself when he is convinced, enlightened, and reaching out for his goal. Only in conviction does he grasp his truth as man. However, for such a conviction to be viable, all the factors that will generate a person's self-realization must work together. In particular, there must be the cooperation of the most imposing factor of all for the development of a person in the direction of his self-realization – the communional dimension, which takes active form, in the patience of time.

e) The Sacrament as Prayer

I would like to mention a beautiful implication of the sacramental factor before leaving the point of the divine reality's self-communication in the Church. Contrary to what many people think, the sacrament is the simplest form of prayer, the form to which everyone can relate. Yet it is commonly thought that it is easier for the person who prays to entrust himself to an immediate, off-the-cuff way of praying – his own spontaneity. This, however, is by definition, precarious because a change of mood – a distraction either melancholic or arid – induces man to forego prayer. It unhinges that attitude of asking which is the supreme expression of man's consciousness.

Let me explain what I mean with this example. Imagine a small agricultural community at the turn of the century where the need for social justice has just begun to make itself felt. A "leader" identifies some grievances against the landowner, his employer, and at a certain point, he is delegated to go to the town and confront the boss. None of the workers has ever been to what must have seemed a great metropolis and, after putting on a show of euphoria at the very idea in front of his mates, who would have given him a hearty and noisy send-off, the delegate feels apprehension creeping over him on his journey. He arrives in the town, and almost forces himself to begin his odyssey and look for the employer's address. He gets lost once, twice, three times before at last he finds the boss's office. He asks to see him and there he stands, before the boss. But all the arguments he has so painstakingly formulated with his workmates cloud over in his mind. He knows he is there for a good reason. He knows and personally espouses the whole cause. However, he just cannot utter a word. So was all the effort – his and his workmates' – just a waste of time? Of course not. His presence there, which was such a rare thing in the whole course of relations between that boss and his workers at that time, had not been futile even though he was unable to articulate what he had come to say. The presence of this man, fumbling, stuttering, standing there twiddling his hat, is still the act of asking. It is a presence which can yet be defined as "asking," and the request is not abstract.

So it is with the sacrament. It does not demand the ability to reflect, to find the right words, to have emotions adequate to the occasion. The catechism in its acute conciseness expressed this well when, for example, it clarified that receiving the Eucharist requires: "knowing and thinking of Him you are about to receive," which means being conscious of the meaning of the Great Presence. A person, then, could still fulfil this act even with a soul brimming with resentment, exasperation, with a cold heart and a blocked mind. What counts is that we freely "approach," that we put ourselves in a position of asking. What matters is our presence before Christ, our conscious presence, which is an act of asking, just like that young farm worker who stood there, tongue-tied, before his boss.

We cannot perceive and experience the operative content of these mysterious gestures, or sacraments by which in the Church the new creature is edified and enriched. All we see of the sacrament is the act we fulfil. If, then, we had to entrust ourselves to the expression of our feeling in order to live our relationship with Christ, we would be prey to emotional ups and downs. However, because the sacramental sign, in contrast, is solidly anchored to its own objective physiognomy, and the Church calls man's attention to this, when man stands before the Great Presence being communicated to him, he responds with his own free presence which is asking for new life. This is the form of prayer most adequate to our nature as individuals, and therefore the simplest in its objectivity.

I believe it is appropriate here to emphasize another aspect of this dynamic of "presence": God leads the world to its total fulfillment by means of the condition the Old Testament calls "election," a mysterious process through which his grace, his word passes. It is the great design by which God's plan unfolds and engages those whom the Father calls. So man's presence at the sacramental act, lived as a prayer, as asking, consecrates his being chosen to be a presence in the history of the world. We must emphasize that the act of an individual drawing near to the sacrament is not a question of pietism. No, it is the participation of a man's life history in God's plan, an individual history within the history of the world, which, in Christ, has already reached its fulfill-ment. And it cannot be denied that the event of Christ has already proven to be so very charged with humanity. How clearly Christ's victory can already be seen! The act of going to receive the sacraments is, first and foremost, the affirmation of Christ's glory, through our presence, our mendicant presence. This formula indicates the good that humanity derives in history from the death and resurrection of Christ, an anticipation of the ultimate glory, of the ultimate happiness. This affirmation reminds us of that phrase in the Gospel so often cited, when Jesus promises those who follow him "the hundredfold on earth" (cf. Matt. 19:29), an abundant measure of life – "glory."

And here we are reminded of Paul's words also often quoted: "What-ever you eat, then, or drink, and whatever else you do, do it all for the glory of God" (1 Cor. 10:31). This is the mark of the Christian con-science – the glory of God in all things, Christ ever-present to man in all things and man ever-present to Christ. It is the type of consciousness no religious experience has ever offered or could ever claim, that touches the very consistency, not of an act or a moment, but of every act and every moment, and as such should invest every action of every day. This is the implication of the sacrament.

Of all acts, the sacrament is the most gratuitous because the only reason for the sacramental act is to affirm the death and resurrection of Christ as the meaning of life and history. It is significant, for example, that in the liturgy of marriage we pray: "God, may they live in their lives, the sacrament they celebrate in the faith." What do we mean when we celebrate marriage as a sacrament? It is as if the couple were saying to each other: "Look, what brought us together was mutual attraction, mutual love, favourable circumstances making us of like mind, body, and soul. But all of this was the discreet declination of the method Christ used to gather us up within his redeeming action. And our unity is more profound, since it has been placed in the perspective of a task that God has given us to do, as a sign that we belong to him in Jesus Christ." Therefore, to live in our life what is celebrated by the sacrament is to base our unity not on grounds of affection or convenience, fragile instruments of that plan, but on God's plan for the world.

Man recognizes through every sacrament, what Christ is. He affirms Christ's glory and bears witness to it before the world, continually proclaiming, in his every hour, with his own present and imploring hu-manity, that perennial source of divine energy.

It must be acknowledged that even for Christians, it is not easy to be ever-mindful of these values inherent in the sacramental gestures.

Through these acts, we are called to recognize the objective meaning of a totalizing value which tends to be censored. How easy it is for us to think that something is valuable "because everybody does it." How easy it is to flounder about in pursuit of a certain fact of life given by public opinion, according to what society decrees as legitimate. In the sacrament, the Church is asking us to affirm the completeness of our act of faith which unity with Christ implies. And as time goes by, grace – that ontological exaltation which baptism generates – shows its efficacy. It begins to build a different conscience in man, the protagonist of that new world to which all human reality aspires and which has already begun with the resurrection of Christ. This man's journey has the life of the Christian community as a visible sign, as a sacrament, as the place where the resurrection, in some way, becomes experience.

Verifying the Presence of the Divine in the Life of the Church

9 The Locus of Verification: Human Experience

Now that we have reached the final stage of our journey, let us retrace our path thus far so that we may address the crucial question that stems from it.

We have illustrated the substance of man's religious sense, its perennial structural dimensions, and its possible declensions, and we have encountered the historical fact of Christ, the incredible announcement of God made man, who entered the history of a humanity pervaded by the longing to see the divine revealed. Moreover, we have asked ourselves: how can such a fact be drawn upon 2000 years later, in such a way as to make it the basis for such an inherently serious decision?

The Christian message announces the permanence of the fact of Christ, as a continuous happening – not something that happened once – but as something that still happens. This is the Christian message indicating the visible, historical face of the Church, which is the people of God from the social point of view and the Body of Christ from the profound, ontological point of view. This is the way in which the Church emerges in history as a phenomenon. It is a community conscious of its exceptional origin, an integral part of life, inherent in the flesh and blood of life. It is a gift from above, which is the Spirit – the energy with which Christ invests history. It is a newness of life, or communion. The profound need for change in human history solicits an ideal, a universal through which everything in human life flows into a unity. Here, this universal is held up and affirmed as the ontological starting point, and therefore, becomes the motive for and source of ethical value, the reason for moral dynamism and the building of a new world, the basis for a different human reality.

We have also noted, however summarily, the terms of the type of self-awareness which this new phenomenon acquired. The Church is perfectly conscious that it is a human reality and so, by definition, it cannot be surprised nor scandalized by the faults it will always be found to have; it is also equally aware that in the midst of all the magma, one must seek – and one finds – the pure gold of truth, the pure gold of definitive reality, of the humanity of the new creature reborn, in grace. This eschatological term indicates something already begun at a precise time and which will appear in all its fullness at the end of time.

And so we come to the question: does all of this, the fullness and peremptory nature of this claim, correspond to the truth? The Church's identity as a phenomenon is unmistakable, but is the message, by whose virtue it claims to have a dimension totally beyond the realms of its verifiable nature as a phenomenon, true or not? Is the Church truly the prolongation of Christ in time and space? Is it the place and sign of his presence? Is the perpetually unfolding event of the Man-God now inevitably present in the world until the end of time?

Firstly, we must clarify the criteria we will use to answer these questions.

I WHAT THE CHURCH DEMANDS AS THE CRITERION OF JUDGMENT

In continuing what Jesus did in his earthly life, the Church addresses our humanity as it is. But its maternal embrace of things human, like the gaze and the acts of the Redeemer, are aimed at sparking in man the most original stirrings of his heart. Like Jesus, the Church makes an appeal to that capacity of man which we called elementary experience, the essential component of the religious sense, the "complex of needs and evidences ... with which the human being reaches out to reality, seeking to become one with it. He does this by fulfilling a project that dictates to reality itself the ideal image that stimulates him from within."[1]

This means that the Church proposes to enter into the drama of the universal comparison to which man is projected when he parallels any element of reality with the elementary experience constituting his heart. The challenge the Church launches can be summarized in this way: it bets on man, so to speak, hypothesizes that the message which it brings will be sifted by man's elementary experience and will reveal the wondrous presence. It also believes that the answer the message holds for the needs of the human heart will be unforeseeably and incomparably greater and truer than the fruit of any other hypothesis.

By entering into this drama of the man who compares everything with his elementary experience, the Church stresses that it is this very experience of man it is addressing and not the masks of humanity which dominate the various forms of society in a vain attempt to cover man's real face or replace his nature with something else. In an essay on the relation between religious experience and the nihilism of the modern world, Bernhard Welte made the following comments:

Despite the immediacy of the factor of experience, it is not at all easy or obvious to recognize true experience and distinguish it from forms of human life which come close to but do not constitute experiences proper. In fact, it is partly true that the immediacy of what we experience is often confused with what might be called public opinion and it can easily happen that there are no clear demarcation lines between the two. In this case, the things that happen come almost inadvertently closer to hearsay pure and simple and this is nearly always completely devoid of experience of any kind. But it is true to say that the immediacy of real experiences is often hidden and repressed and although they are definitely there, they are no longer felt or else they are totally ignored.

This German philosopher of religion adds:

When for purely conformist reasons we simply accept or repeat opinions or expressions taken from the social context in which we all live ... then the immediacy of the fact itself is annulled. Indeed, it does not even take form. So everything comes via something else. Just the words remain and they no longer testify to any experience.[2]

As we already said in the first volume of this trilogy, this is why the complete man, equipped with a critical sense and capable of global judgment, will be the man who has "trained" himself to compare everything with the bundle of profound needs which constitute the core of his true "I," a core uncensored by outside intervention. This is, within Christian tradition, an ascetic task, its reflective element serving "to discover the primary elements often hidden in the depths of our being and ... it therefore serves the immediacy we call experience. In this sense, reflection is not taking the place of immediacy that is no longer there. Rather, it serves to discover immediacy, which is only blocked, repressed or confused. It serves to distinguish it and render it visible in the mists of everyday uncertainties."[3]

It is then, with this supreme critical sense, to be sought and won over and over again, that the Church wishes to measure up, placing itself at the mercy of authentic human experience. It leaves its message to the actuation of our hearts' original criteria. It does not require certain conditions to be mechanically respected. Rather, it entrusts itself to the judgment of our experience and, indeed, it constantly urges that experience walk its path in completeness. Thus does Henri de Lubac warn us: "'Ah, I beg it of you ... Christ would never have said such a thing if he had known how badly it would have been abused' (Tolstoy, *Anna Karenina*). This could be said of every phrase in the whole Gospel both because of the use made of them and because they do not sound "good" to human wisdom. This notwithstanding, *Jesus did say those words*. Let us be careful not to abuse them. But, on the other hand, let us not be persuaded that there is any abuse when those same words wound us and strike us in the heart."[4] And, in this context, the word "heart" is used in its most meaningful, biblical sense, for in Old Testament vocabulary:

The heart's main task is not to represent human sentiment. In contrast to what we always say, it is the spirit which is the seat of feeling while the heart is more the seat of our thinking and judgment. "Heartless" means being unreasonable and lacking in understanding (cf Jer 5:21 etc.). ... [The heart] is the seat of intuition and volition, of our memory of the past and of our planning for the future. It unites our observation and understanding of a fact and our decision-making. ... The heart determines man's exterior and interior conduct. If heart-searching means talking "to ourselves" ... then, in our hearts, we might well adopt a certain position regarding ourselves. ... So the watchword is: keep your heart with all vigilance, for from it flows the springs of life! (Prov 4:23).[5]

2 ON THE USE OF A CRITERION OF JUDGMENT IN ITS UTMOST EXPRESSION

Not only is the criterion of verification through experience, to which the Church wants to submit itself, that of man's original experience, adulterated as little as possible by the false needs induced by the social context. The Church repeats with Jesus that it can be recognized as credible because of its correspondence to man's elementary needs in their most authentic flourishing. This is what Jesus meant by the expression we have already cited, by that promise to his disciples of a "hundredfold" on this earth, and it is as if the Church is also telling man: "With me, an experience of fullness of life that you will not find elsewhere will be yours." It is on the razor-edge of this promise that the Church puts itself to the test, proposing itself to all men as the prolongation of Christ.

After all, is it not true that each one of us, even in the simplest of our daily tasks, seeks just that: greater fulfillment? This is the criterion that guides us even in the least important of our choices. Men accept this or that invitation. They choose to be with this or that person because, in making their choices, they hope for more satisfaction, more intense correspondence with their heart's desire. And since freedom is the power of adhering to the object of our aspirations, man who is made for happiness, steers his free dynamism in pursuit of what Saint Augustine referred to as the "greater fascination." And this means an ever greater fullness of life, ever more total possession of being.

Now, within the history of humanity, the Church proclaims that its only concern is to bring man's supreme yearning to fulfillment without asking him to forget any of his own very real desires or his own elementary needs. Rather, it promises him a result superior to his own powers of imagination – the hundredfold.

Having staked everything on this bet, century after century, the Church cannot deceive. As it emerges from a study of the history of God's revelation in the world, it is already clear, from the time of the people of Israel and their experience, that in revealing itself, God's pedagogy has never shied away from a critical approach. According to Claude Tresmontant:

God did not ask the prophets to believe, and he did not ask the Israelites to believe what the prophets were saying without first discerning and being critical, purely for the sake of the credulity factor. God asked the prophets to believe him because he affected verifiable demonstrations of all that he said – not demonstrations of the type carried out in some secret laboratory but demonstrations out in the open, before the eyes of everyone, in history. This type of demonstration is what the Bible calls *signs*. God gives signs and asks that these signs be read, interpreted and understood. God does not ask the people to believe just any prophet. On the contrary, he provides them with a rule of discernment for distinguishing the false from the true prophet – he whose words come true in history. He is the true prophet.[6]

Nothing is haphazard about this bold challenge launched by the Church. It turns the whole question over to our experience as human beings and goes on to promise, as the Lord did, an experience of fullness unthinkable to our normal existence.

3 OPENNESS OF HEART

For us – just as for those who knew Jesus 2,000 years ago, for the Pharisee or Zachaeus, the publican, the Samaritan woman or Simon, the leper, for those who crucified him or those who grieved for his death, for him who, scornfully nailed the crucifixion order on the cross, just as for him who took pains to lay him in a suitable tomb – for us and for all of these people, the problem of verifying such a far-reaching claim must have as its starting point an "encounter," a physical presence. And the Church is this physical presence: it cannot cheat in making its proposal. It cannot just hand over a book and a series of formulas to exegetes for it is life, and it must offer life, and it must enfold the experience of men deep within the embrace of its claim.

But neither can man attempt to make such a portentous verification without a commitment that engages his entire life. Nor can he reach the end of the journeying that will assure him of the credibility of all the Church proclaims, without first being willing to make a commitment. If the Church presents itself as life, a fully human life charged with the divine, then man must commit his life to be sure of the truth of the challenge. And he will not be able to encounter the truth – of whether the Church's promises are true or not – unless he starts out from what the Church is today, near him. If the Church cannot cheat, then neither can man. Man's prospect is true journeying, but his heart must be willing.

Nothing can predict the steps man will take and the faces he will meet along the way. Christianity, which affirms an incarnate God, has precisely this characteristic. Just as someone might wake up in the morning to find that a husband, a son, a brother has unexpectedly changed their attitude to people or things, so then – if I may make this comparison – God also presents himself in the life story of each one of us by means of the real and changeable face of the community, which nevertheless claims to perpetuate his presence in history.

The minimum requirement for starting out on this journey is the type of willingness to make a commitment that Christian tradition calls poverty of spirit. In his commentary on the first chapters of the *Confessions of Saint Augustine*, Romano Guardini writes:

Then come the immortal words: "since you created us for yourself, and our heart is restless until it finds repose in you." In these words, the Augustinian concept of man touches its deepest core. Man is placed by the Creator inside the realms of true being. He is authorized to keep to his own heart and to press on at his own pace. But his reality is different from that of other creatures. They are rooted in their own natures. Their foundation is self and to self they will always return. The symbol of their existence is the circle which closes on itself, while man's symbol, in contrast, is the arc curving beyond all he encounters, each time he makes an encounter in the world, especially when he encounters another person, "you," and in the final analysis this is the "you" within which God has placed himself for man's sake ... This is the law of his existence and the proof is a profound uneasiness which never calms. It might be misunderstood, but it cannot be banished and when man realizes this it becomes a torment. When he accepts it, it leads him on to the essence of calm, to the fulfilment of his being.[7]

It is precisely this acceptance of the law of existence that the Gospel calls poverty, this willingness to stretch the string of one's bow to reach out, not to self but to another. It might also be referred to as the search for greater richness, although its dynamics rest on that other immortal phrase of Jesus': "Anyone who wants to save his life will lose it; but anyone who wants to lose his life for my sake, will save it" (Luke 9:24). For the focal point of this attitude of acceptance, of poverty of spirit, is a trained eye on all that constitutes the treasure of man, on that gold of a truth and reality so pure that any other image of truth and reality, even our own lives, is humbly recognized as having less value.

To conclude, I would like to reiterate that beginning on the pathway of verification with an open, willing spirit holds the promise of existential fulfillment which the Church declares it can obtain, over and above or in the face of any other proposal. But, naturally, this fullness – the Gospel's "hundredfold" – is just the dawning of the totality. The totality is immeasurably more than we can possibly imagine: it is the "hundredfold." But this hundredfold is the sign that the totality is approaching. It is a hidden sign which makes totality manifest. However, unless he lives this experience, man will never be convinced.

It is worthwhile quoting here the liturgical prayer of the twentieth Mass of Ordinary Time: "God, you who have prepared invisible good things for those who love you, fill us with the sweetness of your love because, by loving you in all things and above all things, we will obtain the good things you promised and which are beyond all desire."

10 "The Tree Can Be Told By Its Fruit"

If, then, the Church is life, we must involve our lives with it in order to judge it. It is primarily a question of living our life with the life of the Church wherever that life is authentically lived, wherever it is seriously lived. This is why the Church proclaims the saints: to indicate how, by means of the most disparate temperaments, in the most variegated historical and social circumstances, with the most divergent of cultural tendencies, it is possible to live the Christian proposal in a serious way. And it is for this reason, too, that the Church, by giving its approval, tends also to prompt associations, movements, and places not only for worship, but also as meeting points. For the conviction which should animate such places of life – if they are lived for what they really are – can impart what a true Christian experience is, a true experience which, however, should always be verifiable wherever there are Christians: in schools, factories, homes, districts, parishes, or wherever, the presence of Christians is called to be seen by the eyes of the world to be participating in the sacrament of salvation. This is to say that they are called to be seen to be a tool for the power of Christ to work in history.

If, having lived all its experiences in a serious way, the Church truly is the continuation of Christ, then we should be able to pinpoint the characteristics that make it effective. The Gospel reminds us of these words of Jesus: "Make a tree sound and its fruit will be sound; make a tree rotten and its fruit will be rotten. For the tree can be told by its fruit" (Matt. 12:33). And on another occasion Jesus said: "You will be able to tell them by their fruits. Can people pick grapes from thorns, or figs from thistles? In the same way, a sound tree produces good fruit but a rotten tree bad fruit. A sound tree cannot bear bad fruit, nor a rotten tree bear good fruit" (Matt 7:16–18).

From the patrimony of Christian tradition, we can distinguish *four categories* of the "fruits" of Christ's presence in the life of the Church: unity, holiness, catholicity, and apostolicity. They are the features of the Church's effectiveness on human life and history and it is through them that Christ continues his action in history. These categories are like the features of the Church's profile, the "distinguishing marks" of its divine value and the Church reminds us of them in every Eucharistic celebration when we recite the Creed, the profession of faith which gained ground in both eastern and western liturgy, after the Councils of Nicaea and Constantinople in the fourth century: "I believe in one, holy, Catholic, and apostolic Church."

I UNITY

When we say "I believe in one ... Church" we are not just affirming our faith in the one Catholic Church. We are also expressing a belief in unity, a fundamental verifiable dimension in the experience of the Church, verifiable because it is the great evidence of what the Church enables us to live. Unity is the principal characteristic of anything that lives, and the dogma of the one triune God introduces us once again to what a life which is consciously lived cannot but evoke. According to Henri de Lubac:

Our reliance on dogma enables us in turn to strengthen and to amplify the initial suggestions furnished by our consideration of experience. Unity is in no way confusion, any more than distinction is separation. For does not distinction imply a certain connection, and by one of the most living bonds, that of a mutual attraction? True union does not tend to dissolve into one another the beings that it brings together, but to bring them to completion by means of one another. ... "Distinguish in order to unite," it has been said, and the advice is excellent, but on the ontological plane the complementary formula, unite in order to distinguish, is just as inevitable.[1]

On the other hand, this characteristic unitary vitality we are called to verify comes directly from what Jesus revealed to us of his nature, and also from what he asked of us in terms of our participation in his Presence, particularly in the Last Supper. Christian tradition has always solemnly remembered the words of Jesus recorded in the Gospel of John, usually called Jesus' prayer at the Last Supper, although much of his message was anticipated the following farewell discourses to his disciples. "May they all be one, just as, Father, you are in me and I am in you, so that the world may believe it was you who sent me" (John 17:21). And in the first part of the prayer he had said: "Keep those you have given me true to your name, so that they may be one like us" (John 17:11b). As Rudolf Schnackenburg observes: "The petitions that the disciples should be kept and sanctified and the desire for their unity come together in the one great intention, that the community of disciples ... should continue in the divine sphere revealed to them by Jesus."

He also observes that: "As long as Jesus stayed with the disciples, he was their bond of unity, but now, after his departure, they are to preserve this unity, because it is the sign and expression of the divine being."

Schnackenburg continues to note that this unity, in fact is "a unity of the kind that exists between the Father and Jesus himself." And he concludes that these words at the Last Supper deal with:

The foundation of divine unity that is manifested and effective in love. ... The unity existing between Jesus and the Father is not only the fundamental model for the unity that should exist among believers – it is the basis for making it possible in their lives. Any explanation that points simply to external harmony, reunion or 'horizontal' oneness is inadequate. The unity to which this text refers is based on God himself and his love. It is a unity that penetrates believers 'from above' and also impels them to be one in brotherly love.[2]

a) Unity of Conscience

Seen from this perspective, unity proves its "fruit-bearing" fertility firstly if it manifests itself as unity of conscience, this is to say, if it appears as a simplicity uniting our perception, feeling, and judgment of life. This is what the individual who seeks with righteousness must be able to find in the Church – proven clarity of the meaning of existence, such that the principle behind our judgment of ourselves and the world is the one unequivocal Presence.

And here lies the genius of the Catholic vision of life. In order to safeguard its unitary formation, the divine in the Church has no need to deny anything. Its very attitude is unity. It looks for the good in all things. It is scandalized by nothing. This is to say that the Church can be certain that it does not have to overlook or renege on any point in order to be faithful to its origins. As the apostle John taught: "For this is how God loved the world: he gave his only Son, so that everyone who believes in him may not perish but may have eternal life. For God sent his Son into the world not to judge the world, but so that through him the world might be saved" (John 3:16-17).

The Church's inner unity of vision derives from its simplicity in adhering to its mission, a mission of salvation which requires not any kind of abstract synthesis, but maternal care. As Guardini exclaims: "That stupendous Fact that is the Church is once more becoming a living reality, and we understand that she truly is the One and the All."[3] It is also a unity of attitude which clashes with all potential forms of compartimentalized thinking, from dualism – that insurmountable temptation to which any culture can fall prey – to divisions which lead to theories of dissolution. The Church is called to affirm and to demonstrate that the value of an action lies in the degree of its connection with totality. That is why a clear criterion is such as the one transpiring from Jesus' words, is needed: "I am the way, the truth and the life" (John 14:6a). As Schnackenburg has commented:

Jesus' answer sounds like an extremely important revelation, a unique statement that has lost none of its sovereign power even now ... "the way" is, in itself, an unusual metaphor to apply to a person, but its meaning is made clearer by the additional statement that "the truth" and "the life" are also incorporated into that person. It almost sounds like a justification, but it is really a clarification: "I am the way, that is, the truth and the life" for everyone who wants to reach that goal. In other words, by revealing the truth that leads to life and mediating that true life to the one who accepts and realizes that truth in faith, Jesus takes everyone who believes in him to the goal of his existence, that is, "to the Father"; in this manner, he becomes the "way."][4]

This word is of the utmost certainty. It is destined to sum up man's whole existence in a unitary attitude. It is also the bearer of a profound possibility of *peace*. Hans Urs von Balthasar commented:

With his incarnation Christ ... broke down the dividing wall between heaven and earth ... Thus for the redeemed all reason for fear is banished: nor can the world, which when Christ came rose up against Him ... but was conquered by Him (Jn 16:33), harm the Christian in any way, just as none of those "worldly elements" according to Paul can be reason for anxiety whatever their dimension. ... Even the last of the enemies to be done away with – death – has been won in this victory (1 Cor 15:26). Anxiety has fled, banished once and for all and not just juridically speaking, by law, but in an essential, substantial way for those who belong to Christ. Such a person *has the power* to be afraid no longer, in that he has the life of the faith. His bad conscience, which makes him tremble, has been overtaken and placed in submission by the "peace of God which is beyond our understanding" (Phil 4:7).[5]

Naturally, this peace, which derives from the certain criterion on which the meaning of existence and the bonds of all things with totality are built, neither contradicts struggle nor shelters us from it. It does not offer a quiet life free of a tension. Again Balthasar remarks:

In asking man to follow Christ, the Church always demands more of him than, by his nature, he can give. Christianity as a whole (as the Church presents Christianity to men and personifies it on their behalf) will always and rightfully appear to them to constitute an excessive claim, excessive tension and, therefore, the threat of destruction for natural man, his laws and measures. But is not this the Church's very goal, that man will dare go beyond his nature in the faith, that in living he try again and again to take this great leap forward? ... This is the paradox of the Church but it was already the paradox of the Incarnation of God ... and yet it is immediately resolved if in faith we think how openhearted the Son of Man was towards the Father and if we consider that all the Church's "instruments of grace" seek only to hold and convey the nearness of our reachless God and his love.[6]

This paradox of peace is beyond comparison, the one antidote to the exasperation of human anxiety when it becomes desperation. And this, in its turn, is the consequence of the tormented wrangling generated by the absence of any point of reference constructive in existential terms. Because of the sublime simplicity of its nature, which censors nothing, this paradox also eludes the Pharisaic attempt into which man is constantly drawn by his anxiety to find some theoretical justification for a way to live his life. The result of this cannot be peace but, at most, a harsh, unbalanced imperturbability.

b) Unity as the Explanation of Reality

In coming into contact with things, with events, with men, this unity of conscience is such that it tends to encompass all it meets, in a way that is open to all possibilities and appropriate to every encounter. And because it tends to be open, it therefore reaches out to find the link bonding all things with their root. For as Saint Paul taught: "Everything there is comes from him and is caused by him and exists for him" (Rom. 11:36b).

And this is how Hugo Rahner refers to how the Christian can bring out the good in every value of ancient culture:

There lies the wonderful certitude of the Christian which resolves all that is tragic in this uncertain life, for, in truth, all has already ended happily in a new beginning that has all the freshness of youth. And because this is so, the Christian can already gaze backwards as one of the blessed and can see all earthly things transfigured and love them as such. For all the things of this world that we really love ... already belong to his "new earth." The whole of creation has become his mystery.[7]

And the same can be said of the Christian's gaze on any element of humanity that comes within his range of vision or of any encounter the circumstances of his life might place on his path. His unitary criterion for interpreting reality is not some intellectual principle. It is a person, and this makes him especially able to meet even with apparently distant realities. He is called not to be shaken, but to affirm those he meets, tirelessly yearning to bring out the best in them. He is called to know how to be enriched by these encounters, just as a healthy body with all the potency of an organic unity is enriched by a genuine personality. As John wrote: "You must see what great love the Father has lavished on us by letting us be called God's children – which is what we are" (1 John 3:1a)! And, in fact, the Christian personality is a true personality, which participates in the divine. Again in the words of John: "Children, our love must be not just words or mere talk, but something active and genuine. This will be the proof that we belong to the truth, and it will convince us in his presence, even if our own feelings condemn us, that God is greater than our feelings and knows all things" (1 John 3:18-19). The mark of participation such as this is the certainty that we are in the hands of someone who is truly great, truly understanding. This is the root which, in this unity of mature conscience, becomes *unity of understanding and all-inclusiveness*. It becomes a *cultural* attitude and principle within which we may experience the *new*.

Life as novelty is experienced much more when something awaited actually happens, rather than in the change wrought between a present and a past. Even in cultural terms this novelty in life is experienced when we discover that there is correspondence, and this is only possible if there has been a "forerunner" – of hope, desire, expectation, need. In this case, the new is the fulfilment of that hope, the satisfaction of that desire, and the answer to that expectation. For the Christian, the new does not lie in change as such, but in the transformation set in motion by the application of this unitary principle of inclusiveness, for which the whole creation "is mystery." As Romano Guardini observes:

True research is guided by an image and its form is a lacking and a need. In reality, we may only seek what our desire has already anticipated so that, more profoundly, real discovery is taking possession and so, also, at the moment of true encounter the feeling is that things "had" to happen the way they did. But what if our research is erroneous? ... In that case, the error will come to light if the living soul is living sincerely. To the degree that one is serious in one's pursuit of life, the truth itself will ensure that it stands out from error. By the enlightening force of life even things clouded by confusion will become clear. ... Acts distinct one from the other and acts that follow one another only ever exist in relation to secondary things and for only a short time. But with the essential, one act sustains another and all of them sustain each other reciprocally; in fact, what counts is the totality of our existence, which is at once given and imposed, and in this state all things are closely linked.[8]

It is from a basis of this "linkage," meant as unity of cultural value, that man is educated to true, critical maturity. Paul gave admirable expression to this in his letter to the Thessalonians: "Test everything and hold on to what is good" (1 Thess. 5:21).

By virtue of the roots from which it draws life, the Church, then, is able to proffer a critical capacity that cannot be found elsewhere. In fact, within the Church nothing is extraneousness, neither people nor things: of itself, it demands an openness to all things, the capacity to become one even with those who are hostile, a sense of forgiveness, all the way to an awareness of the victory over death.

c) Unity as a Way of Life

As we have said, according to the tradition of the Church, there is no thought, however secret, no gesture however insignificant, and no action, however hidden that is not responsible for the universe, that is not an act of eternal value. In theology, this is the thinking behind the concept of "merit." So in every tiny detail, life is given value by the grace of God that allows man to collaborate with his presence in the saving action of his community. In this way, every gesture acquires a communital dimension: action is the phenomenon of the personality, the motive is this profound bond with the presence of Christ in the world. Thus the community becomes the source for the affirmation of the personality, while the Church attributes value – "merit" – to the proportion between Christ's "glory" and the acts of an individual, that is, to the degree that the communital mystery becomes a lived motive. Every gesture, therefore, has eternal value in that it is a gesture responsible for the destiny of the world, in that it is an expression of the individual which becomes a decisive factor for the whole meaning of the universe.

Within this unity of lifestyle, the mystery of communion becomes a factor that determines the community's sense of self. This is to say that it is the originator of its own actions and the form its personality takes. This is a way of life that exalts even the most infinitesimal expressions of the personality. Romano Guardini aptly warns us that this affirmation could seem paradoxical to the mind of modern man: "We must never forget that individualism is perceiving a contradiction, an *aut-aut*, when, in reality, it is structured reciprocity. The more my life is firmly lived within the Church, the more fullness I will have to bring, to be what I must be. But I can only live within the Church, as God and the Church itself require, to the degree that I am mature, mindful of the call of my vocation, and that I have become a personality moulding reality and endowing itself with that reality: one within the other and because of Another."[9]

Never have life and personal responsibility been given so much value than in this vision of man and community.

Physical nature is also assumed into this unity of personality and community, and the supreme paradigm of this is the Church's *liturgy*. Let us listen again to Guardini:

The liturgy throughout reality. It is this which distinguishes it from all purely intellectual or emotional piety, from rationalism and religious romanticism. In it man is confronted with physical realities – men, things, ceremonies, ornaments – and with metaphysical realities – a real Christ, real grace. ... Thus the liturgy embraces everything in existence, ... all the content and events of life. ... Creation as a whole embraced in the relation with God established by prayer; the fulness of nature, evoked and transfigured by the fulness of grace, organized by the organic law of the Triune God, and steadily growing according to a rhythm perfectly simple yet infinitely rich; the vessel and expression of the life of Christ and the Christian – this is the liturgy. The liturgy is creation, redeemed and at prayer.[10]

One of Saint Ambrose's matins hymns features an admirable expression of this praying nature and of liturgy, lived as the redemption of time and space through the consciousness of the new personality.

Hear our praise
O Creator eternal of things,
who, in the night that follows day, makes
time more varied and thankful.

The night is in full dark reign
and already the cock's crowing can be heard,
that glorious presage of light
for the anxiety of the wayfarer.

Then comes the waking hour and in the east appears
the twinkling star of the morning,
the swarm of vagabonds slips away
deserting the alleys of evil.

The cock crows. Its voice calms
the furious crash of the wave;
and Peter, rock foundation of the Church,
washes his sin with bitter tears.

Up, rise up, full of life and ready:
the cock's call wakes the world
accusing the indolent of tardiness
by continuing to sleep under their blankets.

The cock crows. Hope returns:
The sick man feels life flowing back,
The villain hides his dagger,
in the lost, faith lives again.

Lord Jesus, look on us with pity
when, tempted and uncertain, we waver:
your gaze on us wipes away our stains
and sin melts in our weeping.

You, true light, shine in hearts,
banish the torpor of the soul :
untie the tongue devoted to you
for the holy first-fruit of song.

The echo of the liturgy, of the mystery lived throughout our day is the Christian conception of *work*, the expansion of the mystery of salvation in every moment of our lives and in every activity within the context of our personal roles and circumstances.

Work is man's attempt to invest time and space with himself, his plans, his ideas. For Christianity, human work represents the gradual beginnings of man's dominion over things, of a governance to which he aspires by realizing the image of God, "the Lord." Physical reality was originally the instrument for the Spirit's self-realization in a transparent way, directly orientated towards its aim. For Christian tradition, reality became ambiguous and so also the instrument which obstructs the expression of the Spirit in the wake of the illusion that man could be autonomous (original sin). However, Jesus Christ is the moment of history in which reality ceases to be ambiguous, gloriously becoming a bridge to God once again. Jesus Christ is the point in which history and the universe resume their true meaning. Moreover, the Christian community continues this redemption, and we have seen, how, in the sacraments, reality constitutes a pure bridge to God, in that in the sacraments, reality contains its meaning and bestows what it promises. In the liturgy, therefore, matter once again becomes a friend to man, the work of redemption develops, and the universe returns to its origin.

Everything else remains ambiguous to us, including ourselves. But the more we immerse ourselves in the sacramental gesture, the more we feel borne towards that moment in time when human beings will be in their rightful place in the world once more, when they will be before God, and happy. This has already happened in history, and it will happen again for us. It occurred at the moment of Christ's Resurrection and to such a degree that physical laws ceased definitively to be an obstacle to him, becoming instead the simple perpetual instrument of proof of his presence. But this is a prophecy of what will happen for all of us at the end, in the resurrection of the body.

Now, man's collaboration in the work of the community, which communicates Christ's redemptive action through the sacraments, is work. In its slow, weary striving, work is the price man pays for his redemption. It is a collaboration to bring about the ever-brightening dawn of the Resurrection to all the creative relationships that man lives with time and space. In the Christian man's conception, work is the still dusky reflection of the liturgy on the whole cosmos. But, by the operative grace of God's Plan, work fills the space between Christ's resurrection and the final resurrection.

Work is a road signposted all the way along by the proof of God's presence, which the tradition of the Church calls *miracles*. A miracle is the ideal paradigm for man's weary effort in work: it is the prophecy of the final outcome. By miracle, we do not mean here that exceptional something which seems to defy the laws of nature. No, we mean the daily reality which provokes the ambiguity of nature to turn back clearly to its end, the redemption, already beginning to reveal itself in a certain sphere. If the Church truly is Christ present, then just as Christ was recognized by the signs, the Church too must be characterized by the same signs, by miracles. A miracle is an event, a motion of reality which, as a matter of fact, irresistably calls created man back to his Destiny, to Christ, to the living God.

2 HOLINESS

This theme of the miracle, the sign that sustains human work when it is lived as tension towards the final resurrection, introduces us to another great category of effectiveness or dimension, on which any verification of the Church's credibility must focus and that is holiness. In the Catholic tradition, the holy person is a saint, and, in the strictest sense of the word, the saint is the individual who realizes more completely his or her own personality, what he or she is supposed to be. The word "holiness" coincides in the total sense with a true personality. If one is self-fulfilled, he is realizing the idea for which he was created. In fact, for the Church, the concept of sin signifies what first of all obstructs an individual from realizing his personality.

The personality on the conscious path to its realization – that is, the personality, characterized by holiness – is modulated in a clear consciousness of the truth and in its use of its own freedom or self-governance. Within this path, human activity becomes entirely significant: every action, even the apparently least incisive, acquires the nobility of a great gesture. However, this is only possible if an individual acts in the awareness of the ultimate motivation for his action, for this will bring with it a consciousness of self which will facilitate a collaboration with Grace. This is to say, this awareness will facilitate self-dominion and direct freedom, tending the person towards faithfullness to the reason that spurs life on.

And so the saint in the Church makes Christ's presence a presence in every moment, because he, in a transparent way, determines man's action. The saint's self-consciousness is total: he is the master of his action because he has cemented it in the objectivity of God's plan. He consistently governs everything he does in that he seeks to the utmost to adhere to the ultimate reality of things.

The life of Hermann the Cripple, who was born in Von Reichenau and lived in the year 1000 exemplifies how one who lives out the Catholic conception of holiness realizes his personality. Let us listen to a passage or two of Cyril Martindale's touching account of Hermann's life, the incredible rich life

of the little creature who was born most horribly deformed. He was afterwards nicknamed "contracted," so hideously distorted was he; he could not stand, let alone walk; he could hardly sit even in the special chair they made for him; even his fingers were all but too weak and knotted for him to write; even his mouth and palate were deformed and he could hardly be understood when he spoke. ... I tell you he appeared to the judges of 900 years ago what we would call "Defective." His parents sent him away to a monastery where, at the age of 30, he became a monk and where, little by little, that mind believed to be as sclerotic as his body proved to have an extraordinary capacity for expansion. Bertold, his biographer and disciple, began his account of Hermann's life by saying that he was as "expansive" in mind as he was contracted in body.[11]

Martindale continues: "Not once in his life, can he have been 'comfortable,' or out of pain, yet what are the adjectives that cluster around him? I translate them from the Latin biography: 'pleasant, friendly, easy to talk to; always laughing; never criticising, eagerly cheerful... And the result was that *'everybody loved him.'* And meanwhile that courageous youth ... learned mathematics, Greek, Latin, Arabic, astronomy and music." Hermann was just over forty years old when he died surrounded by the love of the monks. He passed away after writing such works as a treatise on astrolabes and a *Chronicon* of world history, after making clocks and musical instruments, and, according to tradition, after leaving us his admirable composition of *Salve Regina* and *Alma Redemptoris*. Martindale rightly concludes his account thus: "In this twisted little fellow from the Dark Ages shines out the triumph of the Faith that inspired love, of the love that acted loyally by faith."[12] He was called "the marvel of his time."

How can a life lived in pain become so rich and attractive? The energy deriving from adherence to the ultimate reality of things means that even what the world around us sees as useless has its use: evil, pain, the fatigue of living, physical and mental handicap, boredom, and even resistance to God. Nothing cannot be transformed and admirably show the effects of that transformation if all life is being lived in relation to true reality – if it is "offered to God," as Christian tradition puts it. In his comparative study of the world of Greek literature and Christianity, Charles Moeller comments: "The frontier between the human and divine has now been crossed: demolished at last is the great wall, clearing the way to the Kingdom of God, to the transfiguration of human pain. ... In truth – and it can be seen clearly – man's sanctification through suffering introduces him, even down here, to a better world – the kingdom of God."[13]

Offering any form of wretchedness to God is the opposite of abdicating. It is the bond, consciously and energetically affirmed, between our particular circumstance and the universal. Father Carlo Gnocchi, who devoted his life to the suffering of others, used to say that the world's happiness derives from human pain offered to God. And this offering holds the key to the meaning of the universe.

It must be stressed that no mechanical, forced acceptance will work the miracle of the fulfilled personality. Accepting is not enough, as Moeller adds: "A Christian cannot be a man *resigned*. He must be a man who takes up suffering in charity and joy. Then the Easter joy will reappear on earth, man's true face will be transfigured in suffering and through suffering: because of sin, pain has become a means of resurrection."[14]

What then is holiness? Holiness, this sign of divine life bestowed on the Church, can be encountered in the form of its three distinguishing characteristics: the miracle, equilibrium, and intensity.

a) The Miracle

I. A miracle may be defined as an event, an experiencable fact by which God forces man to pay heed to him, to values in which he wishes man to participate, and by which God appeals to man to take notice of his Reality. A miracle is a way for him to make His Presence felt. From this point of view, then, all things are a miracle: we do not realize this because it is as if we live outside the original fabric of which we are made. We tend to cut ourselves off from our original bond with objective reality so that we reach a point where we claim to have a critical eye, when it is really only barrenness at play in us.

And so, the more conscious and quick an individual's sense of bond with the Other, who continuously creates this person, the more miraculous everything comes to be for him or her. For the Christian imbued through and through with the awareness of Christ's presence, for the new man, all things are new creation. The Gospel gives us discreet glimpses of the way Jesus looked at nature: when he showed the disciples the flowers of the field, the birds in the sky, the fig trees and vines of his earth, the view of the city he loved. In him, the awareness of the bond between the focus of his gaze and destiny, the Father, was immediately transparent. In him, all things sprang from the Father's act of creation, and so they were miracles each time.

In the same way, the more we live our faith in the presence of Christ in the Church, the more the signs of God will strike wonder in us, even in the most veiled circumstance, even when we are thinking our inmost thoughts. So there is no need for a special "shock" to remind us of the great origin that constitutes life. An instant's normality is enough.

In focusing on a particular point, the eye is designed to take in the whole spectrum and only in this way may the original point be placed in its proper perspective. Similarly, the religious dimension is designed so that it too "takes in the whole spectrum." We often live our lives without this all-embracing vision, as if we had defective sight which reduced the scope of our gaze. Yet, the source of aesthetics, of the *ethos*, of what is true is totality.

II. There are also miracles in a specific sense, particular times when God makes an extraordinary appeal to an individual to heed his presence, to wake up from distraction. These miracles are like a particular emphasis or mark on events, and they call us inexorably to God. It might be unexpected good news, or an unforeseen sorrow that constitutes a miracle for the individual. It is a powerful appeal for the individual, while others interpret it as merely a matter of chance.

For a miraculous event to be considered as a call to God, it must constitute a moral prompting *a priori*. It must prove to be a personal spiritualizing factor. This is the first basic criterion for distinguishing a miracle from the merely extraordinary, from the simply marvellous. In this sense, the condition for perceiving the presence of a miracle is not drawing near to the fact out of curiosity – perhaps even scientific curiosity – but with a religious spirit or with the sense of one's original subjection, which is the opposite of a superstitious spirit. If we are not already open to God, the miracle will confuse us more, and anyone seeking distraction will find even more distraction in the miracle. For the miracle is a comparison between freedom and the God who created it: its discovery as a miracle depends, therefore, on first having solved that ultimate human drama, furtive but very real, of choosing between self-reliance and dependence, between life as self-affirmation and life as the affirmation of Another, between the closed nature of one's own narrow measure and openness to the unfathomable possibility that he has placed at the origin of every life. Without a previous, at least implicit, sympathy for God, we cannot perceive an event as a miracle. And without this sympathy for God, not only can we not perceive the miracle of life, or the miracle in a particular life, we cannot even understand the miracle in its strictest, proper sense.

III. What then is a miracle? It is the place where God intervenes in his creation by means of a fact which no enquiry and no investigative procedure of reason can objectively explain. This happens when God wants to call not just the individual but the whole community to his presence, offering objective, universally verifiable factors for the building of the religious community.

In this sense, the Church does not cheat. As we were saying it subjects itself to being tested by our genuine experience. But neither can man cheat. Man's commitment, his willingness, must induce him, too, to open up to the verifiable existence of an event that cannot be classified in any of the categories known to purely rational or scientific wisdom.

b) Equilibrium

When I define equilibrium as a sign by which we can recognize holiness in the Church, I am not referring to any kind of mechanical stability on the scales of life – between the tensions and passions of life – or any calculation for redressing the forces of instinct and virtue. Rather, the equilibrium we can assume as the distinguishing feature of the presence of holiness in the Church is a richness, that abundance of which Jesus says: "a full measure, pressed down, shaken together, and overflowing, will be poured into your lap" (Luke 6: 38). Utilizing imagery of everyday life, Christ was referring to all that is given by God to those who take up the mercy of the Father as their own criterion of life.

The origin, then, of such richness is a conscience decisively orientated to God. As I have already had occasion to note: "Living the mystery of communion with God in Christ teaches us to see all things in relation to a single value so that all our judgments and decisions start off from a single gauge. From this original, deeper richness springs a vision of life of the utmost simplicity: one sole Reality, as criterion and measure and manner, floods all things with its light so that the 'I' feels one with all things and in all things, even in the face of death."[15]

Holiness in the Church produces a surprising capacity for human understanding and completeness, a capacity to embrace all reality in the light of a single criterion, without terror, without forgetfulness. It is a comprehensive and inclusive propensity whose particular ingeniousness does not ignore but brings out the value in the complementary aspects of human experience. In his commentary on Saint Thomas Aquinas' intellectual attitude in his century, André Hayen, a renowned historian of the Middle Ages, said that this saint's greatest originality lay in just this all-embracing potential: "Saint Thomas ... will not fear that the waters of philosophy can ever corrupt the wine of Holy Scripture. Where he sets himself – within the 'inclusive' perspective of the life of God which takes possession of humanity – the strivings of human reason will never be so intense that they cannot be swept up whole in the 'inclusive' fullness of the Divine Light and of its supernatural revelation." It is an all-embracing upsweeping defined thus: "Saint Thomas' root decision is, simply, to keep faith in his reflections on life with the integrity of life's reality, which offers itself up to conscience in the name of commitment in love (using all the instruments that 13th century life offered to the mind for engaging in this reflection)."[16]

It is then the overflowing richness of being that "takes hold of humanity" which is given to humanity, to be freely accepted as the one criterion of life. This is the source of the equilibrium of Christian holiness. In Christian holiness: "the Absolute is not to be reached by negating the finite condition of the world in various ways. Rather, it is He himself who reaches us, overwhelming us wherever our capacity for imagination is exhausted, which is to say, wherever God is, doing all that man longs to consider doing but cannot ..."[17]

And so there is never a question of restricting the horizon of human experience but rather of expanding it, comprehending, and including every facet of humanity in the name of and, therefore, with the energy of a divine initiative which created all things and whose aim was to save all things. Therefore, the balance struck by Christian holiness derives its originality from a richness that is not of man, but of God, whose desire was to let man share in it. This is not the equilibrium we might attain by utilizing techniques designed cleverly to distribute the weights of forces at play. Rather, this is the equilibrium of the *homo viator* – it is a dynamic destined to make our journeying more concrete and complete, to give more fullness to our pilgrimage on this earth with him, whose fullness is the explication of life, whose fullness he dispenses to overflowing, by our side, journeying with us "Did not our hearts burn within us as he talked to us on the road?" (Luke 24:32), the disciples of Emmaus asked themselves when they recognized their Risen Master in the traveller who had accompanied them part of the way.

c) Intensity

Henri de Lubac, in his reflections on sainthood observes: "Christianity must generate saints, that is, witnesses of the eternal. ... A saint is one who gives us a glimpse of eternity through the heavy opaque veils of time."[18] And in the history of the Church, this penetration of the opaque veils of time has happened at every moment and in all conditions. It has reached us from every continent and in the most disconcerting variety of circumstances.

Throughout history, the forms and proof of holiness in the Church are present in quality and quantity in a way unmeasurable and incomparable to any other locus of religious experience. Let us look back at this moving passage from the writings of Adrienne von Speyr:

The saints are the demonstration of Christianity's potential. So they can be guides along the road to the charity of God that would otherwise be impossible to travel. And God, having established all the forms of saintliness, has created infinite possibilities, some of which at least are also certainly possible for me. In the true following of the saints, Christian charity's need for "still more" is self-evident. In fact, a saint never signifies limitation, a halt. ... The introduction of the saints is a facilitation offered us by the Lord, a means of rendering his commandment concrete, an indication such as to deceive no one. And it will never happen that there will be a sign marking where the road begins so that we might then press on alone with the Lord. The saint is companion in that by his very nature as one who lives in the Lord he becomes increasingly transparent. He does not need to be set to one side. He makes the Lord become increasingly central. For the essence of every holiness consists in living in the Lord until His return.[19]

To the centrality of von Speyr's appeal to the super-abundant experience of holiness in the Church, we could add John Henry Newman's expression of gratitude:

If they were blessed who lived in primitive times and saw the fresh traces of their Lord, and heard the echoes of Apostolic voices, blessed too are we whose special portion it is to see the same Lord revealed in His saints. The wonders of His grace in the soul of man, its creative power, its inexhaustible resources, its manifold operation, all this we know, as they knew it not. They never heard the names of St. Gregory, St. Bernard, St. Francis and St. Louis. In fixing our thoughts then, as in an undertaking like the present, on the History of the Saints, we are but availing ourselves of that solace and recompense of our particular trials which has been provided for our need by our Gracious Master.[20]

Naturally, we might well walk past the miracle, the human equilibrium, the intensity of the experience of holiness in the Church, as if we were perfect strangers to it. But this would mean we lacked the will to allow our genuine experience to assess the characteristics of the Church as the Church itself wants it to. In order to "see" and to believe, our eyes must be trained on their object, and the gaze must be animated by a minimum of sympathy. For, is it not true that this is the natural condition for acquiring any knowledge? As Pierre Rousselot observed: "Love gives us eyes: the very fact of loving makes us see, creates for the loving subject a new species of evidence." And in this our exercise of verification, the dawning of this love is the desire for truth, the desire – if we were to prove the Church's claim true – for access to that "new nature," sanctifying grace, that causes us to believe, i.e. to see signs of the supernatural in the visible world.[21]

3 CATHOLICITY

There was one title of the Church – a title of honour, which all men agreed to give her – . ... It was one which the sects could neither claim for themselves, nor hinder being enjoyed by its rightful owner ... since it was the characteristic designation of the Church in the Creed, ... St. Paul tells us that the heretic is "condemned by himself;" and no clearer witness against the sects of the earlier centuries was needed by the Church, than their own testimony to this contrast between her actual position and their own. Sects, say the Fathers, are called after the name of their founders, or from their locality, or from their doctrine. So was it from the beginning: "I am of Paul, and I of Apollos, and I of Cephas;" but it was promised to the Church that she should have no master upon earth, and that she should "gather together in one the children of God that were scattered abroad." Her every-day name, which was understood in the marketplace and used in the palace, which every chance comer knew, and which stateedicts recognized, was the "Catholic" Church.[22]

In writing of the fourth century Church and its relations with sects and heresy, John Henry Newman thus points to Catholicity, the distinctive characteristic of the community founded by the apostles, the distinctive feature ascribed to it since the second century. For, as the Church gradually became aware of its singularity, proven since its beginnings, it became more and more inclined to express it in such a way that it highlighted its essential Catholic dimensions. This, in fact, was its constant concern. Henri de Lubac points out:

Katholicos, in classical Greek, was used by philosophers to indicate a universal proposition. Now a universal is a singular and is not to be confused with an aggregate. The Church is not Catholic because she is spread abroad over the whole of the earth and can reckon on a large number of members. She was already Catholic on the morning of Pentecost, when all her members could be contained in a small room, as she was when the Aryan waves seemed on the point of swamping her; she would still be Catholic if tomorrow apostasy on a vast scale deprived her of almost all the faithful. For fundamentally Catholicity has nothing to do with geography or statistics. If it is true that it should be displayed over all the earth and be manifest to all, yet its nature is not material but spiritual. Like sanctity, Catholicity is primarily an intrinsic feature of the Church. The Church in each individual calls on the whole man, embracing him as he is in his whole nature."[23]

Catholicity, then, is an essential dimension of the Church, the profound expression of its pertinence to human matters and all the variegated forms they take. That the Church is Catholic means, therefore, that the truth and the spirit of the Church, what it proclaims and the experience to which it introduces us, may be channelled and assimilated by any culture or mentality. History may well have recorded methods which have been dramatically improvident, such as sublime forms of participation and other particular emphases. However, the important aspect to verify is the nature of the human dimension in its entirety, for this is the definition of the Church's catholicity. The Church claims for itself the prerogative of genuine humanity so that any culture or mentality may experience the truth the Church proclaims. Moreover, the experience it proposes is the most suitable form of self-completion, the most suitable fulfillment. In fact, Catholicism declares its simple correspondence with all that comprises man's destiny. On this relationship between the Church and various civilizations, Jean Daniélou observes:

There is always a temptation to turn the idea of unity into that of uniformity; in matters of organization, to think of unity as meaning centralization, and in matters of doctrinal expression to think in terms of terminological identity. On the contrary, there is no real unity without catholicity, which implies a continuing diversity of mentality, culture and civilization, within the single round of one faith, one Church, one dogma, one Eucharist.[24]

This is a variegated, differentiated expression, qualified not by some exterior show of greatness, success, or conquest but as can answer to an inner imperative of the created heart "since," as Karl Adam remarked, "Christ came to redeem all mankind, therefore His body is essentially related to all mankind. ... This world-wide spirit, rooted in the preaching of our Lord has been taken over in its full breadth and depth by the Catholic Church, and by her alone. The Church is not one society or one church alongside many others, nor is she just a church among men; she is the Church of men, the Church of mankind."[25]

Anyone who reads the history of the Church with an open heart cannot but note how the Christian experience has been unceasing in its assimilation and concentration on the value of all things that show an authentically human richness. Jewish terminology and mental categories were immediately set up for comparison with Hellenistic culture. And second century apologists "courageously sought the dialogue with the world around them. ... It is to their everlasting fame that they did not permit themselves to be pushed into a ghetto."[26] Their works gave expression to the aim, which was "to demonstrate the consonance of the Christian message with human reason. This constitutes their special province, and it was in this way that contact was established between the Christian message and Hellenism."[27]

If we also consider one of the most imposing of all the developments in Christian history – monasticism – we will find that it fully exemplifies this capacity to take on aspects of different cultures. As Christopher Dawson rightly notes:

The original institution of Christian monasticism was of purely Oriental origin and came into existence in the Egyptian desert during the fourth century. Almost immediately, the Church accepted this new form of life as an essential expression of the Christian spirit and spread it East and West, from the Atlantic to the Black Sea and the Persian Gulf. As it grew it adapted itself to the life of the different people among whom it came, though it remained fully conscious of its origins and of the continuity of its tradition.[28]

Two Jesuit missionaries, Matteo Ricci and Roberto de Nobili, illustrate this same spirit of adaptation. The first, designated for a mission in China at the end of the sixteenth century, had undergone impassioned preparations for his apostolic work by seeking to learn of the philosophers, the literature, and the religions of the country where he was about to land. He died in China in 1610, honored in the imperial court as an astronomer and mathematician. But he was unceasing in his preaching of Christianity, and he always tried to demonstrate its concrete liveability, even for those who grew up in the shadow of values far removed from those of the west, for primarily Christian revelation would have helped in the understanding of these values, not in the sacrificing of them.

A few years later came the death of the other Jesuit, Roberto de Nobili, who had introduced the same spirit of adaptation during his mission in India. He had earnestly moulded himself to the Indian way of life and pattern of thought and, throughout his life, he sought to introduce the Gospel to the universe of the Indian mind. He knew Sanskrit but he could also preach in the popular dialect, and he recognized the value of all his converts' Hindu customs which were not in open contradiction with the Christian message.

Although it sometimes did happen that objections to such methods of proposing the Christian fact were raised and debated within the Church, they nevertheless bear witness to the multi-form capacity of the Christian experience to address man not as the exponent of this or that civilization but as man. And when, in 1622, in its official role the Church assumed the responsibility of directing missionary activity by establishing the institution Propaganda Fide – it was evident in the instructions it sent to missionaries that it had grasped the importance of all those experiences. In fact, it demanded knowledge of the language and culture of the place where missionaries would preach and live, and it issued fervent reminders to those missionaries that they are in those places to propose the faith, not to impose any particular culture. Henri de Lubac mentions a contemporary missionary, the Benedictine Jules Monchanin, who lived the life of an impassioned participant in Indian culture and who had an ardent zeal for evangelizing:

He would stress that the Fathers often compare the Church with the coat of many colours (Gen 37:3) of the patriarch Joseph, or with the magnificently ornate mantle, *circumdata varietate*, of the bride of Solomon (Ps 45:9). A specific type of Christian spirituality must emanate from the specific spirit of the people of every country. The qualitative universality of the Church, which in no land is a stranger and whose validity nowhere has expired but which is apace with all epochs and connatural with all civilisations, is simply the final attunement and synthesis of all civilisations in the hands of Christ, the Absolute Man, in his theandric pleroma.[29]

And since catholicity, as an intrinsic quality of the Church, must be the personal dimension of every Christian, even of those not called to a specific missionary vocation, de Lubac goes on to outline, with Monchanin still in mind, the indispensable attitude for acquiring this dimension:

He knew how to listen. He listened intensely. He was not listening for the slip where he could introduce a wedge of condemnation, but so that he could grasp all the energy of the hidden spring from which words pour forth. And when he answered, he would unveil prospects that attracted his interlocutor, like a lover, as if to give more complete fulfilment to the other's idea. In devoting himself entirely to what the other was saying, he also gave the impression that the person was fully understood. In a way he would reveal people to themselves by explanation and by transmitting a spark of his own fire to them. On every occasion ... his method (if method there was) was the same as Jesus', as he defined it ... and in which he saw the "genre proper of the mission": "To propose to all a mystery which surpasses even the greatest of us but takes such a connatural form that the most insignificant of us may draw life from it and recognize in it all that in him is most familiar and private."[30]

4 APOSTOLICITY

Just as catholicity is the Church's intrinsic universal nature even giving evidence of itself in its dimension of space – space understood as a category both an interior and exterior category – apostolicity is the characteristic of the Church which signified its capacity to address time in a unitary, structured way. This is the historical dimension by which the Church affirms itself as the only authority to be the custodian of a tradition of values and realities deriving from the apostles. Moreover, just as Christ's will was to bind his work and his presence in the world to the apostles and in doing so he indicated one of them as the authoritative point of reference, so, too, is the Church bound to Peter's and the apostles' successors – the pope and his bishops. This succession, historically provable as far as the bishop of Rome is concerned, is unitary and uninterrupted precisely through the action of the bishop of Rome. It was Irenaeus, who lived in the second century, who would lend particularly strong emphasis to this apostolic nature of the Church.

Thus the thing which Irenaeus threw into bold relief was the pre-eminent role of the Apostles. They are the intermediaries between Christ and the Church, since it was to them that Christ officially entrusted his message ... for it highlights the fact that the Apostles passed on the teaching of the Lord to persons whom they chose for this specific purpose. It is thus a matter of an institutional continuity within which the deposit of faith entrusted to the Apostles is preserved, thus underlining the fact that the Apostles did not rely for the safeguarding of their message on the Scriptures alone, but also on living people. A new feature of the Tradition now emerges: handed down by the Apostles, it is preserved as a deposit by the chain of succession.[31]

What succession, one might ask? But Irenaeus has no hesitation in replying:

Therefore, the Tradition of the apostles, manifest throughout the world, may be seen in every Church by anyone who wishes to see the Truth and we can list the bishops appointed by the apostles to the various Churches as well as their successors to this day. ... But since this exercise of listing the successions in all the Churches would take too long, we will take the very great and very old Church known to all, the Church founded and established in Rome by the two glorious apostles, Peter and Paul. ... In fact, every Church must be in accord with this particular Church by virtue of its most excellent of origins – this Church in which the Tradition that comes from the Apostles has always been preserved for all men.

And in ending his meticulously documented outline, he concludes: "Given such proof as this, therefore, we must not look for the Truth elsewhere. The Truth is easily available from the Church since, in her, and as if it were some precious treasure, the apostles amassed in the fullest possible way all that regards the Truth, so that anyone who wishes may draw the water of Life from her to drink."[32] So if it is true that all the Churches trace their origins to one apostle, then the fact remains that the only one proven to continue that succession is the Church of Rome.

The value of this apostolic succession lies in the nature of the miracle it confers on the phenomenon of the Church itself. And in the Church's historical dimension, the greatest miracle of all is its constructive resilience throughout the centuries, precisely in the expressions of the ideal and in the structures of experience and organization, all of which seem to be (and usually are) essentially contingent. This miracle constitutes the fact that the message of Jesus has taken root in the fibre of history: "In all truth I tell you, whoever keeps my word will never see death" (John 8:51). These are the words which scandalized the Pharisees who were debating with Jesus, and which caused them to be accused of being possessed by a demon. In fact, no man may draw away from the precarious nature of life and when a value emerges, and if it becomes permanently embedded in time, it can only be said to be the bearer of the divine meaning of things. Even in the most ordinary aspects of our lives we believe it a miracle if a sentiment, a bond, a conviction lasts our whole life through, if anything bound up with time manages to endure.

The Church affirms its capacity to address time, not just as a particular strength in which the past is preserved but, fortified by the promises of Jesus, as a challenge to the future. Bringing out the value of our past, faithfulness with our origins, is the sign of the power of a personality whose increasing tendency will be to build its awareness of the traces it leaves in history. But if the intact endurance of the value of the past is a miracle, then how much more imposing is the affirmation of power to bring about such permanence in the future? In fact, the Church's superiority with respect to time is an unimaginable challenge. It is given, and the Church has received it as a gift, as the fruit of the presence of Jesus in the world until the end of time. It is realized by His Spirit which never ceases to assist the sign by which that presence lives.

To conclude, let us now look back at the points we made at the beginning of these brief notes on the Church's fundamental features, for they need to be *verified* in order to discover their divine value. It is important to mention that the category of unity is the horizon within which the other categories we listed are situated: holiness, the energy generating the unity of the "I" within the one Church; catholicity or universality, so that every value flows back into a single horizon embracing all human experience; apostolicity, which sets within the human affair the origin of a new history, unitary in its capacity and experience as the permanent host of the Absolute through time. Thus, each one of these distinctive features opens wide our minds and hearts so that we may drink the rich waters of what is genuinely human, present in all humanity, whose origin is one alone, whose destiny is one alone, whose journeying will take different paths, though the call is to journey in the companionship of the One whose will was to become a human gift to keep us from going astray.

Conclusion

The reflections we have just concluded have been called in the Italian edition a *percorso* (*parcours*) in order to call to mind the idea of a journey and to affirm that these lessons of ours are simply meant to indicate milestones, signposts of the steps we should take if we wish to be reasonable. The value of travelling this particular road – and this is the demand it makes on us – lies in applying our critical awareness of free will, elements without which any adherence or refusal would be stripped of all that makes them effectively human. And since man is *viator* in this world, a wayfarer striving to reach his destination, a traveller, it is better if he knows and loves the road at least enough to save him from wasting time and effort.

Anything that restrains the energy of man's movements, anything that applies a brake to him or blocks him is to be considered as the cause of grave damage to his person.

So as we conclude, let us repeat the warning about falling into the trap of *scandal*, meant here as an undue obstacle on the way. This trap is waiting for anyone at all to fall into it: both for those who must decide on the direction their personal road should take and for those who have already decided and now want to travel it consciously, step by step. On this aspect, Hans Urs von Balthasar makes an interesting point in one of his monographs, on Romano Guardini, where he notes the emphasis this writer places in his work on this mortifying human experience: "'Guardini has often described and defined scandal as using secondary reasons to deny what, for fundamental reasons, should be consented to".[1] And this is precisely what this trilogy has been trying to clarify – the distinction between fundamental reasons and secondary arguments.

Albeit summarily, it has indicated where either is to be found within the Christian experience.

It is always a sign of vulnerability if we allow ourselves to be impeded, scandalized, halted on our road, for this underscores the existence of a wound in the whole question, a wound afflicting every individual. To prevent and heal that wound is the aim of a reasonable method of encountering reality.

The Christian proposal addresses the person directly, and in this individual's particular present situation it invites him to verify it with all the instruments of a fully human experience. And this will be profoundly personal – as in every other case of genuine humanity – and it will be rooted in a social, community relationship. In his consideration of this proposal, past or present, man could be tempted to be swamped by secondary aspects only, which often expose his subjective fragility and do not represent any objective, complete analysis of facts. Moreover, it might be helpful to remember once again how the attitude of "freely offered willingness" is essential on this pathway.

In discussing the roots of European nihilism and the possibility of transforming this into religious experience, Bernhard Welte offers us an interesting note on method:

One cannot be forced to see that this turning point of experience is possible. It is certainly possible at any time but at no time is it necessary. Furthermore, it cannot be produced by any method rationally devised to pursue a target. It is possible to shed light on it, as we have tried to do. It is possible to cite testimonies in favour of it, as we have also done. But there is no obligation inherent in those testimonies. All they do is attract our attention. And the steps we may take to reach some kind of clarification are just pointers to an experience that we may but do not necessarily have to live. ... So in order to live such decisive experiences, there must be willingness, freely offered, to be involved. This willingness, however, can be withheld and it is also possible to refuse outright to be willing. In that case, one takes, at best, superficial note of reflections and testimonies such as these. And if the attitude is a superficial one, then all that is being affirmed will seem improbable. Thus, no personal experience and, more especially, no religious experience is likely to form. The necessary presupposition, then, for attaining the more significant and decisive experiences is a special kind of willingness and openness on the part of our freedom. Without this willingness, it is totally impossible for our freedom to record such experiences.[2]

What the Church intends to teach us to do is to expand our capacity as individuals along a road of freedom, and to seek and experience the truth to which the Church introduces us. This forms the outline in time of the authentic stature of human beings, constantly and ever thirsting for reality, for true being.

Notes

BOOK ONE

CHAPTER ONE

1 Johannes Lindworsky, *The Training of the Will*, translated by A. Steiner and E.A. Fitzpatrick (Milwaukee: Bruce, 1929).
2 Luigi Giussani, *The Religious Sense*, translated by John Zucchi (Montreal: McGill-Queen's University Press, 1997), 57–8.
3 *The Religious Sense, At the Origin of the Christian Claim, Why the Church?*
4 Luigi Giussani, *At the Origin of the Christian Claim*, translated by Viviane Hewitt (Montreal: McGill-Queen's University Press, 1998), 29–35.

CHAPTER TWO

1 Albert Schweitzer, *The Quest for the Historical Jesus*, cited in W.G. Kümmel, *The New Testament: The History of the Investigation of its Problems*, translated by S.M. Gilmour and H.C. Kee (Nashville: Abingdon Press, 1972), 240.
2 Luigi Giussani, *The Religious Sense*, translated by John Zucchi (Montreal: McGill-Queen's University Press, 1997), 3–11.
3 Quoted in John Henry Newman, *A Grammar of Assent* (London: Longmans Green and Co., 1924), 480.
4 Quoted in Henri de Lubac, *Catholicism: Christ and the Common Destiny of Man*, translated by L.C. Sheppard and E. Englund (San Francisco: Ignatius Press, 1988), 401.
5 Newman, *Grammar*, 487–8.
6 Quoted in de Lubac, *Catholicism*, 439.

7 Karl Adam, *The Spirit of Catholicism*, translated by Justin McCann (London: Sheed & Ward, 1929), 59–60.

8 Luigi Giussani, *At the Origin of the Christian Claim*, translated by Viviane Hewitt (Montreal: McGill-Queen's University Press, 1998), 32ff.

9 Giussani, *Religious Sense*, 132–4.

10 C.F. Stäudlin, *De interpretatione librorum Novi Testamenti*, quoted in Kümmel, *New Testament*, 114.

11 J. Weiss quoted in Kümmel, *New Testament*, 279–80.

12 Adam, *Spirit of Catholicism*, 2–3.

13 De Lubac, *Catholicism*, 165, 166–7.

CHAPTER THREE

1 In this chapter, I present in other terms the same reflections which appeared in my book *La coscienza religiosa nell'uomo moderno* (Milan: Jaca Book, 1985), subsequently translated into English as "Religious Awareness in Modern Man," *Communio* 25 (Spring 1998), 104–40.

2 Friedrich Nietzsche, *Beyond Good and Evil* (Hammondsworth: Penguin, 1973).

3 Christopher Dawson, *Religion and the Rise of Western Culture* (London: Sheed & Ward, 1950), 173.

4 Christopher Dawson, *The Historic Reality of Christian Culture* (New York: Harper and Brothers, 1960), 42.

5 Ibid., 37.

6 Henri de Lubac, *Paradoxes of Faith*, translated by Ernest Beaumont (San Francisco: Ignatius Press, 1987), 10.

7 "O novo canto," in *Il laudario iacoponico*, edited by G. Mazzal Bergamo: San Marco, 1960), 9.

8 Dawson, *Historic Reality*, 36.

9 Ibid.

10 Luigi Giussani, *The Religious Sense*, translated by John Zucchi (Montreal: McGill-Queen's University Press, 1997), 36–7.

11 Gilbert Keith Chesterton, *St Thomas Aquinas* (London: Hodder and Stoughton, 1933), 87.

12 Dawson, *Religion and Western Culture*, 164.

13 Henri Daniel-Rops, *The Protestant Reformation*, translated by Audrey Butler (London: J.M. Dent & Sons, 1961), 106.

14 Henri Daniel-Rops, *Cathedral and Crusade*, translated by John Warrington (London: J.M. Dent & Sons, 1957), 594.

15 Daniel-Rops, *Protestant Reformation*, 126.

16 Henri de Lubac, *Pic de La Mirandole* (Paris: Aubier-Montaigne, 1974), 243.

17 "Rime sparse" n. 81, in *Petrarch's Lyric Poems: The* Rime sparse *and Other Lyrics*, translated and edited by Robert M. Durling (Cambridge, Mass.: Harvard University Press, 1976), 184.

18 "Rime sparse" n. 366, in *Petrarch's Lyric Poems*, 582.

19 Dawson, *Religion and the Rise*, 16.

20 Giussani, *Religious Sense*, 57.

21 Charles Moeller, *Sagesse grèque et paradoxe chrétien* (Tournai-Paris: Castermann, 1948), 49.

22 Ibid., 96–7.

23 De Lubac, *Pic de La Mirandole*, 147.

24 Ibid., 148.

25 Ibid., 148.

26 Giussani, *Religious Sense*, 3–11.

27 Karl Adam, *The Spirit of Catholicism*, translated by Justin McCann (London: Sheed & Ward, 1929), 12.

28 Luigi Giussani, "Religious Awareness in Modern Man," *Communio* 25 (Spring 1998): 112.

29 Henri de Lubac, *The Un-Marxian Socialist. A Study of Proudhon*, translated by R.E. Scantlebury (New York: Sheed & Ward, 1948), 292.

30 *Teatro elisabettiano*, edited by Mario Praz (Florence: Sansoni, 1948), 187.

31 Ibid., xvi.

32 Ibid., xix.

33 Christopher Marlowe, *Dr Faustus* (London: Roma Gill, 1959), 68.

34 John Webster, *The White Devil*, act V, scene iv, in *Three Jacobean Tragedies*, edited by Gamini Salgado (London: Penguin Books, 1965), 245.

35 De Lubac, *Pic de La Mirandole*, 400.

36 Henri Daniel-Rops, *The Catholic Reformation*, translated by John Warrington (London: J.M. Dent & Sons, 1962), 360.

37 Louis Cognet, "Ecclesiastical Life in France," in *History of the Church*, vol. 7, edited by H. Jedin and J. Dolan, translated by Gunther J. Holst (New York: Crossroad, 1981), 102.

38 Henri Daniel-Rops, *The Church in the Eighteenth Century*, translated by John Warrington (London: J.M. Dent & Sons, 1964), 13.

39 Oskar Köhler, "Concepts," in *History of the Church*, vol. 7, edited by H. Jedin and J. Dolan, translated by Gunther J. Holst (New York: Crossroad, 1981), 344, 373.

40 Ibid., 343.

41 Daniel-Rops, *Church in the Eighteenth Century*, 43–4.

42 Chesterton, *St. Thomas Aquinas*, 229, 231.

43 Ibid., 243, 245, 246.

44 I have taken my cue for this summary of the constitutive factors of the modern spirit from Henri Daniel-Rops' address given upon his induction into the Academie Française.

45 Hans Urs von Balthasar, *Engagement with God*, translated by John Haliburton (London: S.P.C.K., 1975), 60–1.

46 Henri de Lubac, *The Religion of Teilhard de Chardin*, translated by René Hague (New York: Doubleday, 1968), 171.

47 De Lubac, *Pic de La Mirandole*, 215.

48 Luigi Giussani, "Religious Awareness in Modern Man," in *Communio* 25, 1 (Spring 1998), 123.

49 De Lubac, *Un-Marxian Socialist*, 296.

50 Olivier Clément, *Les Visionnaires* (Paris: Desclée de Brouwer, 1986), 43.

51 Daniel-Rops, *Church in the Eighteenth Century*, 42.

52 Ibid., 23, 41, 42.

53 Luigi Giussani, *Grandi linee della teologia protestante americana* (Milan: Jaca Book, 1988), 67–8. The quotation is from Ralph Waldo Emerson, "Self-Reliance," in *Addresses and Essays* (London: Watts & Co., 1907), 15.

54 W. Gladden, *Ruling Ideas of the Present Age* (Boston: Houghton Mifflin, 1895), 285, quoted in *The Social Gospel in America*, edited by Robert T. Handy (New York: Oxford University Press, 1966), 27.

55 Giussani, *Grandi linee*, 85. Quotation is from J.W. Buckham, *Progressive Religious Thought in America* (Boston: Houghton Mifflin, 1919), 316.

56 Giussani, *Grandi linee*, 90. Last quotation is from Shailer Mathews, *The Social Interpretation of History* (Cambridge, Mass.: Harvard University Press, 2nd ed., 1927), ix.

57 Ibid., 105. Quotation is from W. Rauschenbusch, *Christianity and the Social Crisis* (New York: Harper and Row, 1964), 420–1.

58 Giussani, *Grandi linee*, 106. Quotation is from W. Rauschenbusch, *A Theology for the Social Gospel* (New York: Macmillan, 1919), 158.

59 Ibid., 118. Quotation is from R. Niebuhr, *Faith and History* (New York: Scribner's Sons, 1949), 6–7.

60 Adam, *Spirit of Catholicism*, 7–8.

61 De Lubac, *Teilhard de Chardin*, 189–90.

62 Henri de Lubac, *Catholicism: Christ and the Common Destiny of Man*, translated by L.C. Sheppard and E. Englund (San Francisco: Ignatius Press, 1988), 352.

63 Henri Daniel-Rops was elected to the Academie Française on 3 March 1955 and was received on 22 March 1956.

64 Daniel-Rops, *Church in the Eighteenth Century*, 44.

65 De Lubac, *Teilhard de Chardin*, 36.

CHAPTER FOUR

1 Gustave Bardy, *La conversion au christianisme durant les premiers siècles* (Paris: Aubier, 1948), 5.

2 Luigi Giussani, *At the Origin of the Christian Claim*, translated by Vivianne Hewitt (Montreal: McGill-Queen's University Press, 1998), 49–58.

3 Jacques Leclercq, *La vie du Christ dans son Église* (Paris: Le Cerf, 1944), 92.

4 Luigi Moraldi, *Ricchezza perduta. Quale cristianesimo? Ricerche sui primi due secoli dell'era cristiana* (Cosenza: Lionello Giordano, 1986), 122.

5 Leclercq, *Vie du Christ*, 201.

6 Walter Kasper, *An Introduction to Christian Faith*, translated by V. Green (New York: Paulist Press, 1980), 96–7.

CHAPTER FIVE

1 Henri de Lubac, *Catholicism: Christ and the Common Destiny of Man*, translated by L.C. Sheppard and E. Englund (San Francisco: Ignatius Press, 1988), 76.

2 Gustave Bardy, *La conversion au christianisme durant les premiers siècles* (Paris: Aubier, 1948), 261.

3 De Lubac, *Catholicism*, 61.

4 Mircea Eliade, *A History of Religious Ideas*, vol. 2, translated by Willard R. Trask (Chicago: University of Chicago Press, 1982), 340–1.

5 De Lubac, *Catholicism*, 31–2.

6 Hans Urs von Balthasar, *The Glory of the Lord: A Theological Aesthetics*, vol. 1, *Seeing the Form*, translated by E. Leiva-Merikakis (San Francisco: Ignatius Press, 1982), 52b.

7 De Lubac, *Catholicism*, 269–70.

8 This and the following paragraphs are greatly indebted to the excellent book by Jerome Hamer, *The Church is a Communion*, translated by Ronald Matthews (New York: Sheed & Ward, 1965).

9 Rudolf Schnackenburg, *God's Rule and Kingdom*, translated by John Murray (Montreal: Palm Publishers, 1963), 216–17.

10 De Lubac, *Catholicism*, 62–4.

11 Ibid., *Catholicism*, 226.

12 Romano Guardini, *Vom Wesen des Christentums* (Würzburg: Werkbund Verlag, 1938), 41–2.

13 Romano Guardini, *The Church and the Catholic and The Spirit of the Liturgy*, translated by Ada Lane (London: Sheed & Ward, 1935), 40–1.

14 Pierre Rousselot, "Les yeux de la foi," in *Recherches de sciences religieuses* sept.–oct. 1910: 471.

15 De Lubac, *Catholicism*, 349.

16 Adalbert Hamman, *Vie liturgique et vie sociale* (Paris: Desclée, 1968), 101.

17 Hans Urs von Balthasar, *Two Sisters in the Spirit: Thérèse of Lisieux and Elizabeth of the Trinity* (San Francisco: Ignatius Press, 1992), 249–50.

18 Luigi Moraldi, *Ricchezza perduta. Quale cristianesimo? Ricerche sui primi due secoli dell'era cristiana* (Cosenza: Lionello Giordano, 1986), 88, 91.

19 De Lubac, *Catholicism*, 390.

20 Hamman, *Vie liturgique*, 286.

21 Jacques Vidal, "Rite et ritualité," in *Les Rites d'initiation*, edited by Julien Ries (Louvain-la-Neuve: Homo religiosus, 1986), 39.

22 Enrico Galbiati, *L'Eucarestia nella Bibbia* (Milan: Jaca Book, 1968), 162.

23 Jacques Vidal, *Symboles et religions* (Louvain-la-Neuve: Homo religiosus, 1989), 68.
24 Karl Baus, "The Beginnings," in *History of the Church*, vol. 1, edited by H. Jedin and J. Dolan (New York: The Seabury Press, 1980), 139.
25 Ludwig Hertling, *Geschichte der Katholischen Kirche* (Berlin: Morus Verlag 1949), 34.
26 Henri Daniel-Rops, *The Church of Apostles and Martyrs*, translated by Audrey Butler (London: J.M. Dent & Sons, 60), 13–14.
27 Karl Adam, *The Spirit of Catholicism*, translated by Justin McCann (London: Sheed & Ward, 1929), 87–8.
28 Oscar Cullmann, *Christ and Time*, translated by Floyd V. Filson (Philadelphia: The Westminster Press, 1964), 150.
29 Rudolf Schnackenburg, *The Church in the New Testament*, translated by W.J. O'Hara (Montreal: Palm Publishers, 1965), n.p.
30 Hertling, *Geschichte*, 36.
31 Henri de Lubac, *Le Fondement théologique des missions* (Paris: Le Seuil, 1945), 18.
32 August Franzen, *A History of the Church*, translated by Peter Becker (Montreal: Palm Publishers, 1968), 20.
33 De Lubac, *Fondement théologique*, 40.

CONCLUSION

1 Henri de Lubac, *Catholicism: Christ and the Common Destiny of Man*, translated by L.C. Sheppard and E. Englund (San Francisco: Ignatius Press, 1988), 306–7.
2 John Henry Newman, *Apologia Pro Vita Sua* (London: Sheed & Ward, 1956), 113.
3 Ibid., 133.

BOOK TWO

INTRODUCTION

1 See Luigi Giussani, *The Religious Sense*, translated by John Zucchi (Montreal: McGill-Queen's University Press, 1997), in particular, chapters 10 and 11.

CHAPTER SIX

1 Jean Daniélou, *The Lord of History*, translated by Nigel Abercrombie (Chicago: Henry Regnery, 1958), 284–5.
2 Charles Péguy, *The Mystery of the Charity of Joan of Arc*, translated by Julian Green (New York: Pantheon, 1950, 184.

3 Charles Péguy, *The Portal of the Mystery of Hope*, translated by David L. Schindler, Jr. (Grand Rapids: William B. Eerdmans, 1996), 59–60.

4 Christopher Dawson, *Religion and the Rise of Western Culture* (London: Sheed & Ward, 1950), 107.

5 Henri Daniel-Rops, *The Church in the Dark Ages*, transalted by Audrey Day (London: J.M. Dent & Sons, 1959), 538.

6 Friedrich Kempf, "The Church and the Western Kingdoms from 900 to 1046," in *History of the Church*, vol. 3, edited by H. Jedin and J. Dolan, translated by Anselm Biggs (New York: The Seabury Press, 1980), 213–14.

7 Ibid., 214.

8 Daniel-Rops, *Church in the Dark Ages*, 538–9.

9 W. Brandmüller, "Gregory VII," in Peter Manns, *Die Heiligen in ihrer Zeit*, vol. 1 (Mainz: Matthias-Grünewald-Verlag, 1967), 544.

10 Friedrich Kempf, "The Struggle for the Freedom of the Church," in *History of the Church*, vol. 3, edited by H. Jedin and J. Dolan, translated by Anselm Biggs (New York: The Seabury Press, 1980), 384–5.

11 Roger Aubert, *The Continuation of Catholic Renewal in Europe*, in *History of the Church*, vol. 8, edited by H. Jedin and J. Dolan, translated by Peter Becker (New York: Crossroad, 1981), 84–5.

12 Henri de Lubac, *The Church: Paradox and Mystery*, translated by James R. Dunne (Staten Island, N.Y.: Ecclesia Press, 1969), 2.

13 Kajetan Esser, *Anfänge und ursprüngliche Zielsetzungen des Ordens der Minderbrüder* (Leiden: E.J. Brill, 1966), 224.

14 *The Letters of St. Catherine of Siena*, vol. 1, translated by Suzanne Noffke (Binghamton, N.Y.: Medieval & Renaissance Texts & Studies, 1988), 202.

15 Henri de Lubac, *Paradoxes, suivi de Nouveaux Paradoxes* (Paris: Le Seuil, 1959), 124.

16 Marta Sordi, *Paolo e Filemone, o della schiavitù* (Milan: Jaca Book, 1987), 12.

17 Ibid., 49.

18 Ibid., 55.

19 Ludwig Hertling, *Geschichte der Katholischen Kirche* (Berlin: Morus Verlag, 1949), 92.

20 Hubert Jedin, *Origin and Breakthrough of the Catholic Reform to 1563*, in *History of the Church*, vol. 5, edited by H. Jedin and J. Dolan, translated by A. Biggs and P. Becker (New York: The Seabury Press, 1980), 452.

21 Joseph Lortz, *Geschichte der Kirche in ideengeschichtlicher Betrachtung*, vol. 2 (Münster: Aschendorf Verlag, 1964), 150–1.

22 Jedin, "Origin and Breakthrough," 452.

23 Lortz, *Geschichte der Kirche*, vol. 2, 155.

24 Hans Urs von Balthasar, *The Glory of the Lord: A Theological Aesthetics*, vol. 1, *Seeing the Form*, translated by E. Leiva-Merikakis (San Francisco: Ignatius Press, 1982), 298.

25 Jacques Leclercq, *La vie du Christ dans son Église* (Paris: Le Cerf, 1944), 28–9.

CHAPTER SEVEN

1 Luigi Giussani, *At the Origin of the Christian Claim*, translated by Vivianne Hewitt (Montreal: McGill-Queen's University Press, 1998), 59–79.
2 Hymns on pages 149, 150, 151, and 152 appear in *Mater Ecclesia. Lobpreis der Kirche aus dem ersten Jahrtausend christlicher Literatur*, edited by Hugo Rahner (Köln: Benziger Verlag, 1944), 43, 44, 65, 113, 115, 73, 78–80.
3 Bruce Marshall, *To Every Man a Penny* (Cambridge, Mass.: The Riverside Press, 1949), 293.
4 Romano Guardini, *The Church and the Catholic and The Spirit of the Liturgy*, translated by Ada Lane (London: Sheed & Ward, 1935), 61.
5 Luigi Giussani, *Le risque éducatif* (Paris: Nouvelle Cité, 1987), 64.
6 Henri de Lubac, *Catholicism: Christ and the Common Destiny of Man*, translated by L.C. Sheppard and E. Englund (San Francisco: Ignatius Press, 1988), 141–2.
7 Ibid., 114–15.
8 Guardini, *Church*, 62.

CHAPTER EIGHT

1 Karl Adam, *The Spirit of Catholicism*, translated by Justin McCann (London: Sheed & Ward, 1929), 14.
2 See Luigi Giussani, *The Religious Sense*, translated by John Zucchi (Montreal: McGill-Queen's University Press, 1997), 132–40.
3 Gertrud von Le Fort, *Hymnen an die Kirche* (Munich: Franz Ehrenwirth Verlag, 1924), 15–16.
4 Ibid.
5 Charles Moeller, *Littérature du XXe siècle et christianisme*, vol. 2 (Paris: Castermann, 1964), 405–6.
6 René Grousset, *The Sum of History*, translated by A. and H. Temple Patterson (Hadleigh: Tower Bridge Publications, 1951), 246, 248.
7 Henri de Lubac, *La Révélation divine* (Paris: Cerf, 1983), 173.
8 John Henry Newman, *An Essay on the Development of Christian Doctrine* (London: Longmans, Green, and Co., 1900), 437–8.
9 René Latourelle, *Theology of Revelation* (Staten Island, NY: Alba House, 1966), 265.
10 Luigi Giussani, "Moralità: memoria e desiderio" in *Alla ricerca del volto umano* (Milan: Rizzoli, 1995), 220–1.
11 Joseph Lortz, *Geschichte der Kirche in ideengeschichtlicher Betrachtung*, vol. 2 (Münster: Aschendorf Verlag, 1964), 338.
12 August Franzen, *A History of the Church*, translated by Peter Becker (Montreal: Palm Publishers, 1968), 392.
13 Jacques Leclercq, *La vie du Christ dans son Église* (Paris: Le Cerf, 1944), 116–17.

14 Adam, *Spirit of Catholicism*, 218–20.

15 Newman, *Essay on the Development*, 186.

16 Rudolf Schnackenburg, *The Gospel According to St John*, vol. 1, translated by Kevin Smyth (Montreal: Palm Publishers, 1968), 364.

17 Ibid., 368, 369, 373.

18 Ibid., 373, 374.

19 Mircea Eliade, *A History of Religious Ideas*, vol. 1, translated by Willard R. Trask (Chicago: University of Chicago Press, 1978), 458.

20 Gustave Bardy, *La conversion au christianisme durant les premiers siècles* (Paris: Aubier, 1948), 14–15.

21 See Adam, *Spirit of Catholicism*, 26ff.

22 Hans Urs von Balthasar, *Parole et mystère chez Origène* (Paris: Le Cerf, 1957), 86.

23 Romano Guardini, *The Church and the Catholic and The Spirit of the Liturgy*, translated by Ada Lane (London: Sheed & Ward, 1935), 98–9.

24 Jean Daniélou, *The Lord of History*, translated by Nigel Abercrombie (Chicago: Henry Regnery, 1958), 84.

25 Hugo Rahner, *Greek Myths and Christian Mystery*, translated by Brian Battershaw (London: Burns & Oates, 1963), 101.

26 Jean Daniélou, *History of Early Christian Doctrine*, vol. 2, translated by John Austin Baker (London: Darton, Longman & Todd, 1973), 99.

27 Bardy, *La conversion au christianisme*, 22, 25, 30.

28 Rahner, *Greek Myths*, 84–5, 156, 173.

29 Ibid., 387.

30 Albert Houssiau, "La signification originelle des rites," in *Les Rites d'initiation*, edited by Julien Ries (Louvain-la-Neuve: Homo religiosus, 1986), 424–6.

31 Rahner, *Greek Myths*, 71.

32 Ibid., xiv.

CHAPTER NINE

1 Luigi Giussani, *The Religious Sense*, translated by John Zucchi (Montreal: McGill-Queen's University Press, 1997), 7, 9.

2 Bernhard Welte, *Das Licht des Nichts* (Düsseldorf: Patmos Verlag, 1980), 15.

3 Ibid., 16–17.

4 Henri de Lubac, *Paradoxes, suivi de Nouveaux Paradoxes* (Paris: Le Seuil, 1959), 105.

5 Werner H. Schmidt-Gerhard, *Wörterbuch der Bibel* (Hamburg: Furche Verlag, 1971), 285–6.

6 Claude Tresmontant, *Essai sur la connaissance de Dieu* (Paris: Le Cerf, 1959), 144.

7 Romano Guardini, *Der Anfang. Eine Interpretation der fünf ersten Kapitel von Augustinus' Bekenntnissen* (Kolmar i. Elsaß: Alsatia Verlag, n.d.), 14–15.

CHAPTER TEN

1 Henri de Lubac, *Catholicism: Christ and the Common Destiny of Man*, translated by L.C. Sheppard and E. Englund (San Francisco: Ignatius Press, 1988), 330.
2 Rudolf Schnackenburg, *The Gospel According to St. John*, vol. 3, translated by Kevin Smyth (Montreal: Palm Publishers, 1968), 180, 181, 188, 191.
3 Romano Guardini, *The Church and the Catholic and The Spirit of the Liturgy*, translated by Ada Lane (London: Sheed & Ward, 1935), 26.
4 Schnackenburg, *Gospel*, 64–5.
5 Hans Urs von Balthasar, *Der Christ und die Angst* (Einsiedeln: Johannes Verlag, 1989), 43.
6 Ibid., 92.
7 Hugo Rahner, *Greek Myths and Christian Mystery*, translated by Brian Battershaw (London: Burns & Oates, 1963), 389.
8 Romano Guardini, *Der Anfang. Eine Interpretation der fünf ersten Kapitel von Augustinus' Bekenntnissen* (Kolmar i. Elsaß: Alsatia Verlag, n.d.), 17–18.
9 Guardini, *Church and the Catholic*, 44–7.
10 Ibid., 29, 30, 31.
11 Hermanni contracti, *Vita seu elogium*, P.L. 143, coll. 25–30.
12 Cyril Martindale, *What are Saints?* (London: Sheed & Ward, 1933), 51, 52, 55.
13 Charles Moeller, *Sagesse grèque et paradoxe chrétien* (Tournai-Paris: Castermann, 1948), 265.
14 Ibid., 270–1.
15 Luigi Giussani, "Presentazione," in C. Martindale, *I Santi* (Milan: Jaca Book, 1992), 10.
16 André Hayen, *Saint Thomas d'Aquin et la vie de l'Église* (Paris: Desclée de Brouwer, 1952), 64.
17 Hans Urs von Balthasar, *Christen sind einfältig* (Einsiedeln: Johannes Verlag, 1983), 73.
18 Henri de Lubac, *Paradoxes, suivi de Nouveaux Paradoxes* (Paris: Le Seuil, 1959), 53.
19 Adrienne von Speyr, *Johannes*, vol. 4 (Einsiedeln: Johannes Verlag, 1948), 507.
20 John Henry Newman, *Apologia Pro Vita Sua* (London: Sheed & Ward, 1976), 217.
21 Pierre Rousselot, "Les yeux de la foi," in *Recherches de sciences religieuses*, sept–oct. 1910: 471.
22 John Henry Newman, *An Essay on the Development of Christian Doctrine* (London: Longmans, Green, and Co., 1900), 254–5.
23 De Lubac, *Catholicism*, 48.
24 Jean Daniélou, *The Lord of History*, translated by Nigel Abercrombie (Chicago: Henry Regnery, 1958), 43–4.

25 Karl Adam, *The Spirit of Catholicism*, translated by Justin McCann (London: Sheed & Ward, 1929), 141, 145.

26 August Franzen, *A History of the Church*, translated by Peter Becker (Montreal: Palm Publishers, 1968), 29.

27 Jean Daniélou, *History of Early Christian Doctrine*, vol. 2, translated by John Austin Baker (London: Darton, Longman & Todd, 1973), 31.

28 Christopher Dawson, *The Historic Reality of Christian Culture* (New York: Harper and Brothers, 1960), 118.

29 Henri de Lubac, *Images de l'abbé Monchanin* (Lyon: Aubier-Montaigne, 1967), 44–5.

30 Ibid., 56–7.

31 Daniélou, *Historic Reality*, 146–7.

32 Saint Irenaeus, *St. Irenaeus of Lyon Against the Heresies*, translated and annotated by Dominic J. Unger (New York: Paulist Press, 1992).

CONCLUSION

1 Hans Urs von Balthasar, *Romano Guardini. Reform aus dem Ursprung* (Munich: Kösel Verlag, 1970), 100.

2 Bernhard Welte, *Das Licht des Nichts* (Düsseldorf: Patmos Verlag, 1980), 55–6.

Subject Index

Absolute, the, 25, 57, 152, 224, 232
acceptance, 111
achievement(s), 42, 55, 58; human, 42
act, banal, 39; of creation, 222; Eucharistic, 103
action, 216, 220; Christ's redemptive, 219
actions, man's, 39
acts, 215, 216; of the Redeemer, 204; virtuous, 43, 44, 46
Acts of the Apostles, 68, 69, 72, 73, 76, 82, 88, 92, 93, 100, 101, 110
adhere, 92, 145, 195
adherence, 7, 10, 22, 43, 78, 80, 94, 101, 154, 162, 176, 181, 182, 221, 233
adhering, 27, 70, 80, 89, 137, 173, 186, 107; to Christianity, 90
advent, of Jesus, 59
adventure, Christian, 182
affection, 108, 192, 199
agape, 102, 107; as Church, 102
age, historical, 142

aim, 224, 228; of the Spirit, 218
alertness, 8
Almighty, 165
ambiguity, our original, 173
amen, meaning of, 79
analysis, 57; of an objection, 134-6; scientific, 148
ancients, the, 37
Anglican, 114
Anglicanism, 113, 133
announcement, 182; the Christian, 180; of an ontological exaltation, 182
Another, 149, 152, 161, 195, 209, 217, 223; as the substance of life, 161
answer, 118; to an objection, 195-7
anthropology, Christian, 190, 195; non-Christian, 190
anthropos, 194
antinomies, 30
antinominal elements, 32
antinomy, 53

anxiety, 161, 162, 213, 214, 217
apocalyptic tendency, 12, 13
apostle(s), 68, 72, 73, 84, 86, 100, 101, 102, 104, 105, 106, 107, 110, 111, 124, 125, 138, 170, 213, 226, 230
apostolicity, 211, 230-2
approach, critical, 107
argument, religious, 59
ascesis, 160
asking, 95, 151, 197, 198
assemblies, 85
assembly, 82, 84, 86
assimilation, ontological, 21
atheism, 60, 192
attentiveness, 112
attitude(s), 26, 28, 32, 54, 80, 96, 108, 130, 131, 135, 137, 138, 141, 154, 155, 158, 162, 164, 178, 212, 229; of acceptance, 209; of asking, 197; authentically religious, 156, 157; Catholic, 144; contemporary, 6; critical, 34, 80, 139; cultural, 10, 11, 18, 215; educa-

Name Index